Haiti's New Dictatorship

HAITI'S NEW DICTATORSHIP

The Coup, the Earthquake and the
UN Occupation

Justin Podur

Foreword by William I. Robinson

www.plutobooks.com

BTL

First published 2012 by Pluto Press
345 Archway Road, London N6 5AA
www.plutobooks.com

Distributed in the United States of America exclusively by
Palgrave Macmillan, a division of St. Martin's Press LLC,
175 Fifth Avenue, New York, NY 10010

First published in Canada in 2012 by Between the Lines
401 Richmond Street West, Studio 277, Toronto, Ontario, M5V 3A8, Canada
1-800-718-7201
www.btlbooks.com

British Library Cataloguing in Publication Data
A catalogue record for this book is available from the British Library

Library and Archives Canada Cataloguing in Publication
Podur, Justin J. (Justin Joseph), 1977-
    Haiti's new dictatorship : the coup, the earthquake and the
UN occupation / Justin Podur.
Includes bibliographical references and index.
Co-published by: Pluto Press.
ISBN 978-1-77113-033-2
1. Haiti—History—21st century. 2. Haiti Earthquake, Haiti, 2010.
3. Haiti—Politics and government—21st century. 4. United Nations—Haiti.
5. Nation-building—Haiti. I. Title.
F1928.2.P63 2012   972.9407'3   C2012-903554-8

ISBN 978 0 7453 3258 1 Hardback
ISBN 978 0 7453 3257 4 Paperback (Pluto Press)
ISBN 978 1 77113 033 2 Paperback (Between the Lines)
ISBN 978 1 8496 4782 3 PDF eBook
ISBN 978 1 8496 4784 7 Kindle eBook
ISBN 978 1 8496 4783 0 EPUB eBook

Between the Lines gratefully acknowledges assistance for its publishing activities from the
Canada Council for the Arts, the Ontario Arts Council, the Government of Ontario through
the Ontario Book Publishers Tax Credit program, and the Government of Canada through
the Canada Book Fund.

 Canada Council
for the Arts
Conseil des Arts
du Canada

ONTARIO ARTS COUNCIL
CONSEIL DES ARTS DE L'ONTARIO

 Canada

This book is printed on paper suitable for recycling and made from fully managed
and sustained forest sources. Logging, pulping and manufacturing processes are
expected to conform to the environmental standards of the country of origin.

10 9 8 7 6 5 4 3 2 1

Designed and produced for Pluto Press by Swales & Willis
Simultaneously printed digitally by CPI Antony Rowe, Chippenham, UK and
Edwards Bros in the United States of America

CONTENTS

ACKNOWLEDGEMENTS

I would like to dedicate the book to Samba Boukman, Jean Ristil, and Fr. Gérard Jean-Juste, all of whom were dedicated to trying to get the truth of Haiti heard, all of whose voices are missed.

Patrick Elie is probably the single person who advanced my understanding of Haiti the most, but he is not alone. When I read Peter Hallward's 'Option Zero' in NLR, I felt huge relief that someone at least understood what was going on. I had a similar feeling reading Kevin Pina's articles in the Black Commentator as the 2003/4 coup was unfolding. I also owe huge debts to Paul Christian, Rea Dol, Isabel MacDonald, Isabeau Doucet, Jean St Vil, Kevin Skerrett, Roger Annis, Kim Ives, Brian Concannon Jr, and Marguerite Laurent. Since the earthquake, an indispensable source is Ansel Herz, and I got to spend a week with him in Port au Prince in 2011. Tim Schwartz sharpened my thinking a lot and provided amazing examples. I wouldn't miss anything Paul Farmer wrote on Haiti, though I have never met him. People I disagree with now, but whose writing was a big help to me and whose books I will always recommend, include Amy Wilentz and Alex Dupuy.

I first traveled to Haiti with Andrea Schmidt and Anthony Fenton – Andrea and Anthony were among the first, and most helpful, readers of this manuscript, before it was even a book. Dan Freeman-Maloy helped ensure that it actually got out – and so, in an unexpected way, did Shouri and Fabulous. Michael Albert, Cynthia Peters, Stephen Shalom, Chris Spannos, and Noam Chomsky all supported, inspired, and advised pretty well constantly – sometimes after pestering, sometimes unsolicited. So did Manuel Rozental, Micheal O'Tuathail, Erwin Blanco, Tarek and Mohammed Loubani, Hector Mondragon, Rahul Mahajan, Bob Jensen, Mike Denyszyn, Niiti Simmonds, Naomi Klein, Clare O'Connor, and adopted uncle Badri Raina. David Castle believed in the book and I hope to work with him and Pluto in the future.

I counted on professional support from my colleagues at FES, and York generally, throughout most of these years, but it was the flexibility of my PhD supervisor David Martell from 1999 on that made it possible for me to do this work at all. My family – Varghese and Hilaria, Sunitha and Tyson, Maya and Max – were always there, as were additional extended family like Dave and Lidija, Andrew, Lawrence, Anthony, Uyen, Chris, Brad, Faith, Pete.

Khalida talked me out of giving up more than once and generally inspires everything.

raffazia, I hope you enjoy the finished product.

FOREWORD

In this world of globalized capitalism and U.S.-led intervention, dictatorship is called 'democracy' and enslavement is named 'freedom'. Nowhere is the cynical duplicity of the twenty-first century world order more apparent than in the travails of the Haitian people. This is a people who rose up in revolution two hundred years ago to throw off the shackles of slavery and who have not stopped struggling since to achieve a better life and defend its dignity, all the while in the face of successive dictatorships and foreign predation.

Justin Podur now offers us a study on this struggle in its contemporary manifestations, examining the crucial period from 1991 to 2010. He traces the rise of the Lavalas movement of the poor majority under the leadership of Jean-Bertrand Aristide and the implacable campaigns waged by the United States and other foreign agents to destroy this movement, overthrow Aristide, and reconstitute the power of a tiny local elite. He unmasks the transnationalization of U.S. intervention under the banner of 'donors', the United Nations, other international agencies, and the global media monopoly.

The machinations of power and domination include state and paramilitary terrorism against the popular movement, systematic human rights violations, UN occupation, the orchestration of electoral shams, disinformation campaigns, and economic blackmail. Beyond those interested in contemporary Caribbean affairs, this book is a must read for anyone who wishes to understand the new face of dictatorship in this twenty-first century global order.

Professor William I. Robinson
University of California, Santa Barbara

INTRODUCTION

Haitians have lived under dictatorships for much of their recent history. As dictatorships do, they terrorized the population, bankrupted the treasury, and caused lasting damage to society. Haiti's best-known twentieth century dictators were the Duvaliers, 'Papa Doc' and 'Baby Doc'. Under them, the country was ruled arbitrarily, without a consistent rule of law. Terror was used as a weapon of control against the population, who had no say in their own political or economic affairs. Paramilitaries, called the Tonton Macoutes after a character in traditional Haitian stories, were the ubiquitous symbol of dictatorship. Along with 'Section Chiefs', the Duvaliers used the Macoutes to terrorize and control Haitians' lives in detail. The nightmare of the Duvalier dictatorships ended in 1986, when a popular movement, which came to be known as Lavalas ('the flood' in Haitian Kreyol), threw them out. Among the leaders of this movement was Jean-Bertrand Aristide, twice president of Haiti, twice overthrown in coups.

Haitian scholar Michel-Rolph Trouillot wrote one of the most respected analyses of the Duvaliers.[1] He argued that the concept of 'dictatorship' was vague, insufficient to describe the way the Duvaliers exercised power, as it 'has no comparative value', and that the Duvaliers were worse than just dictators. He conceded, however, that dictatorship as commonly understood had two elements: the use of violence and the centralization of power, and he analyzed the Duvaliers in these terms.

The concept of dictatorship is a useful one, and to Trouillot's two points I would add a few others. In a dictatorship, there is impunity: crimes, including the violation of human rights by the regime and its supporters, go unpunished. Impunity sets the stage for the routine use of violence and terror against the regime's opponents, and as a strategy for controlling the population. There is no effective right to assemble or organize politically.

Dictatorships also have a specific economic arrangement: wealth is concentrated and financial and economic power is wielded in the interests of the regime, not the people. Haiti scholar Patrick Bellegarde-Smith described the economic model under the Duvaliers as being export-oriented agriculture and manufacturing with food (rice) dependence on the U.S., leading to migration from the countryside and a need for docile, cheap labour in the cities to be competitive in world markets, as well as tourism, which leads to the displacement of local cultures. This economic model is inextricably linked to the dictatorship, as 'the net effect of having less than 1 per cent of the population own almost 50 per cent of the national wealth, while simultaneously increasing poverty and wealth differentials, is an increasingly powerful defense apparatus'.[2]

According to these criteria, this book argues, Haiti is again living under a dictatorship. This is true even though there were elections in 2006 and again in 2010/11, even though there is nominal freedom of press and assembly, and even though there is an extensive international aid effort in the country. As I will show, Haitians have no effective say over their own economic and political affairs. Their right to assemble and organize politically is sharply limited. Human rights violations are routine and go unpunished.

Haiti's new dictatorship is less centralized than older dictatorships, because it involves a large number of international actors working in concert with local powers. It also exercises violence in less crude ways. And where older dictators muzzled the press, the new dictatorship outcompetes its opponents in propaganda. The new dictatorship has cost Haitians thousands of lives and years, perhaps decades, of time to develop. The new dictatorship has made every natural disaster, from hurricane floods to food crises to earthquakes, measurably more deadly. And it continues to deny Haitians their fundamental rights to sovereignty and democracy.

This is not inevitable: the new dictatorship has taken tremendous international effort to impose against the will of Haitians. Trouillot argues that, 'In Haiti, as in many peripheral societies, dictatorship ... is the traditional form of government'.[3] Another important Haitian scholar, Robert Fatton, Jr, analyzes 'Haitian despotism' in terms of an authoritarian historical pattern.[4] Based on these scholars, it would be no great leap to argue that Haiti has suffered a continuous set of dictatorships, from before the Duvaliers, to the military rulers of 1986–90, to Aristide, to the interim government of 2004–06, and to the Préval and Martelly governments. Indeed, a recent history of

Haiti argues that Aristide and the Duvaliers are both examples of dictators who mismanaged the country.[5]

But the idea that Haitians have lived under an unbroken line of dictatorships is incorrect. In the 1980s, Haitians made a revolution to overthrow the Duvaliers and built a popular movement to try to overcome the structures of dictatorship, trying to stop the use of violence, challenge the centralization of power, change the concentration of wealth, establish the rule of law, and stop impunity. This movement became the government in 1990 when Aristide was elected, but was violently overthrown months later. Aristide was returned to power in 1994 through a U.S. intervention (whose complex causes I will discuss below), and from 1995 to 2004, the struggle against the deeper structures of the dictatorship (the army, the economic policies, foreign control of Haiti's affairs) won important successes because the movement had links to the government.

But from 2004, when Aristide was overthrown the second time, until today, Haiti's new dictatorship was imposed and solidified, and the popular movement and its representatives in government were exiled, jailed, and murdered in massive numbers. This was done under the control of the U.S., Canada, and France, and with the full participation of the United Nations. How this was done, in the open, successfully silencing Haiti's popular movement, is the subject of this book.

Political contests are in part contests of belief. Communities have ways of sharing their beliefs with one another, creating stories to fit the facts that they observe and, sometimes, their interests as well. Sometimes narratives are created that cannot be reconciled with all of the facts. Which facts are selected, or which facts emphasized, is a matter of ideology. From the facts of Haiti's politics from 2000 to 2010, or 2004–06 in particular, two very different stories have been created, and propagated, in North America. One story is associated with most of the mainstream media, the governments of the U.S., Canada, and France, and a large number of well-funded non-governmental organizations in Haiti and internationally. This is a story of Haiti's President Jean-Bertrand Aristide getting elected, becoming a dictator, and leaving in the face of a popular uprising. The other story is associated with the ousted government of Aristide, its supporters – the majority of the population, proven every time elections were held – and a small number of independent journalists and researchers. This story is of Aristide being undermined, overthrown in a coup, kidnapped, and the popular movement that brought him to power being brutalized.

If resources alone were a guide to the truth, readers should believe the first story.

This book is a telling of the second story. If both stories deal with the same evidence, readers can decide which fit the evidence better. If the stories disagree on the facts, as they sometimes do, readers will have to decide where the balance of evidence rests. If the stories agree on the facts, as they sometimes do, readers can discern differences in values between the stories, and decide which story fits their values best. My hope is that the presentation of the second story as clearly as possible will help readers to make these decisions. Everybody involved with Haiti says they want to help, but these two stories are irreconcilable: if you are helping according to one, you are hurting according to the other.

As a consequence, the stakes are high. I believe that helping Haiti means bolstering its sovereignty: its government's capacity to resist external predation, to enact policies that are in accord with the will of the majority, to redistribute and develop wealth internally. Many of those who I disagree with in this book believe that helping Haiti means putting it under external control.

What follows is an account of the coup/occupation regime that followed the premature ending of the presidency of Jean-Bertrand Aristide in Haiti in 2004. As of this writing Haiti is still occupied by foreign troops in the form of MINUSTAH, the United Nations Mission of Stabilization in Haiti. The country was thoroughly devastated by an earthquake in 2010, an event whose repercussions have only begun to be felt. While the book offers an account of the lead up to the coup beginning in 2000, and of the coup and invasion in 2004, the central focus is the 2004–06 period of Gérard Latortue/MINUSTAH administration, the period of the Préval presidency, from February 2006 to the 2010 earthquake, and the post-earthquake period, 2010–12.

My chronology and analysis of this period has several motivations.

The 2004 coup was justified by claims that Aristide had become an unpopular dictator who was violating human rights. But the coup *resulted* in an actual dictatorship and human rights violations that dwarfed anything that occurred under Aristide's presidency. By every single measure, the 2004–06 regime was far worse than the regime it replaced, and elements of that regime remain in place today. This was entirely predictable, given that its local base was the elite and the military and its enemies were the majority of the population. A history of the coup regime is necessary to establish this important point in the historical record. Those who supported the coup on 'human rights' grounds should not be allowed to rewrite the record to make the coup seem like a liberation from tyranny. It was a delivery into tyranny.

The coup regime was an important international phenomenon. Dozens of countries sent their soldiers to participate in the occupation of Haiti. The diplomacy that occurred between the Haitian business community and other coupster groups, the United Nations and specifically the powerful Latin American countries (especially Brazil) leading MINUSTAH, and the most hardline coupster countries (the U.S., France, and Canada) is of interest to those who are looking to understand how a multilateral violation of sovereignty is organized and carried out.

The 2004 coup was characterized by misinformation that shaped the responses of progressives and the international solidarity community to the coup. The political economy of this misinformation is somewhat complex, but can be simplified as follows. Many non-governmental organizations (NGOs), especially those that are well funded, are an instrument of the foreign policy of powerful countries. These countries use their foreign agencies to fund NGOs in poor countries. These NGOs can do 'development', 'democracy promotion', 'human rights promotion', or any number of very benevolent-sounding activities. The logic of their funding sources pushes their policies and public political statements in the direction of the foreign policy of their donors. These statements are picked up by the press, by official spokespeople, and by progressives in the rich countries as being the voices of the grassroots of the poor countries. Thus, a message that originates in and serves the foreign policy interests of the United States is delivered to a Haitian NGO that rebroadcasts the message, which is then picked up by people in the U.S. as the voice of Haitians. Solidarity movements seeking to follow the lead of the oppressed then follow the lead of these Haitians, ultimately serving U.S. foreign policy.

An even deeper analysis of this phenomenon is provided by anthropologist Erica James in her 2010 book *Democratic Insecurities: Violence, Trauma, and Intervention in Haiti.* James argues that in the 1990s, in the period after the first anti-Lavalas coup, two overlapping political economies, one a political economy of terror and the other a political economy of compassion, took hold in Haiti. The political economy of terror is the more straightforward: the dictatorship of the time used violence and terror in order to control the population and suppress the democratic movement. The political economy of compassion, James describes as follows:

> The opaque and sometimes secret crafts of activists, bureaucrats, and other humanitarian and development experts aiding Haiti made suffering productive. Their labor converted the suffering that embodies individuals after malevolent, inhumane interventions into what I call 'trauma portfolios', the aggregate of paraphernalia compiled to document and authenticate the experience of individual, family, or collective sufferers. The work of conversion created the identity of 'victims' or 'survivors' for individuals who were once [militants or activists]. It was a professional transformation of suffering that fed a growing humanitarian market.[7]

The 'humanitarian market' is a specific way for international aid agencies and foreign governments to relate to Haiti, whether it is to Haitian government or non-governmental institutions or directly with the Haitian clients of these agencies. The nature of the relationship is specified by the terms of the market, and it leaves little room for other ways to relate. Specifically, it leaves little room for a relationship of equality between sovereign citizens of two countries. In the humanitarian market, the recipient of aid, the victim, has no sovereignty and lacks any right to control where largesse is directed. In Haiti, where foreign aid and foreign governments effectively rule the country, the ideology associated with the humanitarian market is a powerful brake on relations of mutual respect and reciprocity.

Another form of misinformation comes from what U.S. filmmaker and Haiti activist Kevin Pina calls a 'disinformation loop': again, a rumor originating in the U.S. is sent to U.S.-friendly Haitian media, where it is in turn picked up by the international press, and the U.S.-friendly Haitian media rebroadcast it as having the additional credibility of coming from the foreign press. This process was documented by Isabel Macdonald in her MA thesis, 'Covering the Coup', and in unpublished research on Canadian media and the Haiti coup by Daniel Freeman-Maloy. Their analyses will be discussed in some detail below as well.

The misinformation was successful and got deep into very

progressive groups and publishers, and made leftists and progressives less credible and less relevant to struggling people. An honest look at what happened could help avoid this error in future coups and imperial interventions.

The occupation of Haiti by MINUSTAH had a very peculiar character and some very strange justifications. In Haiti, an internationalized military solution is being offered for what even the UN admitted were problems of poverty and social crime that occur in many places. The absurdity of this seems to have escaped debate or scrutiny, and worse, the UN occupation, and the justification for it in terms of security from gangsters and bandits, continues even after the rest of the coup was reversed in 2006. I hope that if widespread recognition of its absurdity can be achieved, a change in policy could be affected.

After the earthquake, Haiti was even more completely dependent on foreign aid than it was before. Millions of people who donated to try to help Haiti have questions about where and how the money was spent and why the situation of Haitians does not seem to improve. These questions cannot be divorced from politics or history, especially recent history. Many in the aid community argue that aid is wasted in a country if its government is corrupt or irresponsible. Unfortunately, Haiti's government – the international regime referred to in this book as Haiti's new dictatorship – is both corrupt and irresponsible.

Finally, the story of the heroism and clarity of the Haitian people in this brutal and confusing period deserves to be told as often and as loudly as possible. It is not for an absence of Haitian will that Haiti is under a dictatorship today and not a sovereign government. They did not give up even when abandoned and occupied by most of the world. Their resistance was flexible, relentless, and successful in preventing the coupsters from fulfilling all of their objectives.

The coup did, however, succeed in installing a new form of dictatorship. Instead of Tonton Macoutes and the cult of personality of the Duvaliers, the symbols of this dictatorship are the blue helmets of MINUSTAH and thousands of NGOs. The new dictatorship has already lasted seven years, and Haitians still have no say in their own economic and political affairs. This analysis is offered in the hope that it can help motivate those outside Haiti to support initiatives that strengthen Haiti's sovereignty and weaken the external, dictatorial controls against Haiti's people.

Although I visited Haiti briefly in September–October 2005 and again in October 2011 to investigate some of these problems, my principal sources for this book are published reports from the mainstream and alternative press and from activist groups, especially the Canada-Haiti Action Network (CHAN), the Haitian Lawyers' Leadership Network (HLLN), and the Centre for Economic Policy Research (CEPR).

1 HISTORICAL CONTEXT

Haiti in the Americas from independence to today

Before starting the analysis of the post-2004 period, some historical context is necessary. Most books on Haiti include a short overview of the past, and there are several good histories. This background will emphasize the aspects of history that are important for understanding recent history: specifically, the constraints on Haiti's economic and political sovereignty, imposed from the outside.

HAITI IN THE COLONIAL PERIOD

With the Dominican Republic, Haiti is one of two countries on the island of Hispaniola, whose indigenous inhabitants came into contact with Europeans in 1492 with Christopher Columbus's first voyage to the Americas. Columbus left a settlement behind, and the devastation of the indigenous population through brutal violence, forced labour, and disease began immediately.[1] Over the following century, the indigenous population of many of the new Spanish colonies was wiped out, reducing the forced labour pool accordingly. The Spanish then introduced African slaves in Hispaniola, as they did in Cuba and other colonies. Haiti was thus one of the first terminal destinations for the captured men and women of the transatlantic slave trade.

In the sixteenth and seventeenth centuries, European colonial powers, including Spain, the Netherlands, England, and France, fought naval battles directly and through proxies (pirates) for colonial possessions in the Americas. The Caribbean was the major site of these conflicts. France began to settle colonists in western Hispaniola in the seventeenth century, and by the end of

9

that century the Spanish ceded the western part of Hispaniola to the French, who named the colony St Domingue.

St Domingue became France's most important colony and a major source of its wealth. St Domingue's wealth was from a variety of export crops, especially sugar and coffee, but also tobacco, cocoa, cotton, indigo, and others, produced with slave labour for European markets. In the eighteenth century the colonial capital, Port-au-Prince, was destroyed twice by major earthquakes, once in 1751 and again in 1770. By the late eighteenth century, the slave population was far higher than the white population. The slaves' resistance was constant and, in various ways, successful: they raided plantations, freed others, and, like slaves in Brazil, Colombia, elsewhere in the Caribbean, and the United States, they founded maroon societies of escaped slaves. The history of slavery and of resistance continues to have a powerful resonance in Haiti's culture today.

Unremitting slave resistance meant that the French colonists maintained power through atrocity. Described in detail in C.L.R. James's indispensable *The Black Jacobins*, these atrocities are also summarized in a well-known letter from revolutionary leader Henri Christophe's personal secretary and quoted in Robert Heinl's 1996 history, *Written in Blood*:

> Have they not hung up men with heads downward, drowned them in sacks, crucified them on planks, buried them alive, crushed them in mortars? Have they not forced them to eat excrement? And, having flayed them with the lash, have they not cast them alive to be devoured by worms, or onto anthills, or lashed them to stakes in the swamp to be devoured by mosquitoes? Have they not thrown them into boiling cauldrons of cane syrup? Have they not put men and women inside barrels studded with spikes and rolled them down mountainsides into the abyss? Have they not consigned these miserable blacks to man-eating dogs until the latter, sated by human flesh, left the mangled victims to be finished off with bayonet and poniard?[2]

If slavery, and the atrocities required to maintain it, provided the rage needed to provoke a revolution, the vulnerability of the mercantile economy to a scorched-earth strategy and the fact that the slaves outnumbered the colonists nearly twenty-to-one provided the possibility for success.

THE HAITIAN REVOLUTION

Haiti's revolutionary leaders, Toussaint L'Ouverture, Jean-Jacques Dessalines, and others, were able to take advantage of this possibility. Independence was won in a bitter, brutal revolt against the French colonial masters, the only successful slave revolt in history.[3] Despite Toussaint's willingness to make all concessions except the re-imposition of slavery, including allowing the colony to remain a part of France, the French under Napoleon ultimately decided on a genocidal campaign: if Haiti's population was not to be France's possession, it would have to be utterly destroyed. The Haitian revolutionaries, faced with complete destruction, chose a scorched-earth strategy themselves, as summarized in the instructions Toussaint wrote to Dessalines in 1802 as the French fleet, commanded by Napoleon's brother-in-law, approached:

> Do not forget, while waiting for the rainy season which will rid us of our foes, that we have no other resource than destruction and flames. Bear in mind that the soil bathed with our sweat must not furnish our enemies with the smallest aliment. Tear up the roads with shot; throw corpses and horses into all the fountains; burn and annihilate everything, in order that those who have come to reduce us to slavery may have before their eyes the image of that hell which they deserve.[4]

When the war of independence ended in 1804, Haiti was divided between two revolutionary generals, Alexandre Petion as President in the south and Henri Christophe as King in the north. Haiti was not re-united until Christophe's death in 1820.

HAITI IN THE HEMISPHERE

Toussaint L'Ouverture used the language of the French Revolution (Liberty, Equality, Fraternity) and suggested that the Haitian revolution was only an attempt to live up to those ideals. Similarly, Haiti might have hoped that the United States, upon becoming independent, might embrace its independent neighbour. But the new republic, although in part based also on the ideals of the French Revolution, was also a genocidal settler state and a slave society. These realities coloured the U.S.'s policy toward Haiti much more than any shared revolutionary ideals.

The U.S. refused to recognize Haiti and feared the example of a successful slave revolt.

Jean-Jacques Dessalines, the former field slave who had led the final struggle for independence after Toussaint L'Ouverture was captured, declared himself Emperor upon victory, but was assassinated shortly afterward. Alexandre Petion, President of Haiti after Dessalines's assassination, helped South American Revolutionary Simon Bolivar in the fight for independence against Spain. Bolivar ended up in exile in Haiti twice, in 1815 and 1816. Haiti provided Bolivar first with sanctuary, then with material, volunteers, and transport back to the continent to resume the fight. Petion's condition: that Bolivar free the slaves in the territories he liberated. Bolivar modified the condition in the implementation, issuing a decree that slaves would be freed if they joined his army.

EARLY INDEPENDENCE AND THE INDEMNITY TO FRANCE

In 1825, France issued the Royal Ordinance, calling for Haitians to pay a massive indemnity for winning the revolt and freeing themselves. The indemnity was for 150 million francs, based on the profits that could have been earned by colonists in the period: it represented France's annual budget plus ten years of revenue from the plantations and estates that had been destroyed during the war. On top of this, French ships and commercial goods entering and leaving Haiti were to be discounted 50 per cent. The demands were delivered by heavily armed warships just off of Port-au-Prince. The French promised to recognize Haiti as an independent nation if the indemnity was paid. Haiti had fortified itself against another invasion, but was no naval power. Facing a blockade, the island economy was forced to acquiesce. A French bank loaned Haiti 30 million francs for the first instalment, deducting management fees and charging exorbitant interest: by the time payments were completed, Haiti was 6 million francs deeper in the hole. It took Haiti 122 years – until 1947 – to finish paying the indemnity debt.[5]

The scorched earth warfare, disunity, and indemnity prevented Haiti from establishing itself economically. Haiti's post-revolutionary rulers tried to impose measures to continue commodity agricultural production, but several additional factors worked against this. The lack of international recognition impeded the re-establishment of normal trade. There was no easy way to transition from the plantation economy to an export-based economy that was not based on slavery. The monopoly of skills and organization by the colonists before the revolution meant that after the revolution, when colonists left or were massacred, the country had a shortage of skills.[6] An additional earthquake in 1843, as well as hurricanes and outbreaks of disease, were also devastating. In this period when the U.S. and European countries were undergoing explosive industrial growth, revolutionary Haiti was excluded. Indeed, it continued to be squeezed to enrich the already wealthy with resources it needed for its own growth and development.

Haiti was only officially recognized by the United States during the American Civil War. After the Emancipation Proclamation, the U.S. had no real reason to fear the example of a republic of freed slaves. Haiti's government held a state funeral for John Brown,[7] and allowed the U.S. Navy to operate from Haitian ports to maintain the blockade of the South.

THE U.S. MARINE OCCUPATION: 1915–34

Saddled with these crippling debts, Haiti was hardly able to move forward. The mulatto elite's Liberal Party fought the black National Party for control through the nineteenth century.[8] There were military conflicts between rivals for power within Haiti, local revolts and rebellions, and border wars with the Dominican Republic. As U.S. economic power grew in the nineteenth century, so too did its influence in Haiti. By the 1910s, this influence was symbolized by HASCO, The Haitian-American Sugar Company. Like United Fruit in the Latin American 'banana republics', HASCO was a major player in Haitian politics and a vehicle for U.S. influence in the country.

In 1915, the U.S. Marines invaded Haiti. As always, the U.S. cited local politics and concerns for its business interests (including HASCO) as the reason for invasion. But this was a period in which the U.S. conducted several invasions in the Americas (Nicaragua was occupied from 1912 to 1933, the Dominican Republic from 1916 to 1924, Cuba since the Spanish–American war, and others). The U.S. privatized the National Bank, re-instituted forced labour, tied resistance leader Charlemagne Peralte's body to a door and circulated the photograph. When the Marines left 19 years later in 1934, the U.S. reserved a 'special role' for itself.[9] The U.S. left behind two military forces for use against the population, the 'gendarmerie' and the National Guard, which evolved into the

Haitian Army (renamed Forces Armees D'Haiti, or FADH, in 1958). In 1935, the post-occupation government of Haiti granted a 25-year banana contract to the U.S. Standard Fruit and Steamship Company.[10]

POST-OCCUPATION TO THE DUVALIERS: 1934–57

Two years later, in 1937, the U.S.-supported Trujillo dictatorship in the Dominican Republic massacred thousands of Haitian workers there, in a systematically planned, five-day pogrom.[11] In his history of the period, Matthew Smith argues that the Haitian government may have had sufficient force to stop the massacres from taking place, but was focused on internal threats to its own stability and not the security of its people, who had no international champions either.[12] The Haitian government accepted an indemnity of $750,000[13] for the families of the victims in exchange for cancelling an independent investigation of the slaughter.[14]

In 1941, the Société Haitiano-Americaine de Développement Agricole, or SHADA, was created with a $5 million grant from the U.S. Export-Import Bank. This megaproject, which came to control 100,000 hectares in Haiti, was motivated by the need to produce rubber for the Allied war effort in World War II. By 1944, the project had failed to produce much rubber, left no sustainable infrastructure, and forcibly displaced peasants from their land.[14] The economic failures were accompanied by repression and surveillance: 'A government law insisted on the presence of a police officer at all meetings of workers associations.'[16]

In 1946, a popular movement including workers and students mobilized to oust the undemocratic regime that had ruled Haiti since 1941. The National Guard struck first, ousting the President and promising new elections under a Military Executive Council. In many respects, these events were similar to the 1986 overthrow of the Duvaliers (see below), also accomplished because of popular mobilization but which also ended with the military in charge.[17] The outcome of the elections that followed months later, possibly tampered with by the military regime, were unfavourable to the popular movement. The regime responded to the ensuing protests with further repression.[18] The eventual winner, Dumarsais Estimé, was not the favourite. Elected by the legislature to 'surprise and disbelief' in Port-au-Prince, he found that people 'shouted threats and slurs at him, while many women were, according to one observer, 'on their knees wailing miserably'.[19] Estimé used patronage to win a degree of popular support, brought some socialists associated with the popular movement into his government, and initiated a degree of economic planning. When this caught U.S. attention, Estimé removed the socialist ministers from his cabinet,[20] while attempting a modest programme of reform, including increasing minimum wages, an income tax, new labour laws, labour inspectors, cooperatives, school rehabilitation, and a rural development campaign.[21] U.S. corporations, SHADA and HASCO, labelled Estimé's administration communist; U.S. banks denied the government debt relief and new loans. Estimé successfully waged a public campaign to raise domestic funds to pay off a $5 million loan, but was again rebuffed in most of his efforts to get new loans from the U.S. A poorly planned attempt at nationalizing the banana industry harmed Haiti's market share, its economy, and its government's finances.[22] He was removed in a coup by the National Guard, which he had renamed the Haitian Army (Armée D'Haiti) in 1950.[23]

The post-coup regime of Philip Magloire repaired any strains in relations with the U.S. and created an anti-communist dictatorship allied with Trujillo's Dominican Republic and Batista's Cuba. Like these Caribbean neighbours, Magloire emphasized the tourist industry in his economic plan. But tourism remained ultimately an insignificant contributor to the national economy. The major economic sector, agriculture, declined, subject to boom-and-bust cycles because of over-reliance on a single crop (coffee) and vulnerability to hurricanes. Corruption and nepotism devastated the limited public sector services in the cities; foreign loans and relief funds passed through Haiti without any lasting benefit to its people.[24] Magloire's government facilitated – through massacres in Port-au-Prince, including slums like Bel Air – the rise of presidential candidate François 'Papa Doc' Duvalier, who came to power in 1957.[25]

THE DUVALIERS

Papa Doc, who had campaigned on a platform of economic equality and improvement of the country's devastated infrastructure, was a repressive dictator.[26] He kept the Forces Armees D'Haiti (FADH) divided and under his control, created a parallel personal militia, the 'Volontaires de la Securite Nationale-VSN', or the 'Tonton Macoutes', and crushed the labour movement. This latter act, as well as his anti-communism, kept Papa Doc in favour with the

United States, which had been suspicious of his closeness to the reformer Estimé. The U.S. came to Papa Doc's aid in 1959 when some Haitian exiles mounted an insurrection against the dictator. The U.S. Marines and Navy deployed to help defeat the rebels and end the insurrection.[27]

Papa Doc held elections in 1961 and had eliminated all effective opposition by 1964, naming himself President-for-life in the Constitution and granting himself the right to name his successor (his son, Jean-Claude 'Baby Doc' Duvalier).[28] By the time Papa Doc died in 1971, the regime had killed 30,000–60,000 people (the Haitian population at the time was 3–4 million), tortured and exiled many more, and embezzled $10 million from the small treasury for Papa Doc's personal use.[29] Baby Doc's regime was no different in its abuses or its U.S. support. By the 1980s, however, Baby Doc was facing insurrections, which he viciously suppressed. In 1986 an uprising in Gonaives sparked rural revolts all over Haiti, which eventually reached the capital. By February of that year Baby Doc fled to France on a U.S. Air Force jet,[30] leaving Haiti to the military yet again. Haiti's development was in a disastrous state, symbolized by the fact that there was, at the time of his departure, one school to every 35 prisons.[31]

THE ARRIVAL OF LAVALAS

With the arrival of Lavalas and the overthrow of the Duvaliers at the end of the 1980s, the Haitian people had arrived on the scene – to stay. Their mobilization had finally overthrown the dictator, and their resistance was diverse: armed in some places, non-violent in others. In Port-au-Prince, resistance coalesced around a church and a young priest who had studied liberation theology abroad and put it into practice in the poor neighbourhoods of the city. Jean-Bertrand Aristide had been one of the only church figures[32] to speak out against repression during the Duvalier years, and he used his prestige to organize against the attempts to replace the Duvaliers with another dictatorship, this time by the Army.[33] Aristide's movement evoked the image of many drops of water creating a flood; the Haitian Creole word for 'flood' is 'Lavalas', and that became the name of the movement.

But if the people were coming into their own with Baby Doc gone, the FADH was coming into its own as well – with the help of the U.S. The United States created a National Governing Council

(Conseil National de Gouvernement, or CNG) to rule Haiti in the absence of the dictator and resumed open military aid for the Army. Among the U.S. creations in 1986 was the National Intelligence Service (SIN), a CIA client that received millions of dollars of equipment and training, ostensibly to fight drug trafficking and provide intelligence, but which actually engaged in drug trafficking, torture, and persecution of Lavalas activists and others.[34]

The CNG, under control of the Army, led by Lieutenant General Henry Namphy, wrote a new Constitution in 1987 and scheduled elections for November of that year. Aristide and Lavalas urged a boycott of the elections, which were postponed until January 1988. Turnout was very low.[35] The CNG gave full control to Namphy in 1988.[36] A high priority for the FADH and the U.S. was trying to crush the popular movement. Over the period between Baby Doc's departure and the January 1988 elections, the FADH killed more people than Baby Doc had killed in the previous 15 years.[37] That year, 1988, there was an internal revolt within the FADH, led by General Prosper Avril, who took control from Namphy in a coup.[38] Popular resistance did not stop, however, and in 1990 Avril was forced to hand power over to a civilian member of the supreme court, Ertha Pascal Trouillot, and flee, again on a U.S. aircraft.[39]

The popular movement continued, demanding economic reform, an end to corruption, and justice for the victims of the FADH and the Tonton Macoutes. In response, the Haitian right mobilized as well: Roger Lafontant, former head of the Tonton Macoutes, Duvalierist minister of defence and the interior, held a series of right-wing rallies between July and December of 1990.[40] In the face of an explosive situation, the U.S. Embassy pressured the FADH to allow another election. The election was scheduled for December 16, 1990. The Lavalas movement decided in October to contest the elections rather than boycott them, with Aristide as their presidential candidate.[41] The U.S. sponsored Marc Bazin, a former World Bank employee with a platform based on privatization and regressive income redistribution. Aristide won 67 per cent of the vote in an election acclaimed as free and fair by UN, U.S. and Organization of American States (OAS) observers.[42] Bazin, his closest rival, won 14 per cent.

Aristide's election represented a major change in Haiti's historic pattern. For the first time, the population had at least partial control of some of the mechanisms of the state. This had not been the case during the mobilizations of 1946. The battle had only begun, however: the external powers were just as powerful as they always had been, the Haitian elite was as entrenched and intransigent, and most of the weakened state and military apparatus, including even the parliament, was corrupt or opposed outright to the aspirations of the population. Lavalas might have represented the majority, but against all these forces they had only a fledgling popular organization, or – more accurately – a coalition of diverse popular organizations, hard-pressed to do battle against such wealthy, powerful, organized and ruthless opponents.

THE FIRST COUP: 1991–94

Aristide's inauguration was scheduled for February 7, 1991. In January, the Duvalierist Tonton Macoute leader Lafontant seized the presidential palace, took President Trouillot hostage, and took over the broadcast facilities, anticipating support from the FADH. Lavalas mobilized on the streets and the FADH reversed the coup.[43] Aristide took power as scheduled and nominated René Préval, an agronomist associated with the popular movement in the countryside, as prime minister. When parliament attempted to pass a no-confidence measure against Préval in August, Lavalas mobilized again to protest.[44] Aristide began making moves to dismantle the army, to separate the police from the army, retire the leaders of the officer corps, and create a commission to investigate human rights violations.[45] The commission never began work because Aristide was overthrown in a coup on September 29, 1991. The FADH, seeing the threat to its existence, ousted the civilian government and initiated a three-year-long period of massacre under General Cedras, General Biamby, and Major Michel François (who became the national chief of police).

Shortly after the coup, an officer for the U.S. Defense Intelligence Agency, Col. Patrick Collins, approached a man named Emmanuel Constant and asked him to organize a front to balance Lavalas and do intelligence work against it on behalf of the FADH and the U.S. Constant went on the CIA payroll and formed the Front for the Advancement and Progress of Haiti (FRAPH).[46] As Aristide had moved against the armed groups, the FADH and FRAPH moved against the popular movement. Where Lavalas had tried to use legislation and, to a lesser extent, popular mobilization, the FADH and FRAPH used massacre, disappearance, torture, and rape against the movement. Over the next three years, the International Crisis Group (ICG), a major mainstream think-tank whose board includes former presidents from various countries, estimates that 3,000–5,000 were killed by the coup regime, 100,000 fled into exile, and 300,000 were forced into internal exile. When it caught Haitian refugees, Washington returned them to Haiti to face death and torture, using a 1981 agreement between the Reagan and Duvalier administrations as pretext, but violating international law.[47] Washington did, however, announce an arms, oil, and trade embargo under the auspices of the OAS, which it did not heed. Instead, it sent weapons to FRAPH via the Dominican Republic, including 5,000–10,000 pieces between 1993 and 1994.[48]

There was armed resistance to the regime. In the town of Gonaives, a Lavalas organizer named Amiot Metayer led a community group under constant attack by the FADH and FRAPH. FRAPH committed a major massacre against the group in the area of Raboteau in 1994, killing at least 15 people.[49] This was called the 'Raboteau Massacre', and would become important in Haiti's collective memory.

The coup was also devastating to Lavalas's basic economic programme, which sought to lift Haitians from 'absolute misery to poverty with dignity', and say 'goodbye to American Rice' – both to the company with the same name and to the dominance of imported American rice in Haiti's economy – as journalists John Canham-Clyne and Worth Cooley-Prost revealed in 1995.[50] The government signed import agreements with American Rice's subsidiary 'and soon began operating a rice receiving and bagging facility in a Port-au-Prince warehouse owned by one of Haiti's wealthiest families'.

Aristide, who was living in exile in the United States, faced an impossible dilemma. His movement was being massacred. He was being kept out. At the same time, the United States was offering him a chance to return, in exchange for demobilizing Lavalas and becoming, in effect, an agent of U.S. economic interests; a more efficient one than the generals and paramilitaries who provoked increasingly uncompromising resistance. Compromise was precisely what Washington sought from Aristide, and the only alternative they offered him was acquiescence in the ongoing slaughter. In June 1993, UN diplomat Dante Caputo brokered an agreement between Aristide and Cedras called the Governor's Island Accord. Aristide would name a new prime minister, the sanctions would be lifted, the army would be reformed, the coup-makers would be amnestied, and Aristide would be returned to power on October 30, 1993, with the help of a UN peacekeeping force.[51] October 30 came and went, and the massacres continued. The U.S. tried, unsuccessfully, to get Aristide to sign other plans, in which there would be an even more pervasive amnesty and in which Aristide would 'share power' with a U.S.-selected prime minister. Aristide refused. The military regime was having difficulty holding together without open and constant massacre, which led to increasingly large numbers of refugees and a political problem for the U.S. On September 18, 1994, the Americans sent former President Carter, Senator Sam Nunn, and a former Joint Chiefs of Staff chairman named Colin Powell to Haiti to negotiate Cedras's removal. Cedras agreed to leave on October 15, 1994.[52] As for Aristide, he signed away the right to prosecute many human rights violations; he signed away three years of his presidential term (agreeing that his term would end in February 1995, counting the coup years as if he had been president); he signed away his preference for prime minister, leftist Claudette Werleigh, in favour of neoliberal Smarck Michel.[53]

UNDERSTANDING ARISTIDE'S RETURN

Understanding Aristide's 1994 return as a simple capitulation is an oversimplification. Aristide's popular government made some terrible compromises, but it also had some genuine achievements. Some of the achievements of Aristide's post-1994 regime are easily quantified. Others are not. Respect and confidence and a degree of freedom from terror are all intangible, but expressed in one anecdote: 'A few days before the February 2004 coup, a foreign journalist asked a market woman in Cité Soleil (the largest and poorest neighbourhood in Port-au-Prince) what she thought of the situation in Haiti. She responded: "If it wasn't for Aristide you wouldn't be asking me for my opinion."'[54]

The U.S. certainly did not see Aristide as their agent. On the contrary, they began undermining him as soon as they had installed him. While Washington had turned away, detained, and shipped refugees fleeing the dictatorship to Guantanamo, from now until the 2004 coup those leaving the democratic regime were granted asylum. Among them was mass murderer and lead organizer of the paramilitary organization FRAPH, Emmanuel Constant. He was arrested by the Marines in September 1994, but failed to appear for his hearing two months later. He turned up in New York City on a valid tourist visa granted him by an 'immigration error'.[55]

Like Aristide's 1990 election, his return in 1994 marked another change in the nature of Haiti's conflict. As he had in 1991, Aristide moved quickly against the FADH, this time actually dissolving it in April 1995. But Aristide could no more destroy the FADH and FRAPH with their U.S. and Haitian elite sponsors than these forces were able to destroy Lavalas with its deep roots amongst Haiti's poor. While Aristide had the power to legislate the end of the FADH, the U.S. military was in charge of their disarmament and reintegration. Most of them stayed armed and melted into criminal gangs or private security firms. Others went to the Dominican Republic. Still others were recycled into the police force, some 200 of them moving directly from the FADH to the police.[56]

The Republican Party leadership – more comfortable than the Democrats were with openly supporting dictators – strongly opposed the U.S. intervention to restore Aristide. Seven weeks after the U.S. invasion in 1994, the GOP won control of Congress and soon dismantled the aid programme to Haiti after Aristide refused a massive privatization plan. Per capita aid to Haiti from the U.S. was one-fifth what it was spending in Bosnia and one-tenth what it spent in Kosovo.[57] The Democrats, however, still in control of the White House, were less crude than the Republicans, but still insisted that Aristide implement every detail of the savage programme of the IMF-WB structural adjustment. The newspaper *Haiti Progres* reported in 1995 on then-U.S. Vice President Al Gore's visit to Aristide; the threat was clear in Gore's words: 'We discussed the need for continuing international assistance to meet the developmental requirements of Haiti and the steps the government of Haiti and its people need to take in order to ensure the continued flow of these funds.'[58] Despite this tremendous pressure, Aristide tried to find ways to blunt the effect of foreign intervention and the destruction of the economy, delaying the privatization of the state-run flour and cement mills for two years and refusing to privatize the public utilities.[59] These moves were made against the will of Aristide's unpopular, neoliberal prime minister, Smarck Michel (1994–95),[60] who resigned, after which Claudette Werleigh, Aristide's first choice, was appointed prime minister.

Aristide made other positive changes against the current of foreign pressure. The minimum wage was increased, affecting 20,000 workers. A land reform gave land to 1,500 families (the land was returned to the absentee landlords after the 2004 coup). The government collected taxes from the wealthy (this was, no doubt, the source of at least some of the cries about government 'repression'). Through government intervention the prices of food were lowered (prices doubled after the coup). Malnutrition dropped. An emergency response system was built in collaboration with the Red Cross – a system that could have helped with the hurricanes that ravaged Haiti in October 2004 had it not been dismantled after the coup. Lavalas administrations built more schools between 1994 and 2000 than had been built between 1804 and 1994. School lunch programmes were expanded. 100,000 people were taught to read between 2001 and 2003. An AIDS treatment and prevention programme reduced HIV transmission significantly. In a genuine example of international solidarity, 800 Cuban health workers travelled to work in Haiti and 325 Haitian students went to study medicine in Cuba. With Cuban assistance, Aristide opened a new medical school in the Port-au-Prince suburb of Tabarre, offering free medical training to students from poor communities who agreed, upon graduation, to help fill the desperate need for doctors in Haiti's poor and rural neighbourhoods. (Immediately following the coup, the medical university was converted into a barracks for U.S. marines, and, under Latortue, it was used as a base for Brazilian soldiers. Under Préval after 2006, the building was returned to the Aristide foundation, survived the earthquake, and was used to house earthquake survivors.) The investment in health lowered infant mortality. The Haitian Constitution was printed in Creole and widely distributed. Haiti signed on to the International Criminal Court (the U.S. still has not).[61]

STRUGGLES OVER THE POLICE AND LEGISLATURE

In 1995, having dismantled the FADH, Aristide created a truth commission that issued its 1,200-page report in 1996, recommending reparations and rehabilitation for victims of repression and documenting violations committed under the 1991–94 dictatorship. Unfortunately, the report lacked impact, since it was not made widely available in Creole.[62] The justice system was developed to try to undermine the impunity of the 1991–94 dictatorship era while respecting the rights of the accused.[63] The framework for the Haitian National Police (Police National Haitienne, PNH) was outlined in a Presidential Decree in 1994, when Aristide returned to Haiti with the U.S. invasion. The PNH was made responsible for the coast guard and customs. Now that the FADH was disbanded, the PNH became a battleground between the popular movement's government and the U.S., Haitian elite, and FADH/FRAPH forces. The U.S., with help from countries like Canada, established police training programmes to 'professionalize' the PNH.[64] These programmes were probably as much a source of corruption as they were of professionalization.[65] The U.S. military in Haiti initiated a programme to disarm the FADH and FRAPH, and actually seized several thousand weapons in 1994–95. While the U.S. destroyed 12 per cent of these, the rest were handed over to the PNH. Among the most perverse of the U.S. disarmament programmes was a 'buy-back' operation in which the U.S. collected weapons, paid for them (some $2 million in total), handed them over to the PNH, which then turned them back over to criminals and paramilitaries for further recycling.[66]

In this tug-of-war, the Lavalas government tried to turn the police into a force loyal to it, while the U.S. and FADH/FRAPH tried to turn it into their instrument. The tug-of-war was exemplified with the career of Dany Toussaint, a Major in the FADH under Baby Doc, once exiled by him for refusing to carry out political killings, who was in the palace during the 1991 coup against Aristide and went into exile with him, where he received FBI training in the U.S. Upon their return in 1994, Toussaint became the head of the 'interim police'.[67] Perhaps accepted in this post by Aristide because of loyalty, Toussaint began angling for power himself. After the 'interim police' were replaced by the PNH, Toussaint was ousted and took the job as Lavalas security chief. He organized 'pro-government' armed groups that used terror against the opposition, helped Haiti become a gateway for narcotrafficking, and used police corruption to amass a personal fortune. He openly ran a showroom where he sold badges, handcuffs, and other military equipment.[68]

If Toussaint was an example of a leader of the 'pro-government' armed groups, on the other side, the FADH/FRAPH and U.S. were also organizing armed groups inside and outside the PNH. It was also slowly and inexorably choking the regime of needed financing. By 1996, when Aristide's first term ended, U.S. aid to Haiti was equal to the amount it had provided to the dictatorship that had deposed Aristide. Such aid as did flow went to finance the opposition by reallocating federal funds to Haitian NGOs opposed to Aristide.[69]

A contest for the legislature occurred parallel to the struggle over the PNH. In local elections in June 1995, the pro-Aristide coalition led by the Lavalas Popular Organization (OPL) made significant gains. The OPL took neoliberal stances on many issues, however, and Aristide's supporters broke from the OPL to create the Fanmi Lavalas (FL) in 1996. The FL ran against the OPL in legislative elections in 1997, and the results were not recognized by the OPL, which accused the FL of fraud. This froze parliament and legislative initiatives until 1999. President Préval dismissed those legislators whose terms had expired and organized a new FL cabinet.[70]

FANMI LAVALAS WINS – AND THE DISPUTED SENATE SEATS

It was an impasse. For Fanmi Lavalas, it could be resolved with new elections, planned for May 2000, in which they would, with their popularity, decisively win and finally take control of the legislature. The opposition thus tried – ultimately unsuccessfully – to delay the elections. The plan for delay was exposed, and denounced, by an independent Haitian radio journalist, Jean Dominique, who had tremendous influence and prestige in the popular neighbourhoods. Armed men assassinated Jean Dominique in April 2000. Dany Toussaint, who went on to win a senate seat in the May elections, and who had been close to Aristide before joining the opposition, was suspected of the murder.[71] As a senator, Toussaint was immune from prosecution. He took to entering the Senate with a heavily armed entourage.

In the long-delayed May 2000 legislative and local elections, the Fanmi Lavalas won decisively. The traditional parties had already been thoroughly defeated electorally, but the 2000 elections also wiped out the OPL as Fanmi Lavalas (henceforth Lavalas) winning 89 of 115 mayoral positions, 72 of 83 seats in the legislature and 18 of the 19 Senate seats.

At this point the attack on Lavalas became more intense. The 'Convergence Démocratique', an anti-Lavalas coalition, was formed. The goal was simple: annulment of the elections and refusal to allow Aristide to participate in any future elections. The first step was to discredit the elections, and in this the Convergence was helped by the OAS, who objected to the methodology that the Provisional Electoral Council used to count the votes for eight of the seats in the Senate. The method was to count only the votes cast for the top four candidates in each Senate race. But the Lavalas senators would have won regardless of the method used. Participation was 60 per cent of the registered electorate of 4 million. Lavalas senate candidates received an average 74 per cent of the votes cast.[72]

The European Community responded to this technical dispute over counting methodology by cutting aid to Haiti in 2000. The U.S. began an outright aid embargo on Haiti in that same year, as the Republicans exploited Haiti's 'electoral controversy' as an opportunity to discredit Aristide, who had won a landslide victory in the November 2000 elections with 92 per cent of the votes cast on a turnout of 50 per cent of the adult population. The Bush Administration[73] pressured the Inter-American Development Bank (IDB) to cancel more than $650 million in development assistance and approved loans to Haiti – money that was slated to pay for safe drinking water, literacy programmes and health services, and had serious economic consequences. An IDB report in 2001 stated that 'the major factor behind economic stagnation is the withholding of both foreign grants and loans'.[74]

The 'dispute' over the election was that eight Lavalas senators had won and claimed their senate seats after getting the most votes. The opposition disagreed with the method of vote counting and disputed the elections because there was no runoff vote. The OAS and the U.S. took up the opposition call, though they had expressed no concerns with the electoral mechanisms – known well in advance – before the elections. At any rate, seven of the eight senators resigned in 2001 and the eighth was out shortly after that. The aid freeze continued, further evidence that the dispute over the senators was merely a pretext. The State Department, via the OAS, claimed the aid freeze was a decision of the international community in a declaration on April 22, 2001. There is a letter from the U.S. representative to the IDB asking the loans not be disbursed, dated April 8, 2001. The cancellation of the funds by U.S. order was in violation of the IDB's charter, which states: 'The President, officers, and staff owe their duty entirely to the Bank and shall recognize no other authority. Each member of the Bank shall respect the international character of his duty.'[75]

Despite the cancellations, the IDB demanded repayment, of both old and new loans, to the tune of $1.134 billion, 40 per cent of which was lent to the Duvalier dictators and had gone directly to their personal coffers. This 'odious debt' should not, under international law, have to have been repaid. In July 2003, Haiti sent more than 90 per cent of its foreign reserves to Washington to pay interest on this illegal, odious debt.[76] Haitians were actually paying interest on loans the previous dictatorship had taken out, as well as payments on loans that Washington had blocked them from receiving.

ASSESSING ARISTIDE IN POWER

Some on the Haitian left argued at the time that Aristide had become an agent of neoliberalism.[77] In this argument, what modest gains Lavalas was able to achieve between 1994 and 2004 were a sop, a way of using Aristide's prestige to demobilize the Haitian mass movement, which had overthrown the Duvalier dictatorship, and would have overthrown the paramilitary dictatorship that ruled between 1991 and 1994 as well, had the U.S. not intervened to restore Aristide, the person whose removal they had supported in the first place. The changes to the justice system, the partial privatizations, and the creation of a police force to replace the Haitian military – these were strategies for containing the popular movement. Among those who made this argument were some foreign and Haitian diaspora figures like René Depestre, James Morell, and Christophe Wargny. There were also the peasant groups Tet Kole Ti Peyizan, KOZEPEP, Batay Ouvriye, PAPDA (Haitian Platform for Alternative Development), led by Camille Chalmers, and the MPP (Papaye Peasant Movement), headed by Chavannes Jean-Baptiste.[78] Many of these leaders were later to collaborate with the coup, supporting a cure that was infinitely worse than the disease.

Aristide's options, given the international forces arrayed against him, were very limited. He had disbanded the hated army, but the mass of its soldiers remained at large, with a command centre just across the border in the Dominican Republic and with ample supplies and support from the United States. Meanwhile, problems of social crime and violence – the crime and violence associated with unequal societies[79] – were still present, and Aristide's government, having disbanded the army, had only the inherited and corrupt state apparatus to address such problems. A U.S. embargo meant that the Haitian police lacked the basic equipment, like riot gear, that police forces count on in such situations. Under such circumstances a popular government has to simultaneously try to reform the government apparatus and use the parallel institutions of popular organization to try to overcome difficulties and solve social problems. In Venezuela, Hugo Chávez's government accomplished this by using substantial revenues from petroleum and using the military, which remained loyal, to compensate for the corrupt and uncooperative bureaucracy when necessary. In Haiti, Aristide had neither a resource base nor the military on his side.

In this context, the charges that Aristide tolerated corruption, armed gangs of his supporters, and engaged in financial irregularities can all be understood. A corrupt and incapacitated bureaucracy, a holdover from the dictatorship, could not be tackled directly since the government had neither the means to do so nor the capacity to replace the bureaucracy. Such capacity, for Haiti, could only have come from external aid (whether through reparations or some other mechanism), which was forbidden to Aristide's government. Popular organizations in the poor neighbourhoods, if they supported the government, were likely to come under paramilitary attack, and it should come as no surprise that they would arm themselves for self-defence. As for financing, in the context of an aid embargo closing official channels for finance, a government's turn to unofficial channels to procure fundamental items (such as weapons for the police) becomes understandable. The extent to which Aristide was involved in any of these activities is unclear, and in fact the utter lack of evidence, given the intensity of the search for it by Aristide's opponents, suggests that he was not.

Peter Hallward, reviewing the human rights records of the various dictatorships and comparing them with Aristide's record, found the following:

> Remember the basic numbers: perhaps 50,000 dead under the Duvaliers (1957–86), perhaps 700 to 1,000 dead under Namphy/Avril (1986–90), 4,000 dead under Cedras (1991–94) and then at least another 3,000 killed under Latortue (2004–06). And under Aristide? What sort of numbers might warrant claims of 'continuity' or even 'deterioration'?
>
> [...]
>
> But if reports from Amnesty International can be trusted – and it's telling that as far as I know neither AI nor any human rights organization has yet risked an estimate of the total numbers of people killed under Aristide – then from 2001 to 2004 perhaps thirty political killings can be attributed to the PNH (whose political affiliation was often anti-government) or to groups with (often tenuous) links to FL. Less or differently biased analysts like Ronald Saint-Jean, Kim Ives and Laura Flynn put the real total closer to 10.[80]

Looking at Haiti's history from the perspective of sovereignty reveals how it came to pass that today's Haiti has very little control over its own economic or political affairs. The Haitian revolution that liberated the slaves was a part of a longer, global, and still unfulfilled, struggle for democracy, a state of affairs in which people control their own lives. Haitians have contributed and sacrificed much in this struggle. The struggle is not over, but Haiti's new dictatorship, established in 2004, is a setback.

2 NARRATIVES, MEDIA STRATEGIES, AND NGO STORIES

foolnote

THE U.S., THE UN, THE DONOR COMMUNITY, AND HAITI

Haiti has been called the Republic of NGOs. Second only to India in the number of NGOs operating there per capita, it is probably second to none in foreign-based NGOs, since many of the Indian NGOs are domestic. There are 10,000–20,000 NGOs in Haiti and they provide 80 per cent of basic public services. They are independent, fragmented, and in many ways undercut integrated government programmes. They are also often controlled or funded by wealthy governments, through the U.S.'s USAID and Canada's CIDA. This makes them less non-governmental and more 'other-governmental', offering wealthy countries 'a morally respectable way of subcontracting the sovereignty of the nations they exploit'.[2]

Paul Farmer, a long-time friend of Haiti and sharp analyst of foreign interference,[3] argues eloquently in his 2011 book *Haiti After the Earthquake* that aid should be disbursed in a way that helps the public sector. As a physician and a public health advocate, he argues this for two reasons. The government is the only organization against which ordinary citizens can make rights-based claims: no non-governmental organization has a legal obligation to help anyone in particular, whereas a government has obligations to its citizens. Similarly, a democratic government is (or should be) accountable to its citizens, and not to donors, shareholders, or financiers.

Some of the problems Haiti experiences as a result of having its economy and politics run by NGOs are painfully described in U.S. anthropologist Timothy Schwartz's 2010 book *Travesty in Haiti*.[4] Schwartz describes in detail how U.S. food aid destroys local production capacity, how NGO employees understand this, but how they agree quietly to suppress these basic facts because their employment depends on the food aid continuing.[5] An insider account is not necessary, however, since Special Envoy Bill Clinton admitted the destructive role of U.S. agricultural imports on Haitian production shortly after the earthquake:

> Since 1981, the United States has followed a policy, until the last year or so when we started rethinking it, that we rich countries that produce a lot of food should sell it to poor countries and relieve them of the burden of producing their own food, so, thank goodness, they can leap directly into the industrial era. It has not worked. It may have been good for some of my farmers in Arkansas, but it has not worked. It was a mistake. It was a mistake that I was a party to. I am not pointing the finger at anybody. I did that. I have to live every day with the consequences of the lost capacity to produce a rice crop in Haiti to feed those people, because of what I did. Nobody else.[6]

In summary: Haiti's public services are provided by unaccountable NGOs and not the public sector of a democratically accountable government. Its people depend for survival on food not from the local economy, but from foreign-controlled aid programmes. The same situation applies in health, education, manufacturing, and virtually every other sector. Where services are not aid-controlled, they are controlled by private, for-profit businesses. Private health clinics mean the majority is priced out of quality care. Private schools drain a large portion of poor family budgets.[7]

In the sphere of armed forces, the situation is no different. Aristide abolished the Army in 1995, when the contest for the loyalty of the Haitian National Police began in earnest. After the 2004 coup, the United Nations Stabilization Mission (MINUSTAH) provided the ultimate armed force in the country, while the U.S., Canada, and France exercise important influence over the Haitian Police through a variety of training programmes connected to MINUSTAH's police tutelage arm, UNPOL. Private security firms and their armed agents have proliferated throughout the country. Democratic accountability over police and military forces is very rare, even in powerful countries that have meaningful sovereignty like the U.S. or Canada. If the Haitian Army is reconstituted, as some Haitian politicians have talked about since the election of Martelly,[8] it will likely be as an agent of the new dictatorship, rather than a sovereign instrument. Army

It would be understandable to think that the Republic of NGOs, or what is called here Haiti's new dictatorship, arose from the international community's scramble to respond to the 2010 earthquake. This would be incorrect. The specific form of Haiti's new dictatorship was prepared during the Aristide's second administration, starting in 2000. It was imposed in 2004, and consolidated after the 2010 quake, using a set of political strategies that have been used with varying success elsewhere in the Americas – notably in Venezuela in 2002 (unsuccessfully) and in Honduras in 2009 (successfully).[9]

These political strategies played out in media reporting and depictions, in which NGOs played a very prominent role. What is here presented as a popular movement struggling against foreign-imposed constraints on Haiti's sovereignty was presented in most media outlets as yet another dictator falling because of his own corruption and unpopularity. These depictions had severe political consequences for Haiti's popular movement and its friends outside of Haiti. For this reason, I will describe and try to answer some of these depictions in detail before proceeding with the narrative.

THE CLASH OF NARRATIVES

Sufficient time has passed since the 2004 coup for several book-length accounts to have appeared. These approach the coup from very different perspectives.

Shortly after the 2004 coup, accounts appeared making a very detailed case against Aristide, including accusations from arming gangs to killing babies. Michael Deibert's *Notes from the Last Testament* (2005, Seven Stories Press, New York), which I have reviewed elsewhere,[10] is a book-length argument justifying the coup. Whatever evidence there was to be had against Aristide and Lavalas, Deibert gathered. The book could have been a dossier for the prosecution of the court cases against Aristide and Lavalas government members and activists. Since the book was published, actual court cases occurred and, as we shall see, the charges were dropped for lack of evidence. The factual basis underlying Deibert's argument has collapsed. This could have been predicted from a review of his biased sourcing, unverifiable claims, and low standards of evidence – indeed, I did predict it in my review. But the accusations did not have to hold up in order to fulfill their purpose. Timing is also important. Deibert's book came shortly after the coup, with a left-wing publisher (Seven Stories Press) and confused many people about Haiti and Aristide, people who might have otherwise understood what was going on. In the first year or two after the coup, a reversal might have brought Aristide, and constitutional government, back. Now that moment has passed. Factual errors and omissions can now be corrected without any political consequence. As with books, so with the news media, to which we will return.

More recently, books like Philippe Girard's *Haiti: The Tumultuous History* (2010, Palgrave Macmillan, New York) simply assume all the allegations are true, and treat Aristide and the Duvaliers together. Girard argues that Aristide's attempts to return and the possibility that he might again become president is 'a testament to the ingenuity of Haiti's rulers when it comes to preserving their own rule'.[11] Given that Aristide was overthrown twice and served about six years out of the ten for which he was elected (three years each of two five-year terms), he might be credited with many things, but surely not with ingenuity in preserving his own rule.

Alex Dupuy, who wrote an excellent book on neoliberalism in Haiti years ago,[12] makes a more nuanced case against Aristide in his *The Prophet and Power* (2007, Rowman & Littlefield, New York), as documented by Peter Hallward's review.[13] Hallward's review identifies three criticisms of Aristide in Dupuy's book: that he wasn't conciliatory enough towards his opponents, that he failed to enact real reforms, and that he armed gangs who violated human rights. The second criticism contradicts the first: in seeking real reforms that would benefit the poor, Aristide would be alienating his opponents who were implacably against such reforms, and conciliation with them would involve backing off of needed changes. The third charge, that Aristide armed gangs who violated human rights, was a serious one, requiring serious evidence that is lacking in Dupuy's book, as in Deibert's book and the news reports. Another Haitian scholar, Robert Fatton, makes similar arguments against Aristide in his 2007 book *The Roots of Haitian Despotism*, accusing him of arming gangs, resisting concessions, and corruption, but also of following neoliberal scriptures and doing little to change the inherited authoritarian tradition.[14] These Haitian scholars are also critics of the post-Aristide governments from 2004 on, and I will return to their critiques below.

Not all writers endorse the view that Lavalas in power was no different from the dictatorships that preceded or followed. Some share my view that recent history is better viewed as a history of a popular movement (Lavalas) struggling for democracy and sovereignty against internal and external opponents. Peter Hallward's *Damming the Flood* shows how Aristide's government was destabilized and overthrown through a combination of economic pressure, paramilitary violence, co-optation of civil society organizations, and media disinformation campaigns. Under Lavalas, corruption existed, for example, but it was not built into the structure of government the way it had been under previous or subsequent dictatorships. Likewise human rights violations occurred, but in the pattern you would expect in a poor and highly unequal democracy, not the systematic campaigns of murder and massacre seen in Haiti's dictatorships. Randall Robinson's *An Unbroken Agony* (2007, Basic Civitas Books, New York) is an insider account from a personal friend of Aristide, whose wife, Hazel, worked as a consultant for Aristide's government. To Robinson, Aristide is a saint, as angelic as he is demonic to Deibert. His book offers detailed information on the kidnapping of Aristide from an insider, and can provide some balance against the pro-coup arguments. All accounts have biases. I associate with Hallward and Robinson and disagree with the pro-coup accounts.

MEDIA STRATEGIES

Books play an important role in how events are remembered. While events are ongoing, print, online, and broadcast media coverage can change the course of politics, helping or hurting popular aspirations. Media played an important role in imposing Haiti's new dictatorship, and continue to play a role in upholding it.

Years have passed since the 2004 coup, and the details of its media strategy seem less important than they did in the early days and months when there was a chance of reversing the coup. The strategy included the creation of staged 'incidents', which were used to accuse the government of violations of human rights. Evidence of crimes was scarce, but by the time the first case collapsed, a new accusation had sprung up. Years later, most of these incidents would be disproven, but the damage to the government had been done.

Independent researcher Isabel Macdonald wrote a master's thesis at York University called 'Covering the Coup' outlining media strategies used by the coupster forces and how they played out in the Canadian media, specifically the *Globe and Mail* (Canada's newspaper of record) between January 1, 2003 and March 17, 2004 – during the most intense period of the coup.

Macdonald divided coverage of the coup into two 'frames': the official frame and the critical alternative frame. The frames diverge on six key issues: 1) the 2000 elections; 2) the cause of the 2004 political crisis; 3) the events of February 29, 2004; 4) Aristide's claim to have been kidnapped; 5) Aristide's level of popular support; 6) Aristide's supporters. On each of these issues, the *G & M* overwhelmingly published the official frame. For example, according to Macdonald's counts, the *G & M* published:

1) 18 articles suggesting that the 2000 elections were flawed or illegitimate, 3 that the election was legitimate
2) 8 articles suggesting the cause of the political crisis was Aristide and 2 that it was U.S. policy and opposition intransigence
3) 20 articles suggesting that February 29, 2004 was a resignation or departure, and 1 suggesting it was a kidnapping or coup
4) 11 articles dismissing Aristide's claim to have been kidnapped, 1 suggesting it was valid
5) 6 articles dismissing Aristide's popular support, 0 articles suggesting he had support
6) 34 articles suggesting Aristide's supporters were dangerous and violent, 0 suggesting Aristide's supporters were the majority of the Haitian population.

Macdonald compared how the *Globe and Mail* and *National Post* covered political violence under Aristide and under Latortue/ MINUSTAH governance between January 1, 2003 and April 1, 2004. She compared this coverage on 5 key bases: 1) the quantity of coverage; 2) the status accorded to allegations of government-backed repression; 3) the status accorded to the governments' refutations of allegations; 4) the standards used in the attribution of blame; 5) the quantity of coverage of protests by government critics.

Here, she found that articles in the *G & M* blamed Aristide for violence that occurred under his rule in 17 per cent of cases, and Latortue in 1 per cent of cases. Indeed, 16 per cent of *G & M* articles during Aristide's rule mention government-backed repression, but only 3 per cent of articles during Latortue's rule. She found much the same in the *National Post*.[15]

Official frame spokespeople were cited 111 times in the *G & M* in this period, alternative frame supporters 51 times.

All this proves the perhaps unsurprising conclusion that the *G & M* was not even-handed in its treatment of Aristide and his critics.

Similar studies of other major North American media (*New York Times*, *Miami Herald*, *Washington Post*) in this period, like Jeb Sprague's study published by Fairness and Accuracy in Reporting (FAIR) July/August 2006,[16] find nothing different. If the alternative frame lacks factual merit compared to the official frame, then the media is doing its job. If, instead, the alternative frame has the balance of evidence in its favour, the media is presenting a biased and inaccurate version of events. Macdonald next asks how that came to pass, and analyzes the strategies of the pro-coup forces in disseminating information to the media. Of the 111 citations of official frame sources, 69 of them were non-official critics of Aristide. How were they so effective in getting their perspective into the *G & M*?

First, the owners of Haiti's private media were, by and large, opponents of Aristide. They had access to Haiti's airwaves – and international media would often follow their lead. The National Association of Haitian Media (ANMH) was formally a member of the anti-Aristide opposition. In interviews, they told Macdonald how they used their media as part of the campaign against the government – inflating numbers at demonstrations, providing a constant platform for their messages, mobilizing demonstrations, and repeating accusations of corruption and human rights violations.

Through exchange programmes, ANMH journalists and sources were trained by U.S. and Canadian institutions (NED, IRI, CIDA) on how to influence the international media. They also belonged to the same social circuit, stayed at the same hotels, and spoke the same language as international journalists – advantages that Aristide's supporters disproportionately lacked. To escape from this kind of infrastructure is a real challenge for a Western journalist, and most of them did not do it.

In the narrative, more details will emerge elaborating on the systemic explanation for why media coverage (and related books) in the official frame came out the way they did. But perhaps the alternative frame could be explained the same way? Indeed, Aristide's government spent several million dollars in legal and lobbying fees in the U.S. over several years. This money went to lawyers and consultants who made pro-Aristide arguments, some of whom are among Aristide's most articulate defenders (Ira Kurzban, Aristide's attorney, and Randall Robinson, whose wife, Hazel, was a consultant for the Haitian government under Aristide). But most of the independent investigators who worked on Haiti in this period were not paid – they weren't even salaried journalists like the official frame journalists – but volunteers with other jobs. And neither the money flows from USAID and the IRI nor the fact that Aristide's government paid legal fees for legal work change any of the facts about human rights violations or corruption – facts to which we will turn in the narrative.

Unpublished research on Canadian media coverage by Daniel Freeman-Maloy for the two years after the coup reveals similar patterns. Freeman-Maloy looked at the 300 articles published by the *G & M* in Haiti between 2004 and 2005.

First of all, he notes that many of the facts on which the alternative frame rely are reported in the *G & M* in this period. The *G & M* reported:

- That Canada helped block the crucial IDB loan of $146 million that sealed Aristide's economic fate;
- That Canada's Foreign Affairs Minister met with paramilitary leader Paul Arcelin;
- That Canada participated in a military intervention on February 29, 2004;
- That Canada immediately recognized the Latortue government, helping entrench the coup;
- That Lavalas had won every electoral contest and enjoyed massive popular support.

G & M reported all this from within the official frame, even while repeating allegations of fraud and corruption against Aristide without evidence.

Freeman-Maloy notes especially the timing of the admissions and concessions. Discussing Paul Knox, the *G & M*'s star reporter in the field during the coup, Freeman-Maloy writes:

> Some final comments are in order about Paul Knox, and his gestures of feigned dissent. On March 10 2004, Knox did finally break his silence on the U.S. history of attacking Lavalas. 'The United States,' he explained, 'has much to answer for in its conduct toward Haiti over the past two decades. It allowed Mr. Aristide to be overthrown in 1991 after winning a landslide election, and its agents were linked to organizers of death squads in the next few years. It restored him to power not out of principle but to stem an exodus of boat people. It refuses to extradite death-squad leader Emmanuel (Toto) Constant.'[17]

With these passing admissions (revealing facts directly undercutting the framework he had provided for readers following Haitian politics in preceding weeks), Knox established some limited plausible deniability on his conspicuous silence. As for why he had failed to mention this information in the previous 30 articles he had written on Haiti in the preceding period of that year, he left that unexplored.

The *G & M*'s coverage is similar to the media's strategy in general: inconvenient facts can be mentioned, but better to mention them once it is too late for them to have any effect (after the coup, for example, or when many of those unjustly jailed have been shattered in jail and their followers massacred on the streets). The official frame is most valuable when the coup is in progress, or being consolidated. Once it is too late to reverse the coup, the record can be corrected and 'balance' restored. Take Freeman-Maloy's final comments on Knox:

> Knox's last piece on Haiti in *The Globe* hammered away at the same theme: Things had gone wrong, but only because we were not helpful enough – 'We should have done more to save Haiti from rebellion,' the title read. It opened with a rhetorical question: 'Realistically, could Canada have done anything on its own to prevent the triumph of armed rebellion in Haiti and the overthrow of president Jean-Bertrand Aristide?' Some possible ways aren't hard to think of. It could have refused to back U.S.-led economic destabilization, decided to not deploy forces to help to oust the government, or even supported the diplomatic position of Caricom. But, Knox replied to himself, 'I think the answer is probably no. It pains me to say so, because as readers know, I believe the actions of the Canadian government and others over the past few weeks made a mockery of their solemn pronouncements on democratic rule in the Americas.' A gesture of feigned dissent, conveniently compatible with the Martin government's pledge of 'non-abandonment,' and Knox was off.

Shameful as they are, these patterns point to an important fact: the media were, and are, a part of the coup infrastructure. Because they helped shape people's beliefs about what was unfolding, they helped influence how people acted. By favouring the official frame, they helped ensure the victory of the coup, and the imposition of the new dictatorship, both on the ground and in people's minds.

THE NGO STRATEGY

Haiti's new dictatorship also has a special governance structure, in which many of the functions that are normally performed by government are done by non-governmental organizations (NGOs). Their participation in the coup and in the current dictatorship is worth exploring in some detail.

In Haiti, U.S.- and Canadian-funded NGOs made and repeated false claims about the Aristide government's human rights violations during the coup. These NGOs provided ideal sources for the Western media campaigns and pretexts for military intervention against Aristide's government. There are numerous examples.

The story of a 'Massacre' in La Scerie, in February 2004, was propagated by the National Council for Haitian Rights (NCHR), funded by Canada's CIDA. This story was picked up by other NGOs, like PAPDA, the opposition Group 184, the international media, and finally in books like Deibert's. The story didn't hold up to scrutiny and all of it was eventually dropped – but not before it served its purpose and got several Lavalas leaders in jail for years.

Batay Ouvriye, a worker's organization, was funded by the AFL-CIO Solidarity Center,[18] and accused Lavalas of being corrupt and of capitulating to neoliberalism. No different from those who replaced it, Lavalas's fall from power was no loss to the Haitian people, Batay Ouvriye said.[19]

The IRI provided political training for Haitian opposition leaders in 2002, and urged them not to compromise.[20] The IRI also funded Reporters Without Borders, which gave vastly disproportionate coverage to violations against anti-Aristide journalists while ignoring much worse and more frequent violations against other journalists.[21] The NED, IRI, and USAID funded and organized the anti-Lavalas movement for participation in elections after the coup as well.[22]

Foreign funding is not a guarantee of compromised politics. Nor is independence a guarantee of adoption of the alternative frame. Even independent, membership-based NGOs like Amnesty International had failings on Haiti (although these were not so systematic as the funded government-bound NGOs. See Joe Emersberger's work for an assessment of Amnesty's mixed record in Haiti since the coup).[23]

This raises the point about what it means to help Haiti. Do these NGOs help Haiti? From their perspective, they helped to denounce and remove a government committing human rights violations and corruption. From my perspective, they helped deliver Haiti into a regime that commits much greater human rights violations and corruption.

The new dictatorship features NGOs very prominently in the delivery of what could be government services. To a cynical observer, it would appear that NGOs had an interest in ousting the democratic government and replacing it with one where they play a primary role in governance. But on democratic or efficiency grounds, should those providing services be accountable to their own government, and ultimately to their own people, through some democratic process, which seems to be good enough for countries like Canada (admittedly less and less so in the West as well, as governments increasingly subcontract public services to NGOs and businesses)? Or should they be beholden to other governments who fund them? The distance and unaccountability of foreign-funded NGOs to Haitians leads to distortions that would not be present if the services were provided by a democratic government, as we will see when we discuss Haiti after the earthquake.

It also leads to questions that would never be asked in a sovereign, democratic context. An important book about aid to Haiti[24] asks how much good all the aid dollars have done, stating that Haiti received $4 billion in foreign assistance from 1990 to 2003. This may seem a vast sum, but a few quick calculations suggest otherwise. At the time, Haiti's population was around 8 million. The entire donation amounts to $500 per capita. The period in question is 13 years. That's $38 per Haitian per year, much of which probably went to supporting the 1991–94 dictatorship and supporting the democratic regime's opponents in the years since, to economic programmes to benefit corporations, and to aid dollars that flow back to the donor countries.[25] Later, the same book states that 'between 1998 and 2007, Haiti received about $3.5 billion in foreign assistance … but had little to show for it'. Again, this amounts to $49 per Haitian per year at the most (assuming 8 million Haitians, when there were closer to 9 million Haitians in 2007), much of which probably went to UN soldiers and other dictatorship priorities from 2004 to 2007. The per capita government spending for Western countries is in the thousands, not the tens, of dollars.

These paltry amounts of foreign aid come with very fuzzy

thinking about development economics and the need for an export-oriented, private property-based economic model.

An economy dependent on subsistence-level foreign aid cannot make the investments necessary to develop, especially while constrained by an ideology that states that services are better delivered by NGOs and that governments should stay out of economic affairs. Robert Fatton has argued that this economic model has been disastrous for Haiti: 'To advocate the withdrawal of the state and the supremacy of the market in a country like Haiti is to invite economic, political and social disaster. Such a withdrawal seeks to expose an already devastated society to the harsh rule of unregulated markets, rather than protecting it from further social ravages.'[26]

Beyond the argument about the government's proper role in economic affairs, the point here is that Haitians have never had the power to decide on their development, and so cannot yet be blamed for development failures. When Haiti's development is controlled by a sovereign and democratic government, such blame can be usefully assigned.

My argument can be summarized as follows: there are two conflicting stories about Haitian politics in recent years. One is a story of a leader becoming a dictator and getting overthrown, leaving a basket-case country in a basket-case condition. The second is the story of a popular movement being thwarted in its struggle for democracy and development and ending with a new dictatorship imposed upon it. I have tried to explain who tells each of these stories and why, and to argue for why I believe the second story is the truer one. But perhaps the best way to make this argument is to get on and tell the second story. The narrative resumes with the Aristide government in power for the second time, in 2000, as its opponents prepare for the 2004 coup.

3 THE COUP BEGINS: 2000–04

There were thus, at the beginning of 2004, a number of different factors that made Aristide's government vulnerable. Economically debilitated, the government had little means to deliver its popular programmes. Disbanding the hated military, an instrument of coups and external intervention, did not provide the government with adequate means of defence against paramilitary and external aggression – the U.S.- and Canadian-trained police forces were certainly not created with that end in mind. Politically and organizationally, the government was weakened by trying to hold the empty middle ground between its popular base and the depraved demands of the 'international community'. The wheels of the coup machine had been set in motion years before, and sped up rapidly leading up to 2004.

EARLY COUP ATTEMPTS

In 2000, after the May parliamentary and local elections but before the November presidential elections, Andre Apaid, the Haitian-American leader of the opposition, called Aristide and warned him not to hold the presidential elections until the opposition could prepare a candidate. 'If you hold elections now, you will mortgage the country,' he warned him. Asked later why he thought he could dictate the timing of the election, Apaid replied that he was exercising his democratic right.[1] Apaid owns 15 factories in Haiti, including many garment factories (they could also be called 'sweatshops', since union organizing is violently suppressed on the properties) and was the principal opponent of Aristide's attempt to raise the minimum wage above $1.60 a day.[2]

In February 2001 leaders of the anti-Aristide opposition organization Convergence Démocratique (CD) told the *Washington Post* of their hope for another American invasion, 'this time to get rid of Aristide and rebuild the disbanded Haitian Army', or else 'the CIA should train and equip Haitian officers exiled in the neighbouring Dominican Republic so they could stage a comeback themselves'.[3] While the CD held talks with Aristide's government, the paramilitary insurgency was beginning. On July 28, 2001, these paramilitaries attacked police stations and killed five officers on the Dominican border, taking a cache of small arms with them.[4] When the government arrested 35 suspects, including CD supporters, the CD broke off talks with Lavalas.

The pattern of talk, paramilitary attack, and breaking off of talks by the opposition repeated itself in an assault on the Presidential Palace on December 17, 2001. One of those who participated in the attack, an ex-FADH Sgt Pierre Richardson, was captured on December 20 trying to escape to the Dominican Republic. He told police and the press that former Col. Guy François (arrested the day before on December 19), as well as Guy Philippe (a former police chief of Cap Haitien) and Jean-Jacques Nau (a former police chief of the Delmas neighbourhood of Port-au-Prince), were involved in planning the failed coup d'etat from the Dominican Republic. For his part, Guy Philippe had been shuttling back and forth from the Dominican Republic to Ecuador – in the Dominican Republic in October 2000, back in the Dominican Republic two weeks before the December 17, 2000 coup attempt, and back to Ecuador immediately after the attack. The Haitian government sought his extradition, but did not get him.[5] The CD claimed the attack had been staged, and 'pro-government' groups burned down some CD homes and offices.

From January 31 to February 1, 2003, a group of high-level diplomats from the Americas and France gathered in Ottawa, convoked by Canada's Secretary of State for Latin America, Africa, and the countries of the Francophonie, or French-speaking world, Denis Paradis, to plan regime change in Haiti.[6] It was to be justified with a new Canadian doctrine, the 'responsibility to protect' (R2P), which gives strong countries license to intervene in weak countries. R2P doctrine was developed as an argument that national sovereignty should not be allowed to trump human rights. If Iraq's government was violating the rights of its own people, for example, other countries ought to be able to intervene to protect them. Similarly, if Aristide's government was violating human rights, the international community should be able to disregard Haiti's sovereignty in the interests of Haiti's people. In practice, R2P is inconsistently applied. Instead of intervening in countries where human rights are being most grievously violated, powerful countries apply their own criteria – those of regional control – when deciding where and why to intervene. The human rights violations of allied governments are ignored. R2P offered a pretext for overthrowing an elected government in Haiti and replacing it with an internationally constituted dictatorship.

Another phrase for 'responsibility to protect' was presented by Rudyard Kipling in the nineteenth century, and is called 'White Man's Burden' – the notion that some peoples cannot govern themselves and need to be controlled externally for their own good. One of the diplomats present at the meeting, Luigi Einaudi from the Organization of American States (OAS), was overheard later that year providing another formulation of 'responsibility to protect/white man's burden', when he said at a party (paraphrasing) 'The real problem with Haiti is that the international community is so screwed up that they're actually letting Haitians run the place.'[7] All agreed that Aristide had to be removed and that Lavalas had to be prevented from participating in elections that would follow the ouster. Denis Paradis indicated that Haiti's population growth was a 'threat' to North America, a 'time bomb' that 'must be defused immediately'.

THE OPPOSITION AND THE GANGS OF CITÉ SOLEIL

In July 2003, Haitian-American businessman Andre Apaid, the leader of the Haitian opposition to Aristide and its organization, 'Group 184', met with street leaders from Cité Soleil. Home to 250,000 people, Cité Soleil is somewhat isolated from the rest of Port-au-Prince: the roads to it are easily cut by roadblocks. It is among the poorest neighbourhoods in Port-au-Prince, and Lavalas was very popular there, with a powerful street-level organization and weekly open-air meetings on Saturday afternoons. The Lavalas street leaders of Cité Soleil with whom Apaid met were Amaral, Dred Wilme, Tupac, Billy, and Thomas Robinson, or 'Labanye', who was from the Boston area of Cité Soleil. Apaid asked these leaders to help him crush Lavalas in Cité Soleil. All but one, Labanye, refused. According to two of the others (Amaral and Dred Wilme) Labanye was then 'bought' by Apaid for $30,000. Apaid promised to use his influence to protect Labanye and his men from arrest or reprisal by police or paramilitaries.[8]

ARMED GROUPS IN GONAIVES

For the period before the coup, the best source in English remains Kevin Pina, who wrote a series of articles in the Black Commentator online magazine as the coup plot came to fruition. The first was published in October 2003,[9] in which Pina described 'an increasing barrage of negative propaganda in the U.S. media ... softening the ground for an eventual power grab by the Washington-sponsored opposition in Haiti'. This media strategy depended on international organizations, non-governmental organizations, and journalists. One crucial NGO was, and remains, the National Coalition for Haitian Rights. The NCHR made dubious claims about repression under the Aristide government and was silent on the paramilitary assaults launched from the Dominican Republic that were going on at the time.

The NCHR also told the lie that Amiot Metayer, a popular Lavalas supporter from the city of Gonaives with a long history of community organizing and resistance during the Duvalier and Cedras dictatorships, was the head of the 'Cannibal Army'. In fact, 'Cannibal Army', according to Pina, was the name of a local gang 'Metayer had battled with in the past'. On September 21, 2003, Metayer was viciously assassinated and the opposition suggested Aristide was behind the killing. Pina quoted a Lavalas observer with a different opinion:

> This is part of what has always been the strategy of the CIA and the opposition, to separate the base of Lavalas from its leadership. This was the real reason behind the killing. The U.S. wants Aristide out and a subservient government in place before we celebrate our bicentennial on January 1, 2004. They believe this plan is the best way to achieve that objective. They cannot win elections so they have decided to create conditions for a civil war.

Amiot Metayer's brother, Butteur Metayer, reorganized the armed group into the Artibonite Resistance Front and announced its armed opposition to Aristide's government.[10]

Pina's second article, published at the beginning of November 2003,[11] reviews a set of articles in the *Los Angeles Times*, the *Christian Science Monitor*, and the *San Francisco Chronicle*, all of which described Metayer's assassination in lurid terms and his background inaccurately, and none of which could 'manage a single quote representing the views and opinions of the hundreds of thousands of Aristide supporters in Haiti'. Pina suggested these articles were coming from a familiar playbook: 'As was the case in Venezuela, the strength of the opposition to the government is exaggerated while pro-government support is at best, understated, and at worst, not mentioned at all.' In his third article, published December 4, 2003,[12] Pina described a 'spate of political assassinations of Lavalas militants, charges of government complicity in the killings by the opposition, and the corporate media's constant trumpeting of the evils of "Aristide's Lavalas regime" … climaxing … with the opposition Group 184 holding an anti-Aristide demonstration in front of the national palace with … the international press in tow'. Pina's description of the ensuing clash is worth quoting in detail, since the clash was so obviously stage-managed and intended for international consumption:

> The much smaller opposition Group 184 is overwhelmed and outflanked by over ten thousand angry Lavalas supporters. Group 184 is forced to withdraw as the Haitian police fire teargas and give orders to disperse in an effort to keep the two groups from clashing. Furthermore, two members of Group 184 are arrested for possession of weapons and are immediately pronounced to be 'political prisoners' by the opposition group. Condemnation of the government by the new U.S. Ambassador and the international community is swift as greased lightning. A new round of propaganda begins against Lavalas hammering the theme that freedom of expression is now impossible in Haiti. This media-ready event is touted as further evidence that Aristide is actually a dictator in democrat's clothing. International diplomacy for Group 184 is conducted through the 'Haiti Democracy Project' (HDP), and most of the 184 organizations in the group are funded by American groups: USAID, the International Republican Institute (IRI), or the National Endowment for Democracy (NED).

While the 'Democracy Project' and 'Coalition for Haitian Rights' published reports on the Aristide regime that were eagerly picked up in the international press, paramilitaries were using murder and massacre to destabilize the regime on the ground, as a timeline provided by Pina shows. On September 21, 2003, Jean Tatoune (a former commander of the Haitian paramilitary Front for Advancement and Progress in Haiti – FRAPH – notorious for its massacres and killings during the 1991–94 dictatorship) led a violent demonstration against the government. On October 26, 2003, Tatoune led an attack on a police station in the city of Gonaives, in which three police were wounded and a 17-year-old girl was killed. The police responded the following day with raids and arrests, with more shooting, with one woman killed and two other people wounded. On November 1, a group called the 'Front of Youth for Saving Haiti', based in Port-au-Prince, announced its intention to overthrow the government through 'civil war'. On November 4, another Lavalas leader, Wilson Lemaire, was assassinated. The opposition used Lemaire's assassination to demonstrate for Aristide's resignation, despite the fact that Lemaire had been a Lavalas leader. As the government searched for an electoral solution, the U.S. Ambassador stated that the international community would not accept the electoral results.

The media and paramilitary strategies advanced in step. The local Haitian press, Pina reported,[13] in particular the radio stations, were active members of the coup. The key features of their reporting were exaggerated reports of Lavalas violence, silence on opposition violence, and underreporting of the size and frequency of Lavalas demonstrations. One of the radio stations, Radio Vision 2000, is owned by the same family (Boulos) that funds the Haiti Democracy Project. Tele-Haiti was founded by opposition Group 184's Andre Apaid. Two journalists from Radio Metropole had toured the U.S., funded by the State Department, meeting with editorial boards across the country as part of a campaign against Aristide's government. These journalists were frequent sources for the Associated Press, Reuters, and France's RFI. Haiti's media owners came together in the National Association of Haitian Media (ANMH). ANMH's vice president, Anne Marie Issa, was also active on the opposition Group 184's Steering and Communications Committees. Issa, who believed Aristide's government was a dictatorship, told researcher Isabel Macdonald that she saw ANMH's role as 'using the media against the dictatorship', by ensuring that all opposition demonstrations were covered and opposition activities were portrayed sympathetically.[14]

Journalist Kevin Pina described the feedback loop as follows: 'Here's the way it works: Metropole reports a fabrication; AP and RFI pick it up for their wire services, then Kiskeya and the others report it again in Haiti backed by the credibility of the international press. The positive feedback loop of disinformation for the opposition is now complete.'

Observer Peter Hallward described the effect of the disinformation campaign on public opinion:

> The Western media had prepared the way for another 'humanitarian intervention' according to the now familiar formula. Confronted by repeated allegations of corruption, patronage, drugs, human rights abuses, autocracy, etc., the casual consumer of mainstream commentary was encouraged to believe that what was at stake had nothing to do with a protracted battle between the poor majority and a tiny elite but was instead just a convoluted free-for-all in which each side was equally at fault ... Rather than a political struggle, rather than a battle of principles and priorities, the fight for Haiti became just another instance of the petty corruption and mass victimization that is supposed to characterize public life beyond the heavily guarded gates of Western democracy. Rather than conditioned by radical class polarization or the mechanics of systematic exploitation, the overthrow of Aristide has most often figured as yet another demonstration of perhaps the most consistent theme of Western commentary on the island: that poor black people remain incapable of governing themselves.[15]

DECEMBER 5, 2003: THE INCIDENT AT THE UNIVERSITY

On December 5, 2003, another stage-managed violent incident occurred. Two days before, on December 3, rumours began to circulate that Aristide would be forced to resign on December 5. When the day came, Radio Metropole and Tele-Haiti reported that Lavalas partisans attacked a university – specifically, that they broke in, destroyed computers, and broke the legs of the University Rector. The violence was condemned by both Aristide and Préval, but the incident had already done immense damage to the government's image in the media. By the time the facts of the incident were shown to be false, it was years too late: in 2006, the case came to court, where a medical doctor confirmed that the Rector's legs hadn't been broken. The students who brought the suit ignored summons to appear. Witnesses failed to find any defendants or place them at the scene.[16]

The next wave of demonstrations used this incident as justification to demand the resignation of the government. Ostensibly these were led by 'students': in fact, they were led by the Group of 184.

On December 22, the same sort of drama played out as occurred in Venezuela a year and a half previously: an elite demonstration organized by the media, with help from the U.S. Embassy and the foreign press following, clashing with supporters of the popular government. On December 26, a massive pro-government, pro-Lavalas demonstration took place – but its size and scale, like the other pro-government rallies that were to follow, were minimized in the Haitian and foreign press. Pina appealed to his readers with a simple argument: 'What non-Haitians must try to understand is that if only half of the negative propaganda about Lavalas were true, particularly that President Aristide no longer enjoys wide support in the country, this government would have fallen long ago.' Another, equally simple argument is worth considering: if only half the negative propaganda were true, and Aristide were as repressive as the human rights groups and journalists hostile to his government claimed, would he not have simply crushed the opposition?

RAMICOS IN ST MARC

Starting in January 2004, RAMICOS, a paramilitary organization and member of the CD, began a series of violent demonstrations in the town of St Marc. On January 15, RAMICOS attempted to free criminals in the St Marc prison, set fire to the offices of Radio Pyramide, and burned the homes of several Lavalas activists. In February RAMICOS attacked the police station and looted and burned the customs house. The government took the town back with the support of the local population. The Lavalas prime minister, Yvon Neptune, flew to the town by helicopter and was greeted by cheering crowds.[17]

By January, 2004, and the bicentennial of Haiti's independence, the United States came into the act in a more significant way. Colin Powell began to make pronouncements. On February 9, 2004, the *New York Times* quoted a State Department spokesman sealing the fate of Haiti's democracy: 'We recognize that reaching a political settlement will require some fairly thorough changes in the way Haiti is governed ... I think that could indeed involve changes in Aristide's position.'[18]

Anti-government paramilitaries began an escalating series of murderous attacks, starting in Gonaives, where Metayer had been murdered and where Tatoune had led his assaults in previous months. By February the paramilitaries had achieved military control of Gonaives, having slaughtered dozens of people, including 14 police who were mutilated after death.[19] The paramilitaries had been trained, armed, and organized in the Dominican Republic. Among their leaders: Guy Philippe, former army officer, and Louis Jodel Chamblain, who had been one of the leaders, along with Jean Tatoune and Emmanuel Constant, of the FRAPH paramilitaries who killed so many Haitians between 1991 and 1994. Philippe and Chamblain crossed the Dominican Republic–Haiti border on February 14 with 20 commandos,[20] heading to Gonaives to assume command of the armed factions calling themselves the 'Gonaives Resistance Front' and 'National Liberation and Resistance Front'. American activist Tom Reeves provided some details as to how these paramilitaries were armed:

> Most of the M-1s and M-14s seen in the hands of the Gonaives thugs today have been identified as coming from those Haitian army stockpiles left untouched during the U.S. occupation. A few M-16s, though, have begun to appear in Gonaives as well – identical to those given the Dominican army en masse just a few months ago by the U.S. government, in return for Dominican acquiescence in placing 900 U.S. troops alongside Dominican guards at the Dominican frontier – and for the Dominican agreement never to use the International Court to accuse and try U.S. citizens for war crimes.[21]

The M-16s Reeves refers to were part of a delivery of 20,000 such rifles. The paramilitaries were trained as part of U.S. operation called 'Operation Jaded Task'.[22]

Paramilitary leader Guy Philippe's record as a drug trafficker during his tenure in the Haitian police in the 1990s, along with his second in command, Gilbert Dragon, was well documented by U.S. agencies.[23] The DEA attempted to arrest him in 2007, but he escaped and remains in Haiti as a fugitive.[24]

Given the utility of drug money in funding private armies, connections between drug traffic, arms traffic, and paramilitarism are always present, and are well documented in current wars in Colombia, Afghanistan, and earlier wars like Vietnam.[25] Philippe, who trained in Ecuador and with the U.S. Secret Service in 1995, worked with Colombian drug cartels (who in turn work with army-backed and U.S.-financed paramilitaries to destroy peasant and union movements in Colombia) to use Haiti as a waypoint for drug traffic to the United States.

At this point in mid-February, when in Gonaives – a zone of escalating opposition violence – Lavalas activists raised barricades and threw stones to try to block a demonstration by the opposition, then-Secretary of State for the U.S. Colin Powell denounced the 'pro-Aristide militants' for blocking a 'peaceful opposition demonstration'. Neither Powell nor the mainstream press made mention of the largest 'peaceful demonstration' of this period, which had occurred a week before on February 7 in Port-au-Prince, when hundreds of thousands demonstrated to defend the government, holding up five fingers to signify their determination that Aristide complete his five-year term.[26] The Haitian government, fearing for its international legitimacy, condemned the blocking of the opposition's demonstration in Gonaives (an act that did not, in fact, help its image internationally, since the international media failed to report it). As demonstrations escalated in violence and the Lavalas movement organized counter-demonstrations, the Haitian government ran out of tear gas – and the U.S. refused to allow it access to any more. This ensured any confrontations would escalate quickly to lethal force unless the government backed down and forced its supporters to do the same. Meanwhile, the U.S. Department of Homeland Security announced its preparations for the coup: it had begun preparations for the internment of 50,000 Haitians at Guantanamo Bay, Cuba. By February 23, 2004, the northern city of Cap Haitien was in the hands of Chamblain's paramilitaries.

The military situation was not as dire as it appeared from the outside, however. The group of rebels was small (about 200). Although they were far better armed than any forces the arms-embargoed Haitian government could put in the field, such a group could never hope to control a hostile population for very long. They were able to terrorize the population of northern Haiti, but they would not have been able to take the capital. The reason they were able to take Gonaives was the defection of Butteur Metayer's 'Artibonite Resistance Front'[27] – but even with this gang on their side, they could not take, or keep, the country. Lavalas supporters were preparing barricades in Port-au-Prince, and Aristide himself understood the rebels' limitations. A shipment of small arms, personal protection gear, and non-lethal weapons was on its way from South Africa, and with this resupply, loyal Haitian police would probably be able to hold the rebels indefinitely.[28] U.S. Marines, Canadian forces, and French forces, however, were another story, as we will see.

NGOS AND SUPPORT FOR THE COUP

The disinformation campaign was enjoying success that probably went beyond the planners' dreams. Human Rights Watch, for example, issued a statement criticizing the Haitian government: 'President Aristide must take immediate, constructive steps to reestablish the rule of law and rebuild the country's democratic institutions.'[29] Human Rights Watch, while doing very constructive work in many parts of the world, aided the coup in Haiti with its reporting and is similarly aiding the 'opposition' in Venezuela.[30] A progressive U.S. magazine, *The Nation*, ran a column by Amy Wilentz, who had written a sympathetic book about Aristide in the 1980s but who came out against Aristide as the second coup unfolded. Rahul Mahajan, in his blog 'Empire Notes', noticed that Wilentz's article featured harsh criticism of Aristide but 'manages not to mention the fact that FRAPH, the paramilitary death squad that instituted a reign of terror under the military regime, had ties with the CIA, a fact first reported by Allan Nairn in *The Nation*; that the United States for many years harbored FRAPH's former leader, Emmanuel Constant, in defiance of Haitian extradition requests; or that Aristide's restoration to power had nothing to do with Clinton Administration "good will" but rather with his agreement to institute a raft of brutal neoliberal structural adjustment "reforms"'.[31]

Indeed, various left 'civil society' groups, including Camille Chalmers's PAPDA and Chavannes Jean-Baptiste's MPP, supported the coup as it unfolded. Chavannes Jean-Baptiste's MPP provided both political and paramilitary support. Before the coup Chavannes wrote that '[d]emocracy is not possible with Aristide. It is over. We must remove him from power ... If the [paramilitaries are] the enemy, it is the second enemy ... the principal enemy of the people today is Aristide.' A resident of the Central Plateau reported that Chavannes helped the paramilitaries assassinate the director of police in the local town and that the MPP burned houses alongside the paramilitaries. Chavannes read names of Lavalas activists over Haitian radio, forcing these into hiding.[32] Activist Tom Reeves interviewed representatives of MHDR (Haitian Movement for Rural Development), SOFA (Women's organization), and Batay Ouvriye: women's groups, workers' support groups, and non-governmental organizations who were critical of Aristide's capitulation to neoliberalism, his acceptance of the Free Trade Zones, and his compromises with the U.S. But if capitulation to the U.S. was the problem, why would the leader of the MHDR, Pierre J.G.C. Gestion, proudly describe how USAID 'trained us and taught us how to organize'? Why would the unions of sweatshop workers assist a regime that was going to destroy every institutional gain Aristide had not given in on? These groups had argued that Aristide was the worst in Haiti's history, worse than the Duvaliers and worse than the 1991–94 coup period. Reeves disagreed:

> I met these groups during that time. They were in hiding then, terrified by the very same elements now roaming Haiti freely, committing atrocities now as then. When U.S. and other international delegations visited them a year ago, under Aristide's rule, they functioned openly. They did not appear terrorized. Their most concrete criticisms were that when they demonstrated against the government – during the same period as the sometimes violent demonstrations orchestrated by the 184 and the Convergence, and coming during a time when it was clear that former military and paramilitary (the CIA-funded FRAPH) were entering the country and preparing a coup – police stood by as people they called Lavalas threw bottles of urine and stones at them. All of that is terrible – and should not have gone without a severe criticism of Aristide and Lavalas. But it cannot be compared to the brutal onslaught by the Fraph and former army officers in Gonaives, Cap Haitien and elsewhere after Feb. 5.[33]

International human rights organizations like HRW and progressive funders like Grassroots International accepted and amplified the self-contradictory ideas and arguments of these NGOs, creating and amplifying the 'disinformation loop' even into the spaces of 'alternative' media and progressive activism, making the mobilization of international solidarity and awareness even more difficult.

The Haitian government desperately tried to seek a compromise through the community of Caribbean nations, CARICOM. Diplomatic efforts were scuttled with the help of the U.S. and France. In mid-February, Aristide later told reporter Claude Ribbe, two French emissaries visited him at the National Palace and told him to resign, threatening him with death if he did not.[34] France's Interior Minister Dominique de Villepin called for Aristide's resignation on February 25. As these countries were scuttling diplomatic efforts, they were also planning a military intervention. While Canada, for example, argued for a 'power-sharing arrangement' between the paramilitary killers and the democratically elected government, its foreign minister Bill Graham was meeting with the U.S. and the French to plan an intervention force. Canada's elite special forces/terrorism unit, 'Joint Task Force Two' (JTF-2), had been working in Haiti since the 1990s, training police there.[35] But the U.S./Canada/France force announced its dispatch of troops on February 27.

INTERNATIONAL OPPOSITION TO THE COUP: CARICOM, VENEZUELA, AND CUBA

The Caribbean Community (CARICOM) were involved first in trying to negotiate a power-sharing arrangement, but ran into the recalcitrance of the opposition. As the coup approached, CARI-COM eventually asked for a UN force to intervene. CARICOM wanted a UN force to support Aristide's government – in the words of Bahamas's foreign minister: 'If the international community refuses to act and act quickly, we will be condoning a creeping attempt to overthrow the government of Haiti by force.'[36] The UN eventually came up with the worst of all possible worlds: a multi-national force to consolidate the overthrow of the government of Haiti by force.

Just before the coup, on February 23, Venezuela announced that it would donate a million dollars in aid to Haiti.[37] After the coup, Venezuela's President Hugo Chávez denounced the overthrow of Aristide, refused to recognize the post-coup government, and asked others to follow. Cuba's support for the elected government was, and remained, more low-key, mainly through its medical programme.

Aside from CARICOM and Venezuela, there was little official denunciation of the coup or even recognition of it as such.

THE KIDNAPPING OF ARISTIDE IN FEBRUARY 2004

In the last week of February 2004 the paramilitaries went from massacre to massacre as Aristide and CARICOM groped for a political solution. Under siege in his Presidential Palace, Aristide found himself dependent on a U.S. security detail. That security detail, contracted by the Steele Foundation, was contracted not by

Aristide, but by René Préval, who had been president from 1995 to 2000. The Steele Foundation, which is based in California and maintains an office in Miami, was led by someone who came from the Pentagon's Office of Intelligence.[38]

On February 29, 2004, the Associated Press ran a long story stating that Aristide had 'resigned' and 'fled the country'. The U.S. Ambassador to Haiti, James Foley, said that U.S. forces would 'rapidly be in Haiti' to 'restore order'. Haiti's prime minister, Yvon Neptune, who we will meet again soon, told a press conference that Aristide had resigned to 'prevent bloodshed' and an unnamed 'senior U.S. defense official' told the media that Aristide had 'submitted a formal resignation before leaving Haiti'. Another such 'American defense official' told reporters that three Navy ships were awaiting deployment. The newswires accepted the word of this unnamed 'U.S. official' on this crucial matter. While Supreme Court Justice Boniface Alexandre declared he was taking charge of the country and took the formal oath of office, the voice of Aristide himself, who could have confirmed whether or not he had resigned, was missing from the reports. Instead there were 'senior U.S. officials' reporting that 'Aristide flew from Haiti on a corporate jet that left at 6.45am', accompanied by his security detail. The name of this official was not provided.

Reporters were more diligent in recording reactions in paramilitary-held cities like Cap Haitien, recording touching scenes of the killers yelling 'Aristide's gone!' and 'hugging each other', 'dancing and singing', 'waving at hundreds of people who took to the streets in celebration'. Contrasting with these touching scenes, the reporter described the situation in St Marc (where the reporter, judging from the context, had not been), 'where Aristide militants have been terrorizing opponents, torching homes and executing alleged rebel sympathizers'. Kevin Skerrett reconstructed the clashes in St Marc, where Lavalas militants and opposition members died in fighting, in detail in English.[39] Haitian writer Ronald St Jean analyzed the St Marc incident in a report in French.[40]

These 'Aristide militants' themselves had no voice in the story. Nor did Aristide himself. Had Aristide wanted to resign to prevent bloodshed, it might have been more efficient for him to do so by addressing the nation on television and radio rather than disappearing in the early hours of the morning.

As it turns out, Aristide did address the nation, a little later. He circulated a statement on March 6, 2004, saying: 'During the night of the 28th of February 2004, there was a coup d'etat. One

could say that it was a geo-political kidnapping. I can clearly say
that it was terrorism disguised as diplomacy.' Aristide's statement
described how that night American military personnel went to his
house and told him that those American security agents Aristide
had hired 'only have two options. Either they leave immediately
to go to the United States, or they fight to die.' They told him
that some of his security agents had been interdicted, and that the
paramilitary army, armed heavily, was preparing for a massacre in
Port-au-Prince: 'the Americans precisely stated that they will kill
thousands of people and it will be a bloodbath. That the attack is
ready to start, and when the first bullet is fired nothing will stop
them and nothing will make them wait until they take over, therefore
the mission is to take me dead or alive.' Aristide was convinced it
was no bluff by the fact that the Palace was 'surrounded by white
men armed up to their teeth'. He was bundled on to a plane by the
Americans and not notified 'until 20 minutes before we landed in
the Central African Republic' that that would be his destination.[41]
In an interview with *Democracy Now!* journalist Amy Goodman,
Aristide elaborated on the role of the U.S. The U.S. Ambassador
to Haiti, James Foley, told Aristide that he would be going to talk
to the press 'once they put me in their car ... they put me in their
planes full of military'.[42] The Central African Republic is among
the countries to which the U.S. advises its citizens not to travel. It
has no U.S. Embassy.[43]

Against Aristide's own testimony, there is that of then-Secretary
of State Colin Powell, who has a record of lying and cover-ups
dating back from the American war on Vietnam through to the
fabrication of evidence to prepare for the American war on Iraq.
On March 1, 2004, Powell told reporters '[Aristide] was not
kidnapped, we did not force him on the plane. That's the truth.'[44]

Before this, Powell had told Aristide's friends in the U.S. that
Guy Philippe was going to kill him on February 29 and that the
U.S. would do nothing to stop it, Randall Robinson reported in
his book.[45] Based on long interviews with the Aristides, their helicopter pilot Frantz Gabriel, Steele Foundation security guards and
others, Robinson reconstructed the story of the kidnapping in
detail. In the early hours of the morning of the 29th, the Aristides
were interrupted by a group of fully armed U.S. special forces led
by the U.S. Embassy's Luis Moreno. They were given no time to
gather their things, but were bundled into an SUV and taken to
an unmarked plane. The plane, full of U.S. troops, who changed
into civilian clothing on the plane, flew first to Antigua, with the

passenger windows shuttered (the Aristides were not allowed to open the shutters or know where they were going), and then to the Central African Republic. According to Robinson, the plan for them was likely to have them die there of some mysterious ailment, perhaps malaria, but for a rescue operation by Congresswoman Maxine Waters, Aristide's lawyer Ira Kurzban, journalists Amy Goodman and Peter Eisner, Jamaican parliamentarian Sharon Hay Webster, and Randall Robinson himself. When the delegation met with CAR's president Bozize, after a period of vacillation, he told them, 'You know we are trying to get some assistance from the World Bank. I don't want to do anything that is going to hurt us with the World Bank ... This is very important. If you could help us to get the money from the World Bank that we are negotiating for, that they are promising us, we would appreciate it.'[46]

The kidnapping and the invasion by U.S., Canadian and French troops was the key to the entire coup. Without it, the paramilitary operation would simply have had to wait in the north to be defeated once the small arms shipment from South Africa was distributed to loyal police. The short-term crisis would have been averted, and then the Aristide government would have been able to go about addressing the medium-term crisis of the blocked IDB loans and financing.

But once Aristide was out of the country, incommunicado, his supporters were confused and in disarray. Foreign troops would quickly be able to claim they were invited, and the person they had kidnapped would be nowhere to say otherwise during the crucial moments. As with the many false accusations against Lavalas and Aristide, the lies about Aristide's voluntary resignation had a shelf life, but they did not need to hold up forever: only long enough for the U.S./Canada/France force to take the capital city and install a new government.

When a similar operation ousted Venezuela's President Hugo Chávez in April 2002, there was a powerful outcry not only from the people of the country (which certainly occurred in Haiti) but also at the official level by many countries. Nineteen Latin American countries, including Mexico, Argentina, and Brazil, all refused to recognize the post-coup Venezuelan regime. In addition to the movement on the ground in Venezuela, this international diplomacy was crucial in reversing the Venezuelan coup and restoring democracy to that country. In Haiti in 2004, very few countries were willing to take such a stand. Those countries who stood for Venezuela's sovereignty were silent about Haiti's sovereignty: only Venezuela itself, South Africa, and the Caribbean Community of nations CARICOM, condemned the coup. CARICOM tried to take their demand for a full investigation of Aristide's departure to the United Nations, but recognized quickly that the U.S. or France could easily block such moves in the Security Council. CARICOM was forced to appeal to the Organization of American States (OAS) instead. The OAS deputy secretary general Luigi Einaudi said that the request would be considered 'like all other requests in the organization'. This was the same, unbiased Einaudi who, as noted above, had declared that 'the real problem with Haiti is that the international community is so screwed up that they're actually letting Haitians run the place'.

By this time the AP was reporting that 130 people had been killed in the lead-up to the coup. Aristide no doubt knew the actual number was far higher. From his return to Haiti in 1994 after years in exile, Aristide had a history of being forced to accept the unacceptable in order to try to avert the even worse. Aristide was kidnapped. Whether he was physically moved or just intimidated into acquiescence by the threat of a bloodbath makes no moral difference: a mother who is told to get in the car or her children get killed is no less kidnapped than if she were bodily placed into the car. 'My strategy was then', he told Amy Goodman, 'all I could do to avoid bloodshed.'

It was not avoided.

4 THE SLAUGHTER ON U.S. WATCH: TO JUNE 2004

The new dictatorship was in place. The paramilitaries asserted the new order quickly, starting at Ouanaminthe, a production facility in the free trade zone started up thanks to a $20 million World Bank–International Finance Corporation loan to the Grupo M, a Dominican garment company that does $200 million business annually. The day after Aristide was kidnapped, 34 union members at the Ouanaminthe Grupo M garment assembly factory were fired. The next morning the workforce, 600-strong, went on strike. The strike was broken by the paramilitaries with beatings.[1] Paramilitaries attacked and destroyed over 100 buses that had been purchased and used by the Federation of Public Transport Workers of Haiti under Aristide's government for a bus co-operative.[2] On March 3, they murdered Cassey Auguste, a 20-year-old American citizen, sitting outside his Haitian mother's business in Port Sonde. They said they killed him because the family served Lavalas at their business.[3]

In St Marc, the RAMICOS paramilitary organization began a vengeful massacre against Lavalas, who had repelled their attempt to take the town a week earlier. Refugees later told journalist Kim Ives: 'Seven young people, including two pairs of young brothers, were macheted or shot to death by pro-coup forces. The mutilated bodies were then paraded around the town and dragged by a rope behind a truck to terrorize the rest of the town's population. They were then burned.' RAMICOS proceeded to take the telephone company, tax authority, and port authority buildings.[4]

The paramilitaries also released those who had been jailed for crimes against humanity under previous dictatorial regimes, including former general Prosper Avril, leader of the presidential guard under the Duvaliers and dictator of Haiti from 1988 to 1990. A U.S. District Court had found Avril's regime engaged in systematic human rights abuse and awarded six of his victims $41 million in compensation for his personal responsibility in 'torture and cruel, inhuman, or degrading treatment'. In November 1994, the U.S. Secretary of State told the U.S. ambassador that Avril's 'Red Star Organization' was planning an assassination campaign against Aristide supporters – information that was not relayed to the Haitian authorities. In December, when Haitian police tried to arrest Avril, U.S. soldiers stopped them, allowing Avril to escape, first to the Colombian ambassador's residence, then to Israel. He returned to Haiti and worked with the opposition, openly helped and funded by the International Republican Institute. Finally arrested in May 2001 to the applause of human rights groups like Amnesty International and France's Committee to Prosecute Duvalier, Avril was formally charged on December 9, 2003, and put in prison awaiting further proceedings. He was freed by the paramilitaries on March 2, 2004.[5]

Marines quickly moved on important military targets, for example shutting down the new Faculty of Medicine in Tabarre and occupying the classrooms.[6] The Marines' first shots were fired, however, on Sunday March 7, at a rally organized by anti-Aristide forces. The Marines said they were 'returning fire'. The AP reported that at least seven were killed, including Spanish journalist Ricardo Ortega, and 20 wounded. The French commander, Daniel Leplatois, said 'We're not able to secure the lives of all the demonstrators.' A day later (Monday March 8) the Marines acknowledged their responsibility for (one of) the deaths of the day before. There is reason to believe the Marine operation was a show of force against the paramilitaries who had just overthrown Aristide. First, the shooting did take place at an anti-Aristide rally. There was a pro-Aristide rally the day after (Monday March 8) barely reported, at which no one was killed. Second, the paramilitary leader, Guy Philippe, made a bitter statement after Sunday's shooting, saying the attack never would have happened if his men had not been asked to disarm. Other such actions by the occupiers were to follow, as if to demonstrate that all Haitians, including those who had worked to overthrow democracy and collaborate with occupation, had to remember their place. The U.S. was going to have to assert itself several more times against its armed proxies when they threatened to get out of control.

On that same Monday (March 8), the 'interim' president, Boniface Alexandre, was formally installed as Aristide supporters protested and others looted Port-au-Prince's industrial park, half a mile from the U.S. Marine base at the airport (Aristide's house had long since been trashed and looted, immediately after the coup). With the new president installed, the political wing of the coup's 'Council of the Wise', a panel named by the coup forces three days before Alexandre's installation, interviewed candidates to replace Aristide's prime minister, Yvon Neptune. In doing so it had the support of Neptune himself, who, perhaps confused by events, had helped carry out the 'transition' from a democratically elected to coup-installed regime over the first week of March. Candidates included Smarck Michel, a businessman and former PM from 1994 to 1995, a Haitian army officer Lt. Gen. Herard Abraham, and Gérard Latortue, an 'international business consultant' with a mansion in Boca Raton, Florida. All these had been involved in the planning of the coup, though it was Latortue who was to win and replace Neptune. Neptune did not go into exile, but stayed in the country, silent, perhaps feeling that he had nothing to fear because he had committed no offence.

The next day (March 9) Marines killed a man driving towards a roadblock, a familiar tactic the Marines were deploying at the same time in the occupation of Iraq. Haitian police killed one man and injured two others the same day. Reuters reported the account flatly: 'Marines who saw the incident said the victims were pushing a soda vehicle. One suffered a graze to the head, but was not badly injured and another was shot in the back and taken to the hospital. The U.S. soldiers did not know what happened to the third man but other eye-witnesses said he was killed by police. It was unclear whether the men had been looting.' The Marines also began raids into pro-Aristide neighbourhoods of Port-au-Prince, especially Bel Air and Cité Soleil, killing dozens in each raid, according to witnesses interviewed by activist Tom Driver.[7]

The military forces of the 'international community' were doing more than just shooting Haitians at checkpoints. Canadian Sgt. Maj. Kirby Burgess said, 'We're building a really nice hotel,' describing the military base that was to house some of the 500 troops Canada was contributing to the U.S.-led force (3,000 strong) in Haiti by March to help the coup government establish itself. The Canadian Press story that quoted Burgess noted that in contrast to the Canadian troops' 'really nice hotel', 'Haitians line the streets selling everything from food and clothing to handicrafts and motor oil in an effort to eke out a living. Less fortunate locals compete with dogs, goats and pigs as they scavenge the ever-growing piles of garbage for scraps of food.'[8]

SILENCING LAVALAS

A very few of the voices of Lavalas activists were getting out in the alternative media. 'Johnny', an 18-year-old former youth-reporter with Radio Timoun (Children's Radio) in Port-au-Prince, gave an interview to the Pacific News Service contributor Lyn Duff. Johnny's radio station had been burned, along with the Aristide Foundation for Democracy: 'The U.S. Marines stood by and did nothing while the library at the Aristide Foundation was burned. With my own eyes I saw the American Marines stand and watch while rebels cut a woman and shot her. I yelled at them, "Do something!" and they swung their guns around toward me and yelled, "Get back!"'[9] Jean-Charles Moise, Lavalas mayor of Milo, a city in northern Haiti near Cap Haitien, wrote from hiding about the paramilitary occupation of his town and the return of the hated Haitian army. His report showed that as bad as the situation in Port-au-Prince had grown, the situation in rural Haiti was worse still. 'Those they don't kill', he wrote, 'they lock up in containers, because they burned down the jails. The kind of containers you put on ships.'[10] Moise estimated that these paramilitaries were killing 'about 50 people a day in Cap Haitien'. Other tactics included the imposition of curfew, announced on radio two hours before its imposition. The paramilitaries would then shoot anyone on the street after curfew. Moise also reported seeing helicopters and airplanes being used by the members of the former Haitian military. Still another pattern was described by Tom Driver, a frequent visitor to Haiti. Driver interviewed two men who had been prominent in Lavalas, who described the daily happenings: 'Every afternoon around 4pm. names are broadcast. Perhaps they are on a list of those whom the new government wants to arrest, or perhaps listeners call in with the name of so-and-so. All are linked with Aristide in some way. Some of those named soon disappear.'[11]

In mid-March, two weeks after the coup, Aristide headed back to the Caribbean – to Jamaica. The *Miami Herald* reported that Jamaica's hosting of Aristide, which allowed him to reunite with his daughters after his kidnapping by the U.S., had 'infuriated Bush administration officials'. These officials were gracious under such terrible provocation, however, announcing that 'the Bush Administration will not cut aid to fight AIDS in the region or reduce other kinds of humanitarian assistance', although 'other nonhumanitarian bilateral programs could be slowed down'.[12] General James T. Hill of the U.S. Southern Command warned

Aristide to 'keep his mouth closed'. While the U.S. issued threats and warnings, it was watching the installation of its handpicked 'interim government' on March 17. Lavalas was excluded. The 'Democratic Convergence' and the 'Group of 184' were represented: Yvon Simeon of the former was the new foreign affairs minister, Bernard Gousse of the latter was the new minister of justice. Ex Haitian Army General Herard Abraham, who had been a contender for prime minister, became minister of the interior and began to work on the reinstatement of the Haitian Army.

To celebrate, Canada pledged CAD$1 million to the International Organisation of La Francophonie (OIF) to 'resuscitate and further develop Haiti's fundamental democratic institutions', according to minister for La Francophonie, Denis Coderre. The aid was to be delivered through the Canadian International Development Agency (CIDA), also a major funder of the National Coalition on Haitian Rights (NCHR), which played such an instrumental role in the coup. The Canadian government's press release on the funding noted that Canada had contributed CAD$13 million to the coup, including CAD$5 million through the UN and CAD$5 million through the Organization of American States (OAS).

The U.S. later topped Canada's generosity to the coup administration, pledging $52 million for 'economic development and humanitarian assistance', plus a 'three-year jobs program, which will provide tens of thousands of jobs'; among the tasks was to 'rehabilitate schools and public buildings destroyed by rioting and burning'. Despite these aid announcements, the coup was no job creation project, especially for the public sector. Immediately after the coup, the interim government fired 12,000 government employees,[13] and the state telephone company announced the firing of 2,000 others.[14]

The U.S. also pledged another $9 million for 'elections and democracy building', in addition to $5 million for the OAS Special Mission in Haiti.[15] Senator Mike DeWine encouraged U.S. representatives to sponsor the Haiti Economic Recovery and Opportunity (HERO) Act, which would facilitate the import of sweatshop-produced apparel from Haiti into the U.S. with lower duties, 'contingent upon Presidential certification that the new government is making significant political, economic, and social reforms'. DeWine's office argued that Haitians needed the opportunity because 'the average Haitian lives on less than $400 a year', but did not explain how dismantling the minimal social infrastructure Haiti had left, slaughtering its social movements, was going to mitigate the poverty.

At the same time, persecution of Lavalas and Aristide's officials went international, with Aristide's security chief, Oriel Jean, being extradited and sent to jail in Miami. Jean had been picked up by Canadian immigration authorities while travelling to Toronto a week before, and detained on drug charges. As with so many other cases, the drug charges were a diversion from the real reasons for the detention. This is clear for several reasons. First, even assuming that every single charge against Jean was true, the man had been travelling to Canada for 15 years to seek medical advice for his knees, according to his lawyer – immigration authorities thus had many opportunities to detain him, including in 2002 and 2003. Instead they waited until two weeks after a paramilitary coup had ousted the government he worked for, and charged him with poorly substantiated 'drug links'. Second, Canada knew and had worked with Jean in Haiti, inviting him to the Canadian Embassy in Haiti to ask for advice on navigating traffic in Port-au-Prince. Third, the Canadian government's hard line on Jean's cloudy drug links seems disingenuous given that the paramilitary killers that Canada had helped into power in Haiti, such as Guy Philippe and Louis-Jodel Chamblain, had better-documented and publicly known narcotrafficking careers themselves. The real agenda behind this operation was twofold: first, to demonstrate to everyone that no one from Lavalas or Aristide's regime was safe, anywhere, and second, according to Jean's lawyer, to use the threat of prison against Jean (who, after all, was a security chief in possession of strategic information) to extract information about Aristide and his regime to assist in the repression and destruction of the Haitian political movement, both inside and outside of Haiti.[16]

Outside of Haiti repression was not confined to Lavalas, but to any of those Haitians who wanted to try to escape the violence. These had to be prevented from being seen or heard, at all costs. If the first 1994 U.S. intervention to restore Aristide was prompted in part by the desire by the U.S. to avoid dealing with the Haitian refugees who inevitably resulted from violent dictatorship, the Americans had learned their lesson for the 2004 coup. This time Haitian refugees were systematically and brutally confined to camps and jails, mostly in the Dominican Republic. They were prevented from getting there when possible, and prevented from leaving when they escaped. On March 15, 200 Haitian refugees rioted in a public jail in Santiago, where they were being held.

As with those Haitians who fled the dictatorship in 1991, these refugees were not accorded the status of 'refugees' in the press. They were instead called 'migrants', and pains were taken to clarify that they were 'not fleeing the rebellion, but simply seeking better economic opportunities'. The source for these quotes in the Associated Press story was Sabas Burgos, assistant head of migration in the Dominican Republic: no Haitian refugee was quoted. The same story reported that the Haitian paramilitaries prevented thousands of Haitian civilians from reaching the Dominican border for a cross-border market exchange between the Haitian city of Quanaminte and the Dominican city of Dajabon.[17] By the end of 2004, thousands of Haitians had been detained all over the region. El Salvador's police reported detaining 1,027 Haitians over the course of the year, nearly half of all the 2,223 detained by that country.

Bush had warned before the coup that any Haitians who fled would be returned via 'a [white] picket fence of U.S. Coast Guard cutters'.[18]

'That message needs to be very clear as well to the Haitian people,' said Bush. 'We strongly encourage the Haitian people to stay home as we search for a political solution to this problem.'[19]

Official USCG statistics for 'alien migrant interdiction' indicate 3,078 interdictions in 2004, the highest total since 1994's 25,069. The preventive 'picket fence' measures, combined with statistics that could be drawn from neighbouring Caribbean and Latin American countries, suggests that containment of refugees was a key aspect of U.S. strategy for this coup.

PARAMILITARY VIOLENCE AGAINST LAVALAS

Inside Haiti the paramilitaries were continuing a campaign to erase the steps towards justice for the victims of the dictatorships that had been made under Aristide. The paramilitaries attacked and beat Judge Napela Saintil, chief judge in the trial of the authors of a major massacre under the Cedras dictatorship (the Raboteau massacre of April 1994, in which 20 people were killed), threatening him for his conviction of Louis Jodel Chamblain, a participant in the massacre and a leader of the paramilitaries. Amnesty International received reports of killings and kidnappings in poor, pro-Aristide neighbourhoods. One man was shot on April 3, another on April 4, in the market. The latter's wife was forced into hiding and his house was burned. Two members of the KOMIREP grassroots organization were kidnapped on the street on the same day (April 4). A victim of a gang rape in November 2003 reported being threatened by the police officer who was in prison for the crime and escaped on the day of the coup. The activists being kidnapped and killed were identified by escaped prisoners, working with the Haitian police and international forces to identify Lavalas activists.[20]

Paramilitaries massacred four men on March 30, 2004, in front of Lafanmi Selavi, an orphanage and school founded by Aristide and closed since the coup, according to eyewitnesses who talked to a National Lawyers' Guild (NLG) delegation.[21] The NLG visited the state morgue in Port-au-Prince and were denied the opportunity to view the cadavers or review the record books. The director of the morgue told them that many of the bodies were those of young men shot with their hands tied behind their backs and plastic bags over their heads. They were told by morgue workers that there were 50 bodies there on March 31; the director told them that on Sunday March 7, 800 bodies were dumped and buried by the morgue and another 200 were dumped on Sunday March 28. In another neighbourhood, the NLG heard that 4–60 bodies had been dumped in a field on March 23. They found 'a massive ash pile and pigs eating flesh of human bones that had not burned', and 'photographed fresh skulls and other human bones'.[22] Visiting the town of Les Cayes, the NLG found it in control of 'Ti Gary', an opponent of Lavalas, who admitted committing at least five summary executions in March. One observer stated his belief, based on interviews with families of victims and eyewitnesses to attacks on Lavalas, and the NLG reports, that 1,000 political murders could be documented during March 2004 alone, 40–60 deaths due to U.S. Marine gunfire.[23] In Cap Haitien, the paramilitaries were running a kidnapping and extortion racket with the complicity of the local occupiers, the French.[24]

UNRAVELLING THE JUSTICE SYSTEM

Paramilitaries were aided in their efforts by two 'human rights groups': the NCHR, which put up posters calling for the arrest and imprisonment of Aristide government members, and the Committee of Lawyers for Respect for Individual Liberties (CARLI in French), which produces and reads lists of human rights abusers over the local media based on an anonymous hotline. The condemnations were universally of Lavalas supporters and police. None of the condemnations were for attacks against Lavalas members. The lists and posters were then used by the regime and paramilitaries as arrest and hit lists. The NCHR was funded by CIDA, CARLI by USAID. NCHR told the Quixote Centre Emergency Delegation to Haiti in March 2004 that they were not willing to enter neighbourhoods such as Bel Air and Cité Soleil to investigate reports of massacres carried out by foreign forces and other armed elements.

The paramilitaries also engaged in political theatre. On April 22, 2004, one of the paramilitary leaders, Louis Jodel Chamblain, 'surrendered' to the Haitian National Police at a posh hotel in the presence of the U.S. military and the interim justice minister. Chamblain had been convicted in absentia of responsibility in the 1994 Raboteau massacre, but he was promised a new trial, and perhaps a pardon, for his contribution to 'democracy'. By the time of his surrender, most of the survivors, victims, and witnesses of that massacre were dead or in hiding, victims of the new coup. As noted, the judge in the case, Naipela Saintil, had been beaten up by paramilitaries the month before, and the house of the lead prosecutor was burned down in February.[25] The high-profile surrenders of paramilitary leaders would placate (or at least confuse) international opinion, while preparing the ground for future rehabilitation of the paramilitaries, their incorporation into a returned Haitian Army, and preserve impunity for the crimes of the (previous) dictatorship.

The U.S., in the meantime, was making Haiti the latest site in its global prison system, adding the national penitentiary to its list of international prisons (that includes Abu Ghraib in Iraq, Bagram in Afghanistan, and Guantanamo in Cuba). U.S. officials told Amnesty International that the U.S. Marines controlled part of the prison and were guarding 40 detainees, including the former minister of the interior, Jocelerme Privert, who the new regime arrested in April.[26] Haiti's prisons were handed over to the private consulting firm Advanced Correctional Management's Terry Stewart. Stewart moved to the private sector from a job as director of prisons in Arizona, where he presided over a prison system that was repeatedly investigated for abuse and sexual humiliation of women prisoners. He was sent to Haiti (after a tour helping 'reform' Iraq's Abu Ghraib prison) to help the Americans add Haiti to the American international prison complex.[27] Perhaps it was Stewart's influence that led Jacques Dyotte – a Canadian prison expert who had led the UN mission to reform Haiti's prisons in July 2000 – to resign, which he did in disgust in November 2004.

THE ARREST OF ANNETTE AUGUSTE

The Marines raided the home of folk singer and grandmother Annette Auguste ('So Ann'), a Lavalas activist, on May 10, at 12.30am. They blew the gates to So Ann's house open with a grenade, killed her two small dogs, and ransacked the house. The heavily armed Marines forced every single person in the house – 11 people – to the ground and handcuffed them. Among those handcuffed was a 5-year-old girl, So Ann's granddaughter, Shashou. The grandmother was accused of 'making threats' against the occupying army. All were taken into custody and transported to the Medical University, which the Marines, recall, had closed and were occupying. Two weeks later So Ann wrote a letter from Petionville Penitentiary, where she was being held. After the sham of the 'threats' charge, the Latortue regime had come up with the charge that So Ann was guilty of organizing the (phony) attack on students on December 5, 2003. 'It is clear to me', So Ann wrote, 'that such an accusation is only a small act in this shameful theater.'[28] When independent journalist Kevin Pina passed the restrictive gauntlet needed to visit So Anne in early June, he found her confined to her cell. He saw Louis Jodel Chamblain wandering the prison freely, thumbing through the identity cards of So Ann's visitors.[29]

On May 18, Haiti's Flag Day, tens of thousands of Haitians came out to protest against the occupation. The demonstration was to start at 10am in the neighbourhood of Bel Air and go on until 3pm, followed by a church service. Haitians began gathering at around 8am. As they assembled, U.S. Marines gathered in full gear and shot in the air to disperse them. The crowd dispersed and re-formed in a different part of the city. According to eyewitnesses, the Marines, along with Haitian police, then fired indiscriminately into the crowd, and both groups took bodies away. The Associated Press reported nine deaths from police fire. Kevin Pina reported at least 12 deaths and saw one person shot by a Marine.[30]

International forces – including the French soldiers working with the UN mission – invaded the home of the Mayor of Milo, Jean-Charles Moise, who was one of the few Lavalas activists to get information out (from hiding) about the paramilitary massacres in the countryside. The French soldiers invaded in a convoy of two big trucks, 10 cars, two ambulances, and 80 soldiers, at 4am on June 14. Moise's four children, aged 3 to 9, were asleep at the time. The soldiers kidnapped his wife (they called it an arrest), took her into custody and ransacked the house, presumably to try to force Moise out of hiding. She was eventually released.[31]

In a demonstration of authority over the paramilitaries, Canadian troops raided the home of Dany Toussaint, murder suspect, former senator, and Aristide supporter who had gone over to the coup in 2003. The Canadian troops reported recovering various weapons. While offering no protection to the Haitian population or Lavalas, such raids probably served the purpose of publicly establishing the supremacy of the international forces over the paramilitaries.

The U.S. Marines, with their engagements in Iraq, had not come to stay, however. On April 30, the UN Security Council had announced that the U.S.-led Multinational Interim Force (MIF) would be replaced by the United Nations Stabilization Mission in Haiti (MINUSTAH) starting July 1. MINUSTAH was formally established by Security Council Resolution 1542 on June 1, 2004, with a mandate to provide a secure and stable environment through disarmament, prepare for elections, and monitor human rights. Presented as a transfer of responsibility from one multilateral force to another, it would turn out to be a subcontracting of the occupation from the U.S. to some unlikely countries, led by Brazil. U.S., Canadian, and French troops were still to be part of MINUSTAH, however, and this fact pleased the coup-installed Prime Minister Latortue. 'Even if we have 100 it is better than nothing', Latortue told Florida Congressman Mark Foley on June 10, 2004. 'This is the only force in the world they will respect.' It was clear that Latortue was referring to the Haitian population when he used the word *they*.

In the Free Trade Zone of Codevi, *they* got a taste of what Latortue was talking about when the Dominican garment company Grupo M fired 254 workers from its Ouanaminthe factory and brought the Dominican military in to terrorize the workers, threatening to close the factory down rather than negotiate with the union. Since the sacking of the 34 union workers and the paramilitary repression at the factory in March, the international outcry helped force Grupo M to negotiate an agreement, allowing the sacked workers back by mid-May. On June 4, Grupo M had violated the agreement and the union engaged in a one-hour warning strike. The next day the management called in the Dominican Army to expel some of the union leaders from the zone by force. Workers were locked out on June 7, and on June 9, Grupo M announced that it was abandoning production and laying off all 700 workers.[32] Gildan Activewear, a Canadian-based multinational and one of the world's leading T-shirt manufacturers, announced in July that it was closing its 1,800-employee facility in a 'purely economically driven decision in light of our commitment to constantly driving down our cost structure', the chief financial officer said.

5 INTERNATIONALIZING THE OCCUPATION

The summer 2004 transition

In Brazil, Argentina, and Chile, social movements had, after long travail, elected governments that they hoped would show more independence from U.S. policy and the economics of the IMF than the subordinate governments and dictatorships of previous decades. President Luis Ignacio da Silva (Lula) from Brazil, Nestor Kirchner from Argentina, and Ricardo Lagos in Chile were all leftists. But like the rest of Latin American regimes, these leaders were silent when the Haiti coup happened. They were now to compound their complicity in the violation of Haitian sovereignty as they prepared their troops to take over for the Americans, French, and Canadians as the occupying army.

WHY DID LATIN AMERICA'S 'PINK' GOVERNMENTS SUPPORT THE OCCUPATION?

The people of these countries, with their own living memories of brutal dictatorships, were not so keen on their leaders' positions. A poll in Chile in April 2004 showed that 58 per cent of Chileans were against having Chilean troops in Haiti.[1] Chilean troops had in fact arrived shortly after the Americans, Canadians, and French – 220 Chilean troops were part of the initial coup protection force, on the ground within 48 hours of the coup. Some Chilean troops had been trained in urban warfare alongside U.S. Marines before deploying.[2] In Argentina, there were spirited demonstrations against Argentina's joining the UN occupation.[3]

In Brazil, the Landless Peasant's Movement (MST) were a huge, militant social force and very strong on international solidarity.

The MST were facilitators of a network of peasant movements worldwide, called 'Via Campesina', in which different peasant organizations from different countries could participate. Via Campesina became yet another area of coup operations: the Papaye Peasant Movement (MPP) led by Chavannes Jean-Baptiste, a collaborator in the coup, was Haiti's Via Campesina contact. When the MST was developing its position on Brazilian troops in Haiti, its leadership naturally asked its Haitian counterpart, the MPP, for advice. Chavannes Jean-Baptiste replied with a public letter stating that the MPP 'remains anti-imperialist ... we cannot support the presence of foreign troops in our country'. But, Chavannes wrote:

> at the same time, we consider that ... the presence of armed forces today in Haiti is the direct consequence of the dictatorship of Aristide ... who betrayed his class ... he did everything to destroy the popular movement and used the popular organizations of the cities to assure his despotic power ... so we think that in denouncing the participation of the Brazilian government in the UN force, one must also denounce the dictatorship of Aristide because there is much confusion about Aristide in Venezuela, the U.S., and other parts of the world.

So, several months after Aristide had been overthrown and thousands of activists from his party murdered, jailed, and forced into hiding, Haiti's peasant organization was advocating an even-handed approach, suggesting that criticizing the foreign occupiers facilitating the slaughter be balanced with criticism of those being slaughtered. Like so much of what the MPP and other left organizations did during the coup, this helped to mute, confuse, and demobilize an effective international popular response to the slaughter. Such a response was doubly important since nearly all of the governments of the world and the United Nations were aiding the coup.

Other organizations that had supported the coup, such as the CARLI lawyer's group, were discovering evidence for what they should have known all along – that paramilitaries, horrendous and abusive in opposition, were still worse in power. As their foreign funding dried up, CARLI regained its independence as a human rights organization, and consequently its people came under threat of violent attack and repression.[4] CARLI lawyer Renan Hedouville told the press in August 2004 that CARLI's hotline had received

50 reports of rape by the paramilitaries in that month alone. A Haitian Health organization, GHESKIO (Haitian group for studies of Kaposi Sarcoma and other infections) treated 81 women for sexual assault between July and September. A UNICEF team in Gonaives from October 20 to November 2 found 'a problem of rape of teenage girls'.[5]

With the UN's MINUSTAH mission firmly in place, the Haitian government continued its work of arresting democrats and pardoning killers. The ousted Lavalas prime minister, Yvon Neptune, found his voice and denounced the repression and massacres of Lavalas that were occurring. Immediately, the NCHR circulated rumours that Neptune had been involved in a 'massacre' in the town of St Marc on February 11, 2004. In fact, Neptune had, as outlined above, visited St Marc after a paramilitary attack on the town had failed. The massacre did not occur until the paramilitaries took the town back after the coup, well after February 11. On June 26, the NCHR announced that a warrant of arrest had been written against him. No charges had, in fact, been made and no investigation occurred. He was, however, arrested and imprisoned on June 28 when he turned himself in. So too was former Interior Minister Jocelerme Privert.

In August, Louis Jodel Chamblain, guilty of real massacres, the paramilitary leader who had been convicted of the murder of Antoine Izmery (one of the very few members of Haiti's wealthy business community who supported Lavalas, and whose murder was a major blow to the movement), who had been wandering the national prison freely after his staged 'surrender' to authorities months before, was finally acquitted of the charge of murder. Amnesty International called the trial, which lasted fourteen hours and had one witness who told the court he knew nothing about the case, an 'insult to justice'.[6] Yvon Neptune was in prison. So Ann remained in prison. So did Aryns Laguerre, teenage cameraman for a children's television station.[7] According to an American human rights delegation,[8] U.S. personnel were deeply embedded in the prison system, transferring detainees in U.S. diplomatic vehicles, directing activities, and incarcerating former Haitian government officials on U.S. Coast Guard vessels. Of the 1,000 inmates at the national prison, about two dozen had been convicted of a charge.

THE CONFUSIONS OF THE UN'S
DISARMAMENT PROGRAMME

The dismantling of Haitian society extended into the social infra-structure built by Aristide's regime. In Petion-Ville, the SOPUDEP school for the poor was one of the few such projects to survive the coup in March thanks to international outcry. SOPUDEP was established on the site of an expropriated mansion belonging to Duvalier-era drug dealer and assassin Lionel Wooley and served hundreds of the area's poorest children, providing a hot meal as well. On September 7, the coup-appointed mayor, Figaro, entered the school with his heavily armed paramilitary security force, announcing that they were going to close the school. The rehabili-tation of the Haitian Army proceeded steadily, as paramilitaries took territorial control over various towns. On September 1, they took Petit Goave in southern Haiti demanding the army be rein-stated. The UN mission and government did nothing. Two weeks later, on September 15, the deadline set by the coup-appointed Prime Minister Latortue for all armed factions to disarm, passed without a whimper. Paramilitary leader and former Haitian colonel in Petit Goave said, 'We cannot hand over our arms, and I think the government understands that.' As the paramilitaries marched to greater strength and legitimacy, attacks on the rem-nants of social organization continued. On September 16, masked police commandos attacked the Confederation of Haitian Workers (CTH) local office in Port-au-Prince, arresting a dozen people. On September 18, armed men ransacked the offices of the Committee for the Protection of Haitian Rights, which had taken up the cases of Yvon Neptune and So Ann.

The paramilitaries did not confine themselves to political murder, but extended their activities as paramilitaries often to do 'social cleansing' and the murder of street children. Michael Brewer, of a group called Haitian Street Kids, reported on numerous massacres of street children, 7, 9, 12, 14, and 15 years old.[9]

In September 2004, Haitians had not only to contend with paramilitary massacre, foreign occupation, and economic dismemberment, but also a series of tropical storms and floods that devastated the country. A sovereign country with the capacity to mobilize its own resources is able to reduce vulnerability to natural disasters and generate an effective response, as Cuba's low death toll and rapid recovery from the tropical storms showed. Haiti, by contrast, after the decapitation of its government and the dismantling of its popular movement, was unable to respond. The Civil Protection Bureau, created under Aristide's government to respond to such disasters, had been burned during the coup and its workers driven into hiding. The development aid embargo of the previous years was felt acutely in the lack of environmental and social infrastructure to deal with the floods, and the destruction of the social movement through repression and murder meant there were no social forces that could compensate for the lack of resources. The consequences were tragic. On Saturday September 19, rains from tropical storm Jeanne caused floods across the north of Haiti, with the official death toll rising quickly above 1,000 with hundreds missing. Among the hardest hit was the paramilitary-controlled town of Gonaives. There were also a huge number of secondary victims, precisely because those forces that could have mounted an effective response (government and movement) had been destroyed by violence, and the estimated death toll rose to 2,000, then to 2,500. The U.S. initially offered $60,000 for disaster relief. Venezuela offered $1 million, Trinidad and Tobago $5 million, and the EU $1.8 million – the U.S. then changed its pledge to $2 million for Haiti, and $6 billion for hurricane relief in the U.S.[10] Kevin Pina reported that the floods were used to dispose of victims of political repression, with 'flood victims" bodies being found with bullet holes in them.[11]

On September 30, Lavalas held demonstrations to commemorate the anniversary of the 1991 coup d'etat. In the popular neighbourhood of Cité Soleil, residents began to walk out to join the pro-democracy march near the national palace. Labanye's pro-coup gang[12] fired on the crowd, stopping them from leaving. Many were killed. Public Lavalas meetings in the neighbourhood, which had taken place on Saturdays, were cancelled from then on due to fear.[13]

In the Port-au-Prince neighbourhood of Bel Air, too, pro-democracy crowds were fired upon, this time by police. Unlike Cité Soleil, Bel Air was not cut off from the rest of Port-au-Prince. Also unlike Cité Soleil, the Haitian police did not fear to enter: instead, they entered routinely to conduct massacres, with firepower support from the UN. Like Cité Soleil, however, there is a pro-Aristide resistance to the regime, organized as the Mouvman Resistans Baz Popile (MBRP), including 23 popular organizations from all over Haiti. Among its leaders in September was a young man who went by the name Samba Boukman. Boukman had documented approximately 100 deaths and many more disappeared in police operations since the coup, and over 500 arrests of MBRP members from the summer of 2004 to November 2004.[14]

Also unlike Cité Soleil on September 30, once the police fired on the crowd, the police in turn came under fire. Witnesses saw police fire on demonstrators and collect bodies, and masked gunmen return fire.[15] The government then claimed that the headless bodies were recovered and blamed Aristide supporters for the beheadings, calling them 'Operation Baghdad'.[16] The bodies were never seen, however. Over the next few days, witnesses in the pro-Aristide neighbourhoods of Delmas 19, 30, 32, and 33 reported paramilitaries driving through the neighbourhoods, asking political questions of residents, and shooting those who were pro-Aristide.[17] Confirmed victims of these raids include Marguerite Saint-Fils, shot by police in her home in Bel Air on September 30; Maxo Casseus and Piersene Adema (a 60-year-old woman), both killed by paramilitaries in Cité Soleil on September 30; Wendy Manignat, a child of 15, shot dead by police in Bel Air on October 1; and Ronald Braneluce, shot by police on the same day.[18] At least 80 people were killed on September 30.[19]

Three Lavalas politicians, Deputy Roudy Herivaux, Senator Yvon Feuille, and Senator Gerald Gilles, went on Radio Caraibes FM's 'Ranmase' programme and denounced the violence, condemning the police for firing on the demonstrators on September 30. The regime quickly arrested them – with heavily armed police officers moving into position around the radio station before the programme had even ended – and charged them with the 'intellectual authorship' of the violence on September 30. During the long standoff in which the Station Manager refused to allow the police entry (they eventually obtained authority from Judge Gabriel Amboise to cut the locks) former Deputy Axene Joseph arrived on the scene to protest the arrests. He was then arrested himself. On October 4, the government announced they would free Gilles, citing a lack of evidence, but the Minister of Justice continued to maintain that Herivaux and Feuille were intellectual authors of the violence that occurred on September 30. Lavalas activists in Bel Air threatened to take to the streets, demanding the return of their leaders. From October 2–4, the Haitian National Police cordoned off the area and attacked Bel Air. People in the neighbourhood fired back, and the police retreated. The police returned to Bel Air on October 6, with MINUSTAH this time, and conducted a total sweep, including mass arrests and house searches.[20] On October 5, the police 'swept' the western neighbourhood of Martissant. In Cité Soleil, the police intervened at a hospital to prevent a man who had been shot in the stomach from receiving medical treatment – something that was reported to have occurred frequently. By the end of the week, the United Nations were using Armored Personnel Vehicles, helicopters, and attack dogs to besiege Bel Air, with 200 UN troops and 150 Haitian police conducting raids, detaining hundreds and arresting dozens in a single day. Still the raids continued.

On October 13, armed paramilitaries marched on Port-au-Prince and announced their intention to take action against Lavalas, probably a power move to pressure the occupying forces into more raids. The United Nations did nothing. By November, these paramilitaries had taken up residence in the Petionville suburb, the richest neighbourhood in the Port-au-Prince area. The paramilitaries displayed uniforms, heavy weapons, and openly called themselves the 'Haitian Army'. In November, 300 such soldiers were headquartered at the Petionville base, carrying not only heavy weapons, but swords and gas masks. The leader of the 'Haitian Army', Remissainthes Ravix, supposedly the subject of an arrest warrant and a nationwide manhunt, was giving in-studio interviews at radio stations around the capital with impunity. In a press conference in November, 'General' Ravix threatened the Latortue regime, accused it of weakness, and demanded that it recognize the Haitian Army's authority and its right to recruit Haitian youth. The second-in-command, Commander Jean-Baptiste Joseph, said that there were 5,000 such soldiers on 'active duty' throughout the country.[21]

On October 15, thousands of Bel Air residents took to the streets to demand the return of Aristide. Police fired at them yet again, and gunmen fired back, yet again. While Reuters estimated on October 6 that 45 people had been killed over the course of the first week of raids, on October 15 the morgue at the General Hospital issued an emergency call for removal of the 600 bodies that had piled up there over the past two weeks, stating there was no space for corpses, as the morgue had reached full capacity.[22] At dawn on October 24, the UN conducted a massive raid, called 'Clean Sweep Bel Air', with 100 police officers from Canada, Benin, France, and Spain, advancing into Bel Air behind ten Brazilian armoured cars with mounted sub-machine guns.[23]

On October 22 in the neighbourhood of Martissant, Lavalas supporters created a barricade in the street, carrying weapons and firing at Haitian police who had arrived for one of their 'operations'.

The police called MINUSTAH, and two tanks arrived. The armed Lavalas supporters fled, but other demonstrators continued to throw rocks. A MINUSTAH tank fired on and killed 26-year-old Carlo Pierre, who was taking aim with a rock at the time.[24]

ROOTING OUT LAVALAS IN CITÉ SOLEIL

In Cité Soleil the pro-Aristide street groups who had refused to take up Apaid's offer the year before now organized for self-defence against Labanye under Dred Wilme and Amaral, calling themselves simply the 'security force'. Dred Wilme, still a youth, had resided at Lafanmi Selavi, a shelter for street children founded by Aristide years before. Both of these leaders swore to bring Aristide back to the poor or die trying.[25] When Labanye's Boston group cut off the exits to Cité Soleil, the 'security force' established martial law in their own regions, preventing commercial traffic into the entire neighbourhood of Cité Soleil.

The resistance took both the regime and the UN by surprise. The Haitian police refused to enter Cité Soleil, while the United Nations would only enter in force, with machine guns and armoured personnel carriers. According to Dred Wilme, these UN incursions actually prevented Labanye from completely wiping out the pro-Aristide forces in Cité Soleil. Unfortunately, the UN seemed committed to wiping out the same forces themselves.

The responses to the media by government and UN figures demonstrated their contempt for the Haitian people and their flailing in search of a scapegoat. Latortue reached for South Africa's president Thabo Mbeki, accusing him of using South African territory to help 'organize violence' in Haiti. Latortue evidently preferred that violence in Haiti be organized from Miami, Washington, Montreal, Ottawa, New York, Santo Domingo, or Brasilia. The Brazilian general Augusto Heleno blamed U.S. Senator John Kerry, who was campaigning for the U.S. presidency that month and had made some criticism of the Republican's irrational hatred of Aristide. Heleno told the Brazilian news agency that '[s]tatements made by a candidate to the presidency of the United States created false hopes among pro-Aristide supporters ... that should Mr. Kerry win the U.S. election in November the former Haitian president might be restored to power'. Heleno's troops proceeded to act to ensure that hope was absent for Haitians. His policy, as he said on the radio on October 8, was simple and bloody. But the general intended to discriminate between victims: 'We must kill the bandits [i.e. Aristide supporters] but it will have to be the bandits only, not everybody.'

THE ARREST OF JEAN-JUSTE

The regime responded to its own violence and to the unexpected resistance with another high-profile arrest of a well-known peace activist, after So Ann's early arrest. This time it was 57-year-old Catholic priest Gérard Jean-Juste, arrested at his parish of St Claire in the neighbourhood of Petite Place Cazeau on October 13 while feeding neighbourhood children. The regime accused the pacifist priest of importing arms and harbouring gunmen. He told the Haiti Information Project: 'Everyone who knows me knows that I do not support violence. This is a desperate move on the government's part to frighten people into silence who they believe do not support them. This is sad day for democracy in Haiti because without freedom of speech there can be no democracy. I will pray for them from my prison cell.'[26] Although government officials had publicly accused Jean-Juste of gun-running, when lawyers obtained the official government documents after Jean-Juste had spent a week in jail without a hearing, it turned out he had been charged with disturbing the peace, which carries a fine of about 40 cents.

Jean-Juste's arrest might have been an extraordinary case of government impunity, but he was not alone. At the end of October the regime published an 'arrest list', offering tens of thousands in rewards for 32 individuals. Months before, the list had contained 37 individuals: 5 of them had been killed in the meantime.[27] At the end of October, the U.S. lifted the arms embargo that had been imposed on Haiti since the first coup in 1991, in order to get more weapons into the hands of the regime.[28] The regime was making good use of the weapons it already had. On October 26, Haitian police in black helmets entered the neighbourhood of Fort Nationale, rounded 13 young men up, lined them up, forced them to the ground, and executed them one by one. Eight of these turned up at the morgue.[29] On October 28, another five young men were murdered in the same way in Bel Air.[30] In November, Reuters broke a story that 19 police officers were plotting to assassinate Lavalas political prisoners in Port-au-Prince. These police were punished with a slap on the wrist: special orders to appear at the general inspection office until the allegations were resolved.[31]

Those same days (October 27–28), a delegation of human rights observers affiliated with Harvard University were interviewing MINUSTAH commander Augusto Heleno Ribeiro Pereira and his first assistant, Carlos Chagas. The observers complained that MINUSTAH, whose mandate included monitoring human rights, had not published a single human rights report since its mission began. They were surprised to learn that the commanders of the mission did not see such investigations as part of MINUSTAH's mandate. The delegates used a bucket and a stick to unearth a mass grave in Titanyen outside Port-au-Prince, and delivered the remains of a small child to CIVPOL officer René Leclerc. Several months of inaction later, the Harvard delegates were told by CIVPOL Commissioner Beer that Titanyen was 'not an active case being investigated'.[32]

At the same time as the massacres were taking place, Canadian corporate representatives invaded Haiti to sign trade agreements. Businessmen from New Brunswick and Quebec representing 12 companies in the Francophone Business Forum were in Haiti to discuss contracts in 'road infrastructure, telecommunications, energy, urban planning, waste disposal, sustainable development, agroindustry, manufacturing, fishing, fish farming, the environment, renewable energy, water treatment, education and training'. Latortue commented that '[i]t is [in?] trying times that one finds out who one's true friends are'.[33] Another 'friend' from Canada, Prime Minister Paul Martin, visited Haiti a week later, on Sunday November 14, three days after police arrested Jean-Marie Samedi, a popular Lavalas leader in Bel Air who was caught and beaten while riding a scooter.[34] Martin declared on the visit that 'there are no political prisoners in Haiti'. Perhaps to try to give the impression of a more friendly Haiti to these international investors, the regime freed Father Jean-Juste on November 29. Jean-Juste spent the next few months travelling in the United States and in South Africa before returning to Haiti in 2005.

The police and UN conducted frequent incursions into Bel Air. On November 8, Samba Boukman, a spokesperson for pro-Lavalas resistance group MRBP, sent a letter to MINUSTAH requesting protection for a demonstration on November 10. On that day, demonstrators gathered to call for Aristide's return. MINUSTAH was on hand, as requested, and proceeded to watch as the Haitian police arrived on the scene, killed seven people, and seized 180 more.[35] On November 18, a national holiday, a major police operation in Bel Air was observed by a human rights delegation. Police helicopters hovered over the target neighbourhood. Police officers gathered in trucks, dressed in black, with black helmets and face masks, with high-powered weapons. MINUSTAH soldiers in Armoured Personnel Carriers (APCs) accompanied the police, blocking off entry or exit by journalists, investigators, and civilians. Gunfire began. The police left some bodies behind, and took others with them. The human rights investigators found the bodies of a middle-aged woman who had been shot in the abdomen, and the bound and partially burned body of a man who had been killed by gangs as a suspected police spy. They encountered wounded Hercules Lefevre, who had been shot in the shoulder by a MINUSTAH APC, and Inep Henri, 35, who had been shot in the head and was refused medical care at various hospitals in the city.[36] Many who were shot avoided hospitals, for fear of being marked for death by the police.[37]

On December 1, U.S. Secretary of State Colin Powell visited the new Haitian President Boniface Alexandre. At the same time, in the national penitentiary, in one of the cell blocks, called 'Titanic', prisoners rioted. Prison guards called in a special police unit to suppress the riot. The police proceeded to massacre Lavalas prisoners, according to eyewitnesses who told reporter Reed Lindsay about the massacre. One witness saw 60 prisoners killed, with police going from cell to cell executing them. Another witness reported being forced to cart bodies from the Titanic to another part of the prison. Lindsay visited the prison weeks later and found that estimates of the death toll ranged from 40 to 110, though prison officials gave a figure of seven. An ambulance driver told Lindsay he had personally transported 30 bodies from the prison to a dumpsite which, fearing for his life, he refused to show Lindsay.[38] The United Nations responded with a proposal to provide $50,000 to repair cells and another $15,000 for the women's penitentiary in Port-au-Prince. The director of Haiti's penitentiary system, Claude Theodat, refused. Perhaps Theodat, unlike the UN, understood the real purpose of the prison system, which most certainly was not to provide a comfortable experience for the prisoners, 17 of whom among the 1,100 had been convicted of a crime and all of whom, since the paramilitaries had freed the criminals in February 2004 and the regime had replaced them over the months that followed, were Lavalas.

Also in December, a document prepared by the 'Canadian Foundation for the Americas' for the Canadian parliamentary

Foreign Affairs committee summarized the intentions of the 'international community' towards Haiti.[39] Like so many such documents, it was a perfect inversion of reality. Rather than discussing the ways in which the U.S. and Canada destabilized Haiti, the document called Haiti a 'destabilizing influence on its neighbours'. Rather than talking about how Haiti's people and social organizations were victims of massive crimes, it called Haiti a 'transnational crime base'. Rather than mentioning the aid embargo, destabilization campaign, and disinformation, the report said previous situations had failed 'through a combination of Haitian truculence, corruption, donor fatigue, and impatience'. Calling Haiti a 'failed state', it proceeded to suggest a 10-year-long occupation, with Brazilian troops, American funds, and Canadian leadership due to its prestige in the international community. The authors of the report were banking on an international prestige based on Canada's relative lack of colonial history. That was rapidly being eroded as Canada engaged in occupations and assaults on the sovereignty of other nations.

The pattern of UN-police-paramilitary raids in the pro-Aristide neighbourhoods continued, and would be continuous over the months to follow. In Cité Soleil, the UN provided the backup for paramilitary incursions to murder and massacre. The mutilation of victims was a tactic used by the paramilitaries.[40] At 3am on December 14, Brazilian and Jordanian troops in armoured personnel carriers conducted an incursion into Cité Soleil. Among the victims of their APC fire was 2-year-old Herlens Henri, who died in his mother's arms in bed.[41] Eyewitnesses reported heavy gunfire lasting three hours.[42] That incursion was probably to try to deter the anniversary celebrations and demonstrations that would have taken place, since December 14, 2004 was the 14th anniversary of Aristide's first electoral victory. The assault did not stop Haitians from demonstrating. Two days later on December 16 in Cap Haitien, Haiti's second largest city, over 10,000 Haitians demonstrated to demand Aristide's return, chanting: 'We will never accept the kidnapping of our president!'. The demonstrators were briefly joined by Jean-Charles Moise, the former mayor of the town of Milo, who came briefly out of hiding.[43] The regime tried a sop to the growing resistance, releasing some of the prisoners whose arrest had galvanized the movement after the September 30 massacre. Yvon Feuille, Rudy Heriveaux, and Lesly Gustave were freed on December 24.

HAITI'S ARMED GROUPS

Much less of a sop was the regime's compensation payments to the paramilitaries. Former soldiers who participated in a takeover of Aristide's residence on December 15 were 'convinced' to leave by the UN, then trucked to a police academy to prepare for a ceremony. Thirty-three of these received the first of a series of checks that will total $5,000 per soldier, and the regime said 6,000 former soldiers would be eligible (for a total of approximately $30 million). This money had symbolic value as well: it was back pay for the ten years the Haitian Army had been dissolved. The paramilitaries, composed in the first place of the former army of the dictatorship, were being absolved, rehabilitated, and re-absorbed into the Haitian police force.[44]

This created some tension between the different officially sanctioned armed groups in Haiti. First, there were the paramilitaries, composed of the former army of the dictatorship and the FRAPH paramilitaries who had terrorized Haiti during the years 1991–94. These paramilitaries had been re-organized and re-armed in the Dominican Republic, and set upon the Lavalas regime. Now that they had achieved victory, they wanted full integration, promotion, and a return to power.

The second officially sanctioned armed group was the Haitian National Police. Within this group there were three subgroups. First, there were those who had been trained in 'professionalism' by U.S. and Canadian police forces as part of various aid missions, and wanted to remain above politics. Second, there were those who, during the coup, opted to defect from Lavalas and join the coup. Third, there were those who remained loyal to the Lavalas government as the coup unfolded. The main armed activity of the paramilitaries during the early stages of the coup consisted of killing members of this third subgroup. After the coup, 500 police officers, most probably from this subgroup, were purged from the police force.[45] The first subgroup of police, however, were resentful over issues of promotion and professionalism: officers expressed dismay that paramilitaries with no police training or professional standards were being promoted into positions of authority in the police force because of connections to the post-coup regime over those who had trained under U.S. and Canadian police in 1995 and since to become 'professional' officers.[46]

The third officially sanctioned armed group were the armed gangs, such as that of Thomas 'Labanye' Robinson in Cité Soleil. These gangs were recruited and organized by members of the Haitian elite like Andy Apaid, and operated with impunity, police protection, and financing. Their mission was to physically eliminate Lavalas's street and community organizations and networks. Of the 13,000–18,000 illegal weapons MINUSTAH estimates are in Haiti,[47] most of these are likely in the hands of this type of armed gang, as well as narcotraffickers, paramilitaries, and police-affiliated groups.

The final officially sanctioned armed group was the international forces. Judging by their behaviour, the U.S. Marines had a clear sense of their mission, as did the Canadians and French who arrived with them. The MINUSTAH and CIVPOL missions, however, had stated aims that were mutually contradictory. CIVPOL was supposed to be helping to professionalize a police force that was integrating paramilitary murderers to the top ranks of its power structure. MINUSTAH was supposed to be disarming gangs and supporting the coup regime, while some of the gangs were working for the coup regime. MINUSTAH and CIVPOL were also there to support the coup regime, however, which meant providing backup for the paramilitaries and police.

Facing this diverse array of armed forces was the essentially defenceless Lavalas street and community organizations. Its leaders, at every level, were either dead, in hiding, or in the process of being liquidated, with the high-profile leaders having been eliminated first. Loyal police had also been killed in the early stages of the coup. Lavalas street organizations were being systematically cut off from their political leadership, and as a result increasingly resorted to armed self-defence, facing opponents with far better armament and international support.

By the end of the year thousands more Haitians were seeking to escape. But they would be denied refuge outside as well as inside Haiti. Rony François, a 30-year-old Haitian-American bus driver and father of a 10-month-old child, was stopped on Christmas Eve 2004 by authorities in Miami and thrown in jail. Agents in Haitian neighbourhoods in Miami were asking for identification at bus stops and on buses, arresting undocumented Haitians. Haitian-Americans started staying at home, but even that was little protection. One Haitian-American youth pastor in West Palm Beach was arrested in his home. In Orlando federal agents arrested a handful of Haitians at a grocery store. Immigration officers denied an increasing trend of deportations, stating that from October 1, 2003 to September 31, 2004 (fiscal year 2004), the U.S. deported 753 Haitians, compared to 1,019 in fiscal year 2003.[48] Those statistics did not count pre-emptive deportations like the Coast Guard's returning of 208 Haitians to Port-au-Prince after catching them on a 30-foot sailboat en route to Florida on December 29, 2004,[49] nor similar denial of asylum by Haiti's neighbours like Jamaica, which denied asylum requests from 281 Haitians in September of 2004.[50] Haiti's National Office of Migration said that 2,000 Haitians had been repatriated, or denied asylum, in 2004.

6 OCCUPATION YEAR TWO: 2005

The New Year in Haiti began as the last one had ended, with murderous incursions into poor neighbourhoods and Haitians struggling against all odds. In Bel Air, thousands marched on New Year's Eve to demand the return of Aristide.[1] In Cité L'Eternel, another neighbourhood of Port-au-Prince, police officers killed a 28-year-old man and a 13-year-old girl and arrested several others in a raid on January 4.[2] Police also raided Cité de Dieux and killed six people, including a 16-year-old girl, on the same day.[3] The next day, January 5, 400 troops from MINUSTAH joined the Haitian National Police in a raid on Bel Air, killing five and arresting nine people. Afterwards, they posed for photos removing garbage and wrecked vehicles from the streets.[4] Among those arrested that day outside his home in Fort National by MINUSTAH was Jimmy Charles, a Lavalas activist who was handed over to the Haitian police anti-gang service to be imprisoned. Just over a week later, on January 15, Jimmy Charles's body turned up at the morgue, riddled with bullets, a day before his court date. Police spokesperson Jessy Cameau Coicou told reporters that Charles had been killed in a clash with police. The NCHR said he had been released before being killed.[5] On January 6, armed gangs attacked a mission of the Sisters of St Vincent de Paul in Cité Soleil. On January 7, MINUSTAH and the police invaded Cité Soleil and arrested dozens of people in connection with the attack. Members of the community claimed Labanye's gang was responsible for the attack on the mission, but the community did not fight back. Instead a peaceful demonstration was quickly organized to protest the raid.[6]

THE MURDER OF ABDIAS JEAN AND POLITICAL CLEANSING

On January 14, journalist, law student, and correspondent for WKAT 1360 radio in Miami, Abdias Jean, witnessed a police operation in the Port-au-Prince neighbourhood of Village de Dieu. The police killed two young people in the sweep. Abdias Jean left the scene. The police followed him to a house and killed him there.[7] The police spokesperson Coicou eventually admitted that Jean was killed by police. She only denied that his murder was ordered by high command.[8]

On January 16, police attacked a peaceful pro-Aristide demonstration in Bel Air. MINUSTAH secured the area, throwing riot-control grenades and firing warning shots at random through the afternoon.[9]

Police spokesperson Coicou also tried to explain the murder of Ederson Joseph, the sixth-grader shot dead on January 17 by police officers in the Avenue Pouplard neighbourhood of Port-au-Prince. Joseph's grandmother, Regine Poteau, was unimpressed with Coicou's allegation that the child was a bandit.[10]

On January 18, police killed four youths and set fire to several houses of Lavalas members in Corridor Bassia in Port-au-Prince.[11] On January 21, Lavalas leaders Paul Raymond, René Civil, and Clifford Larose were arrested in the Dominican Republic. Larose had been the head of the National Penitentiary under Aristide[12] and was accused of human rights violations as Yvon Neptune had been, but the evidence did not hold up in court and a Dominican judge ordered him released on January 26. He was freed on January 28.

In the countryside a pattern of violence and displacement – 'political cleansing' of Lavalas from paramilitary controlled towns – continued. In the paramilitary stronghold of Petit Goave, Lavalas members in hiding kept lists of those dozens of activists forced into hiding and records of beatings, looting, and the burnings of houses of those who spoke to reporters or human rights delegations.[13] There was also some tug-of-war between the Lavalas movement, MINUSTAH, and the paramilitaries in the countryside. On January 19, in the city of Cap Haitien, armed paramilitaries marched through Cap Haitien as a demonstration of strength. Chilean MINUSTAH troops stopped them, disarming some. On January 21 they marched again, unimpeded by MINUSTAH, and entered the popular neighbourhood of Lafocet, killing a woman and wounding many others. MINUSTAH, who had arrived on the scene too late, responded by announcing on the radio that the paramilitaries were not allowed to bear arms or make arrests, and prohibited these former Haitian army paramilitaries from entering Lafocet. On February 1, the paramilitaries disobeyed the prohibition and arrested two men wearing Aristide T-shirts. On February 4, paramilitaries assassinated Antonio Renaud, member of the peasant movement in Milot and a close associate of the ousted mayor, Jean-Charles Moise.[14]

Social cleansing continued. A practice of paramilitaries dating back to the Duvalier dictatorship, the murder of street children, had declined under Aristide, who initiated prosecution of adults who mistreat children, supported children's radio stations, and created centres like Lafanmi Selavi for street children in Port-au-Prince. Now Lafanmi Selavi was closed and children were targets again, with a five-fold increase in targeted beatings and killings of street children. One missionary said that she had seen three murdered street children between 1995 and 2004 and 150 such murders since the February 29 coup.[15]

THE FINANCIAL COUP

As the police, the paramilitaries, and the UN were raiding the neighbourhoods, the World Bank was raiding the treasury. On January 4, Haiti gave $52.6 million to the World Bank in service payments on the debt, unblocking the way for Haiti to go into further debt: the World Bank had suspended loans since January 30, 2001. Of the $52.6 million, $12.7 million came from Canada. The other $40 million came from Haiti's own reserves. The World Bank had big hopes for the coup government, according to its Economic Governance Reform Operation Project agreement, which said: 'The Transitional Government provide[s] a window of opportunity for implementing economic governance reforms ... that may be hard for a future government to undo.'[16]

As it had in the past, the United States competed with Canada for generosity. Canada had sent $12.7 million to the World Bank so that that institution could take another $40 million from Haitians. The State Department gave its largesse to the Fluor Corporation, to the tune of $72 million, for a new U.S. Embassy in the capital.[17] Canada was outdone again. In November 2004, it had sent Hydro-Quebec to Gonaives for a $4.5 million electrification project,[18] which paled in comparison. Its embassy, completed by engineering firm SNC-Lavalin in September 2004, cost only $20 million.[19] Land for the Canadian Embassy had been purchased from Gilbert Bigio, one of Haiti's wealthiest men. Brazil, wanting to show its largesse as well, announced later that year that it had sent 235 tonnes of food and medicine to Haiti and would send 28 more tonnes by airlift.[20]

The United States also sent members of the 372nd Military Police Company – the unit publicly associated in the sexual humiliation, torture, and murder of Iraqi prisoners at Abu Ghraib prison – to Haiti to provide security for the various international missions there. Staff Sargent Edwin Ramos, commenting on this, said: 'They want to show the world they have a big heart. The way I see it, they live up to the Army values of honor, courage and selfless service.'

EMMANUEL CONSTANT'S DAY IN COURT

Haitians kept seeking avenues to fight impunity. A group of Haitian women served paramilitary leader Emmanuel 'Toto' Constant with papers in a U.S. court charging torture, crimes against humanity, and the systematic use of violence and rape. Constant, with Guy Philippe and Louis Jodel Chamblain, had been the leader of the FRAPH (Revolutionary Front for the Advancement and Progress of Haiti) paramilitaries who terrorized Haiti and killed thousands of Haitians from 1991 to 1994. Constant, who was still living in Queens, New York, was charged by three women who were survivors of gang rapes and attempted murder by Constant's paramilitaries. The women who brought the suit were not only seeking justice for past crimes: they were explicitly hoping to deter current crimes. One of them said of the current violence: 'We hope that the suit will deter at least some of the violence, by sending a message that anyone who commits atrocities will no longer be able to visit or live in the U.S. with impunity.'[21] In the end, Constant did end up in jail – for mortgage tax fraud, in 2008.[22]

One paramilitary who was not allowed to live in the U.S. with impunity was Butteur Metayer, leader of the 'Front of Resistance of Gonaives', one of the paramilitary groups that murdered and massacred their way to power and ousted Aristide. Metayer had been imprisoned in Florida for nearly two months under accusations of arms trafficking and human rights violations. He was repatriated, free and clear, to Gonaives and to his paramilitary followers, on January 21.[23] Rather than living in the U.S. with impunity, Metayer was to live in Haiti with impunity.

A year of massacre had still failed to break resistance to the coup, and the coup regime recognized this, though it tried to divert this resistance. Latortue announced that the regime would send an envoy to South Africa to negotiate with Aristide to 'find a solution to the violence', according to a report by Guyler C. Delva, the Reuters correspondent for Haiti and the secretary general of the Association of Haitian Journalists (AJH).[24] Such 'negotiations' missed the point. Even though a key demand of those resisting the coup was the restoration of Aristide, the resistance was not, despite the fantasies of those who had made the coup, a tap that Aristide had turned on and could turn off at will. It was the inevitable resistance to a murderous regime intent on liquidating and dismantling a popular movement. Such resistance could be crushed, and the regime was trying to do so. It could be placated by returning to a constitutional regime and disarming the paramilitaries. But it could not be negotiated away.

At any rate Latortue was soon to reject any such negotiations and issue a veiled threat against the journalist who had published them. In a press release of January 23, Latortue called Delva's report a 'shameful machination' and accused the journalist of preaching 'disinformation about Haiti [...] to his own political clique'.[25] Delva was stunned: he had given Latortue the opportunity to reply, and Latortue had done so, saying that while he was not negotiating with Aristide, he was encouraging others to do so. Delva read Latortue's statement as encouragement and incitement to violence against Delva and journalists more generally, by paramilitaries and police who had only weeks before murdered journalist Abdias Jean.

Latortue had nothing to say about Abdias Jean's murder, but perhaps he was preoccupied with the important scandal that wracked his government in late January. This scandal had nothing to do with the raids in poor neighbourhoods, murders of journalists, rehabilitation of the paramilitaries, or even the World Bank raid on the Haitian treasury. Instead the scandal was over 15 bags of rice. Two members of Latortue's cabinet, Raymond Lafontant, and his spokesperson Michel Joseph, authorized the non-governmental organization (NGO) Food for the Poor to turn over 15 containers of rice to the deputy mayor of Port-au-Prince, Jean Philippe Sassine, without consulting Latortue. He suspended them. The spokesperson for the Council of the Wise, Anne Marie Issa, expressed shock at the corruption of the government in the rice scandal.[26] Latortue got set to make some cabinet shuffles in February, perhaps in response. To the Interior Ministry, Latortue planned to appoint Michel Bernardin, a Duvalierist with family ties to the dictators (Bernardin's cousin, Army Colonel Max

Dominique, was Papa Doc Duvalier's son-in-law). Latortue had second thoughts, however, and cancelled his swearing in the next day.[27]

THE SLOW ROAD TO ELECTIONS

Latortue's main move for legitimacy, however, was the announcement of elections. Local and municipal elections were scheduled for October 9, legislative and presidential elections for November 13, 2005. Among the strategies for gaining democratic legitimacy was the ridiculous proliferation of parties, with 91 parties registering and 100 candidates preparing to contest the elections immediately after the announcement. At the beginning of January Latortue promised that the elections would be fair, and that he would not remain in office after February 2006. 'It is out of the question for me to remain even one hour longer,' he said.[28] These elections were the subject of a great deal of controversy within the coup camp. Andy Apaid, one of the principal private financiers and organizers of the coup regime's bid for power, had tried the year before to put forward an electronic voting scheme for $112 million. The scheme involved the purchase of thousands of laptop computers that would be acquired by one of Apaid's companies. Electronic voting in Haiti was, however, somewhat impractical, since most of Haiti's capital does not receive more than six hours of electricity per day, to say nothing of the rural areas. Apaid's scheme was frustrated at the eight-member Provisional Electoral Council by the council's president, Roselor Julien. Julien countered Apaid's scheme with a cheaper, $51 million, paper-voting scheme, which won support from international donors and broke the consistent 4–4 deadlock at the council. Apaid and other business groups then lobbied the Supreme Court to appoint a ninth member to the council, destroying what independence it had. Julien resigned in November 2004.[29]

Marc Bazin, leader of the Movement for the Establishment of Democracy in Haiti (MIDH), former World Bank employee, and the U.S.-backed candidate defeated by Aristide in the 1990 elections, was sceptical about the planned elections. 'I could act like certain other political leaders, but I myself am a realist, I am willing to see the reality in front of me,' he said. The reality, he elaborated, was that the majority of people in the country were sympathetic to Lavalas and no serious election would be possible in Haiti without them.[30] Because of the likelihood of very low voter turnout for the post-coup elections, the government planned to tie social services to voter registration. In February, Justice Minister Bernard Gousse explained the plan for the voter card: 'It would not be a voter registration card but a digital national identity card with the fingerprint, photograph and other information of the voter,' Gousse boasted. 'Initially, this card will make it possible to identify all adults through the data collected. Later, it will make it possible to identify all citizens,' including children, presumably.[31]

For all the regime's manoeuvring, voices that had opposed the coup could not be completely silenced. On February 1, Lavalas announced it would not participate in elections so long as government terrorism against them continued. The Caribbean Community of Nations, CARICOM, announced on January 7 that CARICOM would not recognize Haiti's regime until democratic elections were held and democracy restored. By the end of January Brazilian parliamentarians like Ivan Valente were calling Brazil's involvement in Haiti a 'quagmire'.[32] Thousands signed a statement calling for the restoration of the democratic government of Haiti at the World Social Forum in Porto Alegre, Brazil, at the end of January. Called the 'Porto Alegre Declaration on Haiti', the statement also called for the freeing of political prisoners, asylum for refugees, and an end to UN support for the police and paramilitaries. The international response against the coup was further developed at a conference in Washington, DC. The Congress Bwa Kayiman, from February 5–7, 2005, brought Haitians from the diaspora and activists together to gather a 'movement of solidarity with the struggle of the Haitian people' to 'win back national dignity and the return of democracy in Haiti'. It was sponsored by organizations like the Institute for Justice and Democracy in Haiti, the TransAfrica Forum, and the Let Haiti Live Coalition, as well as many Lavalas-affiliated organizations in Haiti.

Within Haiti, some of these groups demonstrated against the coup. On February 7, the anniversary of the fall of the Duvalier dictatorship in 1986, the National Popular Party (PPN) and the Confederation of Peasant Groups of Borgne (KGPB) held a 20 km march of hundreds from Petit Bourg au Borgne to the town of Borgne.[33] On the same day, thousands of Lavalas supporters marched in Port-au-Prince. Scattered armed resistance to the coup regime occurred around this time as well. On February 5, a guerrilla group called the Dessalinien Army of National Liberation (ADLN) described an attack they had made on a police station two days before in the countryside town of Plaisance and told resistance fighters all over the country to stand firm.

POLICE AND PARAMILITARY VIOLENCE

The police were simultaneously conducting another round of raids in and around Bel Air. On January 30, police raided Korido Bassia and Mon St Michel (a neighbourhood located between Bel Air and Fort National), shooting five men. The police dragged two of these (one of them a 17-year-old youth) into the street and executed them.[34] On February 4, police officers in black uniforms and bala-clavas shot and killed a 14-year-old child. On February 5, they killed a 21-year-old. They killed three more people on February 6, leaving them on the Rue de Peuple near Bel Air for some time before returning to pick up the bodies: when they found one alive, they killed him.[35]

Haitian Carnival weekend, which took place from February 6–8, saw four police and six civilians killed. The four policemen were killed by former army/paramilitaries while on patrol near the airport. On February 7, the Carnival parade in Port-au-Prince was attacked by gunmen, later identified by police (who returned fire) as paramilitaries and former soldiers.[36] Perhaps in reprisal for these paramilitary attacks, police, with UN backup, stormed a compound in Port-au-Prince on February 10, ostensibly to arrest paramilitary leader Remissainthe Ravix, who had spent the previous month (and would spend future months) openly patrolling the streets of the capital, calling himself 'commander' of the Haitian Army, and demanding – and receiving – back pay for his soldiers. No shots were fired by the UN. Ravix, who was not apprehended, later quipped: 'Who could dare arrest a military commander?'[37] A young girl, however, was shot and killed as she left school a block away from the raid.[38] Despite the ineffectiveness of the raid, it demonstrated continuing divisions between the police and the paramilitaries, just as the killings of the police officers had demonstrated the paramilitaries' willingness to use violence even against their allies. They continued to issue warnings and threats to the coup government. Paramilitary Clement Mathurin Etienne told reporters, 'This life is in our blood. It only took us a few months to get ready to fight Aristide, and now we are ready for whatever comes … It would be difficult for any force to make us disarm because this is our home.'[39]

Meanwhile, Labanye's government-backed Boston gang was terrorizing Cité Soleil, battling the pro-Aristide gangs. On February 13, a person from the Boston area, Rosemond, was killed in another area. On February 14, the Boston gang crossed into Soley 9 and killed a man named Emmanuel and wounded a 10-year-old orphan, a girl named Natalie, whose mother had been killed by the Boston gang.[40]

Detention and prison remained constant. In early February immigration officials from the Bahamas, who had deported 3,000 immigrants – mostly Haitians – in 2004,[41] reported that 400 Haitians had been caught trying to enter that country already in 2005.[42] The Jamaican government caught 58 Haitians in a rowboat on February 17.[43] In Haiti's prisons, thousands of prisoners were 'languishing in squalor', according to a *Globe and Mail* reporter who interviewed the imprisoned Prime Minister Yvon Neptune on February 7.[44] Neptune told the reporter he was concerned about being assassinated inside the prison.

THE ASSASSINATION ATTEMPT ON YVON NEPTUNE

His fears were nearly realized on February 19, when four commandos dressed in black and armed with assault rifles attacked the prison. They killed a prison guard and sent other guards fleeing. The gunmen took Yvon Neptune and former Interior Minister Jocelerme Privert away in their jeep.[45] Hundreds of police moved in to secure the prison shortly afterwards, but not before some 480 prisoners escaped. UN sources suggested the prison break could not have occurred without collusion from within the prison.[46] The regime blamed Lavalas, but Bel Air resistance leader Sanba Boukman dismissed the allegations. 'It's a simulation', he told a reporter. 'They say it was Lavalas activists, but it was the government who did it.'[47] French reporter Claude Ribbe suggested a different story, based on his sources. The prison break, Ribbe wrote, was the work of a group in the Haitian Police, who were working on a $150,000 contract with narcotraffickers to liberate their accomplices. The prison guard was killed because he had recognized the commandos as police. The attackers took Privert and Neptune as an attack of opportunity, since these Lavalas leaders were enemies of theirs. One of the commandos, Arnold Bellizere,[48] changed his mind and dumped Privert and Neptune in the street, where they sought refuge in a nearby house. Privert and Neptune then contacted the UN, who brought them back to the prison.[49] Several days later, on February 24, when he realized that even these dramatic events would not see them brought before a judge, Neptune went on hunger strike. In a letter explaining his hunger strike, Neptune wrote the following:

> With hopes that strong and sincere voices of moral authority and the partisans of justice will say unequivocally to the Government that it must cease to ally itself with delinquents, vandals, notorious assassins, and discredited organizations which shamelessly persist in trying to make me out to be a murderer so they can justify for the benefit of the Government my eventual lynching. I am sure that the spectacle of my slow and certain death would be much more palatable to the Government and its cohorts. To facilitate their purpose I have undertaken a hunger strike so that one day my brothers and sisters who are made to wallow in abject misery will no longer be disdained, starved, scorned and ostracized.[50]

The UN, meanwhile, continued to act as an occupying army, committing crimes against the civilian population. A 23-year-old woman reported being raped by three UN peacekeepers at a banana plantation. 'The foreigners grabbed me and pulled my pants down, had me lie on the ground and then raped me,' she told a reporter. The peacekeepers claimed they paid the victim for sex,[51] and MINUSTAH, investigating the claims, cleared the UN troops of the rape charges. Certainly the UN had no monopoly on generating rape allegations. Journalist Lyn Duff recorded testimonies of political rapes of children, girls of age 9 and 14.[52] Duff suggested a pattern of rapes by paramilitaries against children and family members of Lavalas activists as well as Lavalas activists themselves.

The first anniversary of the coup was the occasion of so much violence that it caused another brief fissure between the paramilitaries and their UN backers.

Reuters published an estimate that at least 28 people had been killed in the slums from February 23–28, with a total death toll of 278 since September 30, 2004.[53] On February 22, one of the high-profile Lavalas leaders of the resistance to the coup, Sanba Boukman from Bel Air, a public youth activist with Lavalas, was arrested by MINUSTAH Brazilian troops. He was on his way home from a meeting where demonstrations commemorating the coup of February 28–29 were being planned. Boukman was released the next day, but on February 25, the Haitian Police and the UN conducted another massive raid into his community of Bel Air, where they killed at least six people.[54] A gang had killed at least ten people in the Village de Dieux neighbourhood the day before.[55] On February 28, while Brazilian MINUSTAH troops watched, Haitian police fired on the peaceful Lavalas march of about 2,000 people in Bel Air that Boukman had been planning when he was arrested a week earlier. The police killed three people in the shooting[56]: Dieudonne Juste (16 years old), Alexandre François (18 years old), and 'Chichi' (23 years old).[57] The UN was 'furious': UN Ambassador to Haiti Juan Gabriel Valdes told the *Miami Herald*, 'We cannot tolerate executions. We can't tolerate shooting out of control. We will not permit human rights abuses. We believe that all we have done in Bel Air is seriously threatened by this incident.'

In fact, the UN was embarrassed enough to prevent one police massacre in Bel Air. When thousands of Lavalas supporters in Bel Air demonstrated again on March 4, MINUSTAH was present but the Haitian police were not: they were instead forbidden by MINUSTAH to approach the demonstration, which consequently occurred without any violence.[58] This upset the coup regime's Justice Minister Bernard Gousse, who went on Haitian radio to accuse MINUSTAH of violating its mandate by excluding the police.[59] But MINUSTAH excluded the police again on March 8, as 3,000 women marched, again in Bel Air, for the return of Aristide, on the occasion of International Women's Day. Once again, the march occurred without violence.[60]

A similar pattern occurred in the northern city of Cap Haitien, where 10,000 demonstrated on February 27 for the return of Aristide. They were flanked on all sides by UN and Haitian police. The Lavalas mayor of Milot, Jean-Charles Moise, came out of hiding to join the demonstration. When Chilean MINUSTAH troops moved into the crowd, Moise fled, and people in the crowd threw rocks, fearing that MINUSTAH had arrested Moise (they had not).[61] On the military front, the city's only independent, Lavalas-affiliated radio station, Radio Etincelles, was fired upon by paramilitaries and its transmitter damaged. As Latortue gave a conference at the law school in Cap Haitien on March 6, police and paramilitaries attacked the nearby town of Milo, raiding and searching houses, probably looking for ousted Lavalas mayor Jean-Charles Moise, who had joined the previous week's demonstration but returned to hiding. The aggression was, again, moderated by the Chilean MINUSTAH group, who sent a team into Milot and patrolled the town for the next several nights, during which the paramilitaries were inactive.[62]

Latortue returned from the countryside to Port-au-Prince for meetings with the World Bank vice president for the region, Pamela Cox, who announced $75 million in financing – $37 million of which would have to be paid back, with interest.[63] The World Bank had recently raided the treasury to the tune of $40 million. A week later (March 16–17) Canada's foreign minister, Pierre Pettigrew, went to Port-au-Prince to announce $17 million for the coup regime, $2.9 million of which was actually paid to the Caribbean Development Bank, to get Haiti into another debt relationship.[64] Canadian coupster Pettigrew and World Banker Cox were allowed into Haiti. Aristide's American lawyer, Ira Kurzban, was not. Kurzban was travelling with U.S. Rep. Maxine Waters D-Cal to visit Lavalas Prime Minister Yvon Neptune and Interior Minister Jocelerme Privert, both of whom were in prison. He was told that he could be arrested if he tried to enter the country.[65] Waters tried to convince Neptune to end his hunger strike and accept exile, but Neptune refused.[66]

Meanwhile, the incomplete and somewhat theatrical split between the UN and the paramilitaries continued. For a brief moment in Cap Haitien, MINUSTAH seemed to be acting to disarm the paramilitaries, rounding up 300 former army soldiers – most of whom voluntarily surrendered, some of whom were found with help from the civilian population – on March 13 and putting them on a bus. Latortue was with MINUSTAH, however, and he made sure the bus actually headed to the police academy in Port-au-Prince where the soldiers were given their $5,000 'back pay', re-trained, re-armed, and re-deployed as part of the Haitian police, after a ceremony at which they returned seven weapons.[67]

MINUSTAH also moved on Petit Goave, 70 km west of Port-au-Prince on March 20, actually engaging in a firefight with the paramilitaries who had taken over a police station. MINUSTAH killed two paramilitaries and wounded seven, losing one soldier and two wounded. Taking control of the police station, MINUSTAH detained 20 people, among them paramilitaries and civilians.[68] Among the victims of this operation was journalist Laraque Robenson, 25-year-old reporter for Tele Contact radio. He, along with other journalists, was watching the battle from the balcony of Tele Contact's offices when he was hit in the head and neck. He died in hospital weeks later.[69] MINUSTAH also raided the town of Terre-Rouge, 40 km northeast of Port-au-Prince, the following day, on March 21. Two paramilitaries and two UN soldiers were killed in the fighting: the paramilitaries fled and the UN took control of the area.[70]

On March 23, word hit the streets that Thomas 'Labanye' Robinson, head of the coup government-backed Boston gang in Cité Soleil, had been killed by a rival gang leader that night. Spontaneous demonstrations of celebration broke out on March 24. Haitian police fired on the demonstrators, killing at least one person and wounding several others.[71] Some 1,000 MINUSTAH troops cordoned off Cité Soleil, set up road blocks, and swept their way through the community. The gang dynamics in Cité Soleil were changing, and MINUSTAH was in the battle. On April 3, MINUSTAH left five purported gang members injured or killed in an operation.[72] On April 4, Dred Wilme, leader of the pro-Lavalas armed resistance in Cité Soleil, was wounded.

As MINUSTAH made its way into Cité Soleil to disarm gangs, Latortue was complaining about the poor armaments of his own gang, the Haitian police. On March 31, he urged lifting the arms embargo on Haiti, which he said was impeding his police: 'As prime minister, I cannot stand by and watch police die,' he said, succinctly expressing his priorities.[73] He may have had reason to worry. Two days before, on March 29, a group of police were ambushed in the Delmas neighbourhood of Port-au-Prince: two police officers and a driver were killed.[74] UN officials suggested the paramilitaries were responsible: 'It seems like the attackers knew the police's route and were waiting for them,' one said. The complexity of both paramilitary and police organizations invites several possibilities for the killings: fights over spoils or territory, some specific vendetta, or some kind of frame-up. The same day, thousands of Lavalas supporters marched in Hinche and in Cap Haitien.

Latortue need not have worried too much about the arms embargo. In fact by the time he made his statement on March 31 the arms embargo had already been lifted and shipments of arms delivered. Robert Muggah of the Swiss-based Small Arms Survey showed in a report based on his field research that the U.S. had sold thousands of weapons, worth $7 million, to Latortue's government.[75] A State Department official admitted later that the shipment, in August 2004, had included 2,657 weapons, including M-14 rifles, sub-machine guns, and 2,000 revolvers.[76] Another deal had been brokered six months before by a Haitian American Florida Republican named Lucy Orlando and an arms dealer named Joel Deeb, an associate of the late Pablo Escobar, head of Colombia's Medellin narcotrafficking cartel until his death in 1996.[77] Deeb told the UK newspaper *The Independent* that he had been given $500,000 by Latortue's nephew, Youri (who is also his uncle's security chief), and told to buy arms. 'Everybody is saying I have done something with the money, but it is still there,' he told the paper.[78] Orlando, with her Republican affiliation and her Florida location, was very close to Florida's governor Jeb Bush, who Latortue visited in Florida on April 11. The occasion was the launch of Haitian-American Chamber of Commerce of Florida along with a 243-page report by a special task force on Haiti set up by Jeb Bush himself. 'You're a hero in my eyes, Mr Prime Minister,' Bush said. 'We welcome you back to Florida.'[79]

Latortue was in Florida and the UN Security Council was in Port-au-Prince. All 15 members sent representatives from April 12–16 to review the progress of MINUSTAH. The head of Haiti's UN mission, Juan Gabriel Valdes, said that 'a true dialogue is essential'. The preceding weekend (April 9–10) saw MINUSTAH and the Haitian police in firefights with the paramilitaries. On April 9, they killed three people – including the famous leader of the reconstituted Haitian army, former sergeant Remissainthe Ravix. They arrested 18 others. On April 10, they fought another battle and killed seven others, including ex-soldier Jean René Anthony.[80] Indeed, as Valdes was making his declaration that a dialogue was needed on April 15, a MINUSTAH soldier was killed in a gunfight at a roadblock in Cité Soleil,[81] and thousands turned out in Bel Air to demand the release of political prisoners and a return to constitutional rule.[82]

MORE REVERSALS OF JUSTICE

On April 18, the coup regime finally brought formal charges against ousted Interior Minister Jocelerme Privert, who had already been in prison for ten months without charge.[83] The next day the coup regime arrested Ginette Apollon, president of the National Commission of Women Workers (CNFT), at the airport. Her crime was attending a solidarity conference in Venezuela, celebrating the reversal of the coup against Venezuela's President Hugo Chávez three years before. Paul Loulou Chery, coordinator of the Confederation of Haitian Workers (CTH), and his brother Lamour Chery were at the airport to greet Apollon. They were also arrested. The police accused her of receiving money abroad to finance violence in Haiti. Police found about $30-worth of this financing on her person. They were released, but told to return to the police station days later.[84]

On April 17, ousted and imprisoned Lavalas Prime Minister Yvon Neptune briefly ended his hunger strike and allowed himself to be taken to a MINUSTAH-managed hospital. He continued to warn that the coup regime wanted to assassinate him after smearing him as the author of the 'St Marc massacre'. On April 21, MINUSTAH took him to a 'Prison Villa' in Pacot, very close to the Haitian police headquarters. He tried to warn the UN officials that this was a trap that would lead to his assassination, and returned to his hunger strike in protest. On April 22, between seven and ten paramilitaries who Neptune recognized from the prison system forcibly dragged him into a vehicle and drove him to Saint Marc, where they tried to organize a 'trial'. When the judge, Cluny Pierre Jules, did not show up, the paramilitaries were at a loss. MINUSTAH sent a helicopter to pick Neptune up and returned him to the prison in Pacot, where he kept wasting away on hunger strike.[85] A week later on May 1, the Associated Press repeated reports from Haitian radio that Neptune had fled to exile. The reports were completely false – Neptune was still in prison,[86] and even MINUSTAH's own human rights division chief Thierry Fagart, a French lawyer, criticized the situation on May 5. 'Since the beginning of the procedure until today, the fundamental rights, according to national and international standards, have not been respected in the case of Mr Neptune and Privert,' Fagart said.[87]

While Neptune and Privert languished in prison accused of a fabricated massacre, Haiti's Supreme Court was overturning convictions in a real massacre. On May 11, The Haitian Supreme Court absolved 1991-coup leaders Raul Cedras and Philippe Biamby, ex-police chief Michel François, and paramilitary commanders Emmanuel Constant and Louis Jodel Chamblain.[88] They had been convicted of a massacre of some 15 people in Raboteau, Gonaives, which occurred on April 22, 1994. Their trial and conviction in 2000 under Aristide's government was a landmark in Haitian history, proof that impunity would not reign and that massacres would not go unacknowledged and unpunished. The symbolism of the final reversal of that decision and the imminent release of Jodel Chamblain from prison was clear. Perhaps coup PM

Latortue had a guilty conscience. He told the AP that '[n]o orders were given, no instructions. If the results have been annulled, the judges have decided to annul them independently.'[89]

Two days before the Raboteau massacre conviction was overturned, on May 9, the National Coalition for Haitian Rights, NCHR, that 'human rights organization' that had played such an instrumental role in the coup – and in the imprisonment of Neptune, Privert, and other political prisoners – changed its name to the 'National Network for Defense of Human Rights' (RNDDH).[90]

Haitians got no relief from crossing the border into the Dominican Republic. In May, when a Dominican woman was murdered and Haitians accused of the murder, the Dominican government expelled thousands of Haitians and mobs attacked Haitian ghettoes in agricultural towns where Haitian farmworkers were trying to earn a living as seasonal labourers.[91] This story repeated itself in December, when a murder and machete attack on Dominicans was attributed to Haitians, followed by armed bands of machete-wielding Dominicans vowing to kill any Haitian they met, killing one, and forcing others to flee.[92]

Back in Haiti, Lavalas kept fighting. On April 25, a group of demonstrators felled a telephone pole in Port-au-Prince's wealthiest suburb, Petion-ville, causing a traffic backlog lasting six hours. A spokesperson told the Haiti Information Project:

> We are not gangsters, we are not criminals. We did not use guns to perform this act. Many of the elite who sponsored and supported the coup of February 29, 2004 must use this road to return home to their families. We want to create a traffic jam to force them to sit and reflect upon what they have done to this country. You can see them finally acknowledging the poor market place women who line the roads to their homes. Today, U.N. forces that are ready to kill us surround Cité Soleil and Bel Air. Maybe now they will see how vulnerable they really are. The poor who supported Jean-Bertrand Aristide live among them, in their communities. We demand the return of our constitutional president and only after that can we can have free and fair elections.[93]

On April 26, some 10,000 Lavalas supporters marched again, from Bel Air to Cité Soleil, first to demand Aristide's return and the release of political prisoners, and second to break the siege of Cité Soleil and give what little food and water aid they had in Bel Air to the even harder-hit inhabitants of the besieged neighbourhood.[94]

When demonstrators came out again the next day, April 27, the Haitian police fired on them, this time outside MINUSTAH's headquarters in Bel Air. They killed at least five people on the scene and at least four others died later from their wounds.[95] MINUSTAH watched.[96] Bel Air's Lavalas organization was undeterred, and thousands mobilized again on May 4. This time, MINUSTAH forced the Haitian police to back off and perhaps averted another massacre.[97] On May 18, Haiti's Flag Day, MINUSTAH also provided security at the front and back of a huge pro-Aristide demonstration. Haitian police made numerous attempts to attack the demonstration. Pro-Lavalas American journalist Kevin Pina was on the scene with a video camera, announcing his presence and his camera aggressively when police threatened the crowd. He filmed a Brazilian MINUSTAH soldier telling him: 'You are always making trouble for us. I have taken your picture and I am going to give it to the Haitian police. They will get you.'[98] The police began the killings after the demonstration had ended, when they killed three people in Cité Soleil.[99]

The Flag Day murders marked the end of the fissure between MINUSTAH and the Haitian police. The Haitian business community threatened to form its own private militias and go on the offensive against the poor neighbourhoods. The United States threatened to bring the Marines back. Facing these sources of pressure, MINUSTAH capitulated, joined the Haitian police, and embarked on a bloody summer campaign in the poor neighbourhoods. This campaign was basically unopposed militarily: the pro-Lavalas movement was not an armed one and, despite the smears, was basically political and democratic in character. There were some armed groups in armed resistance, such as the rural 'Dessalinien Army of National Liberation', but these were no real military threat to the coup regime or UN forces.

On May 25, the police shot a 15-year-old girl and an 11-year-old boy on their way to school.[100] On May 31, MINUSTAH and the police raided Cité Soleil, killing at least three people.[101] A firebombing in a market in Bel Air on the same day, by unknown assailants, killed ten others.[102] Latortue went on the radio to promise revenge for the fire.[103] Also on May 31, French consul for Cap Haitien, Paul Henri Mourral, was assassinated in his car, again by unknown assailants.[104] On June 3–4, the police and MINUSTAH committed major massacres in Bel Air, killing some 25 people and setting over a dozen homes on fire.[105] U.S. Secretary of State Condoleezza Rice suggested these massacres could be a reason for more U.S. troops: '[We] need to look hard at whether or not the force posture there is adequate,' she said. 'It may be not just a matter of force posture. It may be a need for more election help.'[106] The coup regime's Prime Minister Gérard Latortue agreed, and asked the UN Security Council for more force during a trip to New York on June 7.[107]

The U.S. Secretary of State had one proposal to deal with the poor neighbourhoods. The Haitian Chamber of Commerce and Industry's Dr Reginald Boulos had another. Just before the MINUSTAH attacks, on May 27, Boulos met Haiti's Chief of Police Leon Charles, where he argued that the business community should have legalized, private militias armed with heavy weapons. He also suggested the business community could buy heavy weapons for the police on the international market, if only the arms embargo on Haiti could be lifted. 'If they don't allow us to do this then we'll take our own initiative and do it anyway,' Boulos said.[108] The security agendas of the U.S. and the Haitian Chamber of Commerce converged on June 8, when the U.S. government announced its intention to lift the arms embargo against Haiti – an embargo imposed during the first coup against Aristide and the military junta that followed it in the 1991–94 period. The U.S. Embassy donated $2.6 million in hardware to the police on June 8.[109]

The fissure that had opened up between the UN forces, commanded by Latin American countries, and the Haitian Police, which answered basically to the U.S. and Canada, had been closed. The rapprochement was announced on the radio on June 11 by the head of the UN Mission, Juan Gabriel Valdes, who compared Haiti to Chile under Pinochet and said that 'compared to that experience, there is no political persecution in Haiti'.[110] It was not persecution, but security, that the UN and the Haitian Police were bringing. And the price of insecurity, MINUSTAH and the coup regime argued, was high.

Insecurity was among the arguments of first resort in the continuing delay of elections. When the coup occurred in February 2004, the coup regime had promised to hold elections within the year. But despite the ongoing destruction of the Lavalas movement, electoral delays had to continue, for the results of elections were still unpredictable. Nor was insecurity the sole stated reason for delays. The international community organized the elections as if they were inventing them for the first time (despite their allocating substantial amounts of money for post-coup elections – $17 million from Canada to that point, for example[111]). One of the members of the coup regime's electoral commission, Patrick Fequiere, told American reporter Reed Lindsay in June that because of inexplicable firings of dozens of employees, only 60,000 of Haiti's 3.5–4.5 million voters had registered. 'The damage has already been done. Even under the most idealistic conditions, the elections will happen only after 2005,' Fequiere told Lindsay.[112] Conditions were not idealistic, though they were adequate for multinational corporations to gather biometric information from Haitians. Cogent Systems, a corporation based in California, won a $2.5 million contract from Haiti's Provisional Electoral Council to provide fingerprint identification technology for the elections.[113] Offered as a way of assuring electoral results in a context of illiteracy, such systems also provided a means of establishing a database that would help monitor Haiti's voting-age population. They did not, however, stop a massive attempt at fraud when the elections finally did occur, a point to which we will return. In addition to justifying electoral delay on the basis of 'insecurity', the coup regime began floating the idea of not opening registration offices in poor neighbourhoods. These neighbourhoods happened to be the most 'insecure', the most pro-Aristide and the most opposed to the coup and the coup regime.

The various insecurities suffered by the majority of the population, from unemployment and underemployment to hunger through to imprisonment and terror at the hands of MINUSTAH and police, were less important to Haiti's custodians than problems like kidnapping, which did reach serious proportions under the coup regime. The Canadian press reported on a 65-year-old Haitian-Canadian, Huguette Goulet, who paid a ransom of $300,000 to her captors and was released in June.[114] Goulet was one of hundreds kidnapped over the summer of 2005: estimates were of half a dozen kidnappings a day in the worst periods.[115] Foreign Affairs ministries from the coup-sponsoring governments (Canada and the U.S.) issued travel advisories entreating their citizens to avoid the violence and the Peace Corps suspended its operations.[116] The International Crisis Group produced a report at the end of May called 'Spoiling Security in Haiti', identifying groups that might benefit from Haiti's 'insecurity' and suggesting that a more unbiased, fair, and transparent UN mission and coup regime could better stabilize the country. Their 'spoilers' included criminal groups, former military personnel, politicians who feared yet another Lavalas victory, the business community jealous of their privileges, and perhaps – a claim offered without evidence – Lavalas partisans in the poor neighbourhoods. But which of these 'spoilers' was responsible for the kidnappings? Certainly it was organized crime and business that could provide the infrastructure for a kidnapping ring, military and police that could provide the muscle and the impunity. Lavalas, and the pro-Lavalas youths in the poor neighbourhoods, would then take the blame and the brunt of the attacks done to stop this 'insecurity'.

The coup regime's justice minister, Bernard Gousse, resigned on June 15,[117] around the time of another deadly police raid into the poor neighbourhood of Bel Air. On June 17, the Haitian police attacked, exchanging fire with gunmen in the neighbourhood, killing three and wounding four.[118] Abuses like these only strengthened the coup regime's resolve to have even more police. The very day of the massacre, Haiti's foreign minister, Herard Abraham, announced a plan to train 2,000 more police in advance of elections and to seek an 'ideal' target of 18,000 police (up from the 5,000 Haiti had at the time).[119]

On June 22, the UN Security Council renewed MINUSTAH's mandate in Haiti, to the surprise of no one.[120] MINUSTAH's mandate would continue regardless of what happened. If there were violence, rather than it being evidence of failure, it would be evidence that MINUSTAH was needed and should be expanded. If there were not violence, MINUSTAH was succeeding and why mess with success? The UN settled into a situation where it could lightly criticize the coup regime while enabling it to continue its human rights violations and suppression of the popular movement. This occurred on June 24, when UN envoy Valdes criticized the Haitian Justice system for not releasing Yvon Neptune. 'We believe that serious attention should be given to Neptune's release,' he said.[121] But on June 29, the UN was back to attacking the poor neighbourhoods with the police. That morning MINUSTAH troops assaulted Cité Soleil again for eight hours, killing at least six, arresting 13 and turning them over to the HNP, and taking no casualties itself.

As of July 1, 200,000 of Haiti's 4.5 million eligible voters had registered; 100 of 424 planned voter registration sites had opened. Journalist Sue Ashdown wrote in the *San Francisco Bay View* that '[b]y the end of May, out of 436 planned registration offices, the Organization of American States admitted that only 14 had been set up. The 436 offices, were they to exist, would still stand in sharp contrast to the Haitian elections of 2000, when more than 12,000 registration centers and polls served the Haitian people.'[122] The UN special envoy to Haiti, Juan Gabriel Valdes, added the insightful comment: 'These are not Austrian elections, these are Haitian elections. These elections are not going to be in a country which is in absolute tranquility.' But, Valdes added, 'There is no alternative to elections except chaos.' Valdes's two alternatives, elections and chaos, were not mutually exclusive. Rosemand Pradel, secretary-general of Haiti's Provisional Electoral Council, announced the possibility of delaying the local and regional elections and floated the idea of not having the elections in the pro-Aristide slums of Cité Soleil and Bel Air, until these areas 'cool down'. American 'expert' Dan Erikson of Inter-American Dialogue suggested that the 'kid gloves' strategy of handling pro-Aristide groups in the slums was to blame for the turmoil: 'The possibility for good elections in Haiti decreases with every day that the security situation remains unchecked.' Bus driver Frantz Isidor speculated to AP reporter Stevenson Jacobs as to the kind of 'good elections' Erikson sought: 'I really don't know how we're going to have elections ... Unless it's just going to be a smoke screen and the next day we're going to wake up and hear on the radio who won.'[123]

UN Secretary General Kofi Annan went to the United States, pleading with Condoleezza Rice to send some American 'boots on the ground' to occupy Haiti. Annan specifically wanted American firepower to face down the lightly armed pro-Aristide gangs in the neighbourhoods, because Haitians 'respect the U.S. military'. Another UN official put it still more directly: 'We want scarier troops.' The U.S. Ambassador to Haiti, James B. Foley, who had helped orchestrate the coup and personally threatened Aristide, agreed. Formal requests for a show of force were being 'evaluated' by the Pentagon, Canada, and France – the original triangle behind the 2004 coup.[124]

The alliance of forces maintaining the occupation of Haiti included the U.S./Canada/France, the Latin American countries in charge of MINUSTAH, various armed elements from the police, military, and paramilitaries, and the Haitian business community. Some of the armed elements, led by Remissanthe Ravix, had committed excesses since the coup and paid the price in shootouts with MINUSTAH. But MINUSTAH itself was disciplined by warnings from the Haitian elite, and more importantly, by declarations from the U.S. By July these problems had been resolved, and the solution was simple: MINUSTAH would back the police up in a series of spectacular raids against Lavalas partisans in the poor neighbourhoods.

THE JULY 6, 2005, RAID ON CITÉ SOLEIL

On July 6, MINUSTAH and the Haitian police conducted a massive raid, with 400 soldiers and police attacking Cité Soleil. Among those they killed was Dred Wilme, one of the pro-Lavalas gang leaders who had emerged since the coup.[125] An American delegation reported the raid as follows, based on accounts from journalists and members of the community:

> Two helicopters flew overhead. At 4:30 AM, UN forces launched the offensive, shooting into houses, shacks, a church, and a school with machine guns, tank fire, and tear gas. Eyewitnesses reported that when people fled to escape the tear gas, UN troops gunned them down from the back ... Multiple community people indicated that they had counted at least 23 bodies of people killed by the UN forces. Community members claimed that UN forces had taken away some of the bodies.[126]

The aftermath of this raid was filmed by some Haitian and American journalists. Footage from the raid can be seen in Kevin Pina's film, *We Must Kill the Bandits*. The story of the massacre began to emerge the following week, with Reuters publishing an estimate of 25–40 killed in the raid.[127] The UN eventually investigated the raid and exonerated itself, stating that UN forces 'did not target civilians', but that 'the nature of such operations in densely populated urban areas is such that there is always a risk of civilian casualties'.[128] General Augusto Heleno Ribeiro, answering the criticisms in Brazil in November 2005, said the accusations of executions were made by 'gangs linked to Aristide'.[129] Six months after the raid, the UN did admit in an internal report that civilians may have become 'collateral victims' of the July 6 raid.[130] With other Haitian occupiers making inflated comments about 'urban warfare', however, the UN was sending contradictory messages. If it was warfare, after all, did the rules of warfare and the Geneva Conventions – meant to be enforced by the UN – apply? If it was not warfare but some sort of police action, then why the APCs and heavy weaponry? Because Haiti has so many weapons? 200,000 weapons in a population of 8.5 million – compared to the U.S., which has about one weapon for every single American? Because Haiti had exceptional levels of violence and murder? With lower murder rates – even in 2004 and 2005 – than the Dominican Republic, Guyana, Trinidad, and Jamaica?[131] Should all these countries be occupied by the UN? This was a fundamental contradiction of MINUSTAH's behaviour in Haiti.

Haitian police followed the July 6 raid up with a raid in Bel Air where they killed ten more people,[132] and another six a week later in the neighbourhood of Solino.[133] In between, on July 14, 5,000 people demonstrated against the MINUSTAH/police raids in Cité Soleil.[134] As the police were killing, its leadership was rotating: Mario Andresol replaced Leon Charles as police chief on July 19. Charles went off to the Haitian Embassy in Washington, DC. This had no discernable effect on police behaviour.

As another hurricane (Hurricane Dennis) struck Haiti's devastated environment and infrastructure, killing at least 40 people in rural areas, the coup regime returned to its political persecutions, beginning another campaign against Fr. Gérard Jean-Juste. Having been freed in November, Jean-Juste travelled back and forth to Miami. In mid-July he was briefly detained, and released, upon his return to Port-au-Prince. As frequently occurred with Lavalas activists, he was arrested on the basis of accusations made against him on pro-coup radio, again of gun-running. He was quoted in an AP report saying that he would consider running for president if asked to do so by his party.[135] It may have been this announcement, along with Jean-Juste's popularity in Port-au-Prince, that led to the pattern of harassment and detention that was eventually to return him to jail.

Haiti's insecurity claimed the life of another journalist, poet Jacques Roche, who was found dead on July 15 after having been kidnapped and unable to raise the ransom.[136] The government accused Lavalas of the murder, but produced no evidence for the accusation.[137] Haiti's 'Council of the Wise', the group that appointed the coup regime, asked its appointees to clamp down on the press, in response. Reuters journalist Guyler Delva protested this suggestion on constitutional grounds.[138] The Council, undeterred, proceeded to recommend that Lavalas be barred from elections on grounds of 'encouraging violence'. The Council's appointed government had unleashed tremendous violence on Haitians, especially targeting Lavalas. Haiti's electoral council said they would not ban Lavalas. Jean-Juste said the council was 'scared of us. They are afraid we are going to win'.[139]

Jean-Juste's story crossed Jacques Roche's at the murdered journalist's funeral on July 21. Because Roche's memory had been claimed by the coupsters, Jean-Juste's presence at the funeral was viewed as provocative (he was there with a group of priests participating in the service). Coupsters at the funeral shoved, spit on, and cursed him. Police took him from the service, later to imprison him on the accusation of involvement in Roche's murder. The same day, July 21, two pro-Lavalas leaders who had fled the 2004 coup and were in the Dominican Republic, Paul Raymond and Mario Exilhomme, were deported to Haiti, where they were promptly jailed. The Haitian coup regime had submitted a list of exiles they wanted to add to the 1,000 political prisoners they were holding, and the Dominican Republic was complying.[140]

Haiti's police chief acknowledged that a quarter of his force was corrupt.[141] Police raids kept up through August, with those killed classified either as 'bandits' or as regrettable victims of such operations in urban areas. On August 10 police killed five people in a raid on Bel Air, including a pregnant woman and a teenage boy, according to witnesses interviewed by an Associated Press reporter.[142] On August 11, Louis Jodel Chamblain, a leader of the FRAPH paramilitaries that had killed and tortured thousands of Haitians from 1991 to 1994 and organized the armed rebellion against Aristide in 2004, was released from prison. His conviction for the Raboteau massacre had been overturned long since, but he was still being investigated for other charges. The courts decided there was no evidence to hold him. Even U.S. Ambassador Foley disagreed with the Haitian court, and linked Chamblain's release with the constitutional Prime Minister Neptune's continuing imprisonment.[143]

THE MASSACRE AT MARTISSANT ON AUGUST 20, 2005

The summer ended with another major massacre. On August 20, at the 'Summer Camp for Peace' programme in Grand Ravine, a soccer game was underway as part of this USAID/Haitian government-sponsored programme. The game was attacked by masked police and civilians with machetes, who killed an unknown number of people, at least 20. On the following day, some of the killers returned to the neighbourhood, this time with Haitian police, and burned the houses of some Lavalas supporters.[144]

Also at the end of the summer, Fr. Gérard Jean-Juste announced, from prison, that he would have no objection to being the Lavalas candidate in the presidential elections.[145]

7 THE ELECTORAL GAME OF 2006

The Haitian forces behind the coup regime – the business community and the various armed factions – were not content with an appointed regime working with a UN army. They wanted the neighbourhoods cleared, Lavalas finally defeated, and a stable, elected government that would rule in their interests. The various international bureaucracies that had settled in to work on elections plodded along in their technocratic ways, supporting the destruction of the popular movement. But Haitians' aspirations to be free of foreign occupation and interference did not disappear, even when many of their movement leaders were being disappeared or murdered. If an election were to happen, how could the outcome be guaranteed for the coup supporters? Perhaps if turnout could be made low enough and enough people disenfranchised? But that would lead to another illegitimate government, which would continue to go unrecognized by CARICOM and Venezuela – not the most powerful countries on the world stage, but important enough in the region and to Haiti. What's more, the Haitian pro-coup forces wanted to be loved, indeed had no idea they were not loved, and they were to learn as much when they put themselves forward as presidential candidates. Guy Philippe, Dany Toussaint, Charles Baker – Apaid's brother-in-law and a fellow sweatshop-owner – and other coupsters registered as candidates, and were no doubt genuinely surprised and disappointed in winter 2006 with the miniscule numbers of people who voted for them. In the fall, they were still telling themselves and the world the story of how they had freed their country from a dictator and deserved a reward – power – for doing so. But beyond the fact that the electoral council and the international electoral specialists that had descended on Haiti were organizationally unable to meet the one-year deadline or even the fall deadline, there were potentially also political reasons for the delay. Lavalas leaders had been jailed and hounded, but had they been jailed and hounded enough? The Lavalas grassroots had been massacred and terrorized in their poor neighbourhoods, but they were not truly pacified. If the elections were permitted they might take on a life of their own, bringing another popular leader – perhaps Jean-Juste – to power, and then the coupsters would have to start all over again.

The organized popular movement had its own dilemma. Its leaders in jail, dead, exiled or being hunted, its people left without protection, it recognized that elections were being set up to be a sham. But if elections were at all fair, then the coupsters would lose and a more legitimate government would be in power with a mandate from the people – something far better than this appointed coup regime. But how could the movement know before it was too late? And how could a movement based on democratic legitimacy tell the people not to vote in elections, even if these took place after a coup and under an occupation? It was not the popularity of Lavalas's platform that had been eroded by the coup and the political persecution under the coup regime, but its organizational capacity. Did it have enough capacity to organize a boycott of elections? It is not much harder to organize a boycott of elections than it is to organize to win elections. And if they could do the one, why not do the other? To survive through to the elections, the movement needed to be able to communicate, to call attention to the abuses and human rights violations committed against it, and to fight against the smears and slanders. In all these, the movement had partial success.

VOTING CARDS AND CANDIDATES

This was the game that played itself out in the fall. At the same meeting where they announced the candidacy of Jean-Juste, Fanmi Lavalas leaders called on their people to register to vote and get the national identification card.[1] Aristide announced his intention to stay in South Africa through to the elections and not try to return, as this might provide an excuse to destabilize the election.[2] On September 4 the electoral council announced the first and second rounds of legislative and presidential elections would be held on November 20, 2005, and January 3, 2006. Municipal elections were to be held on December 11, 2005, and the new government would be inaugurated February 7, 2006. By late September, 2.4 million

people had registered to vote out of 4.5 million eligible adults –
but a new demographic study circulated among the international
experts suggested that due to outmigration there were fewer eligible
voters than originally thought, just 3.5 million instead of 4.5. The
proportion of registered voters thus took a quantum leap over the
course of a single study.[3] By late October, 3.04 million voters had
registered – and were waiting for their voting cards.

A few days after Jean-Juste's candidacy was formally announced,
on September 9, pro-Lavalas journalists Kevin Pina and Jean
Ristil got a tip that the Haitian police were searching Jean-Juste's
church. They rushed to the scene, suspecting that the police would
plant weapons there as they had seen the police do in the past to
incriminate their victims in poor neighbourhoods. If police could
'find' evidence that Jean-Juste was a gun-runner, this might make it
easier for the coup regime to paint the Lavalas priest as a common
criminal and not a political prisoner. Ristil and Pina were arrested
at the scene and put in jail, briefly, themselves.[4] That day police
also issued a decree forbidding any demonstrations from September
9–16. Forbidding demonstrations on security grounds was a tactic
increasingly resorted to by the police throughout the fall.

As for Jean-Juste, his candidacy floundered on the Haitian
bureaucracy. In late September the list of 54 presidential candidates
(later pruned to 32) was produced by the electoral council. Jean-Juste
was not on the list, because he could not present his registration in
person, which is a requirement of the electoral council. According
to the Haitian constitution, individuals can designate two lawyers
and a justice of the peace to present their registration as candidates
– but Jean-Juste's designated proxies were rebuffed by the electoral
council. Others trimmed from the list: a Texas millionaire named
Dumarsais Simeus and an ex-Lavalas senator named Louis
Gerard Gilles. With their chosen candidate in Jean-Juste rebuffed,
a regional Lavalas organization endorsed Marc Bazin, who ran
against Aristide in 1990 and lost. Other candidates included Dany
Toussaint, Charles Baker, and Guy Philippe. The pruned electoral
list also included an important name, one that had been a Lavalas
name but was now linked to a new party called Lespwa (Hope):
René Préval. Préval had a strong base in rural Haiti, a record as
the only Lavalas president to ever finish his term, and no blood on
his hands.

The election had already been rigged. Brian Concannon Jr, one
of Aristide's lawyers, called this 'electoral cleansing'. Haiti's 'ballots
are being cleansed of political dissidents, its voting rolls cleansed

of the urban and rural poor. The streets are being cleansed of anti-government political activity.'[5]

Despite this, with Préval the popular movement had a chance. Leaders like Annette 'So Ann' Auguste endorsed a strategy of calling on people to register, thus leaving open the flexibility to call for a boycott or unite behind Préval and win the election at the last minute, which is what had occurred with Aristide in 1990 – and would occur again when the elections finally did take place.

They were not going to occur in November. The electoral council's president Patrick Fequiere announced at the end of September that it was not ready to hold elections on schedule. The more difficult deadline was February 7, which was an important symbolic date for Haiti,[6] when the new government was supposed to take power. It ended up being the date of the elections themselves.

Although it took several months, and although blame was still misplaced, a human rights scandal was developing over the July 6 Cité Soleil raid and the August 20 soccer stadium massacre in Martissant. The head of a UN human rights team, Thierry Fagart, pronounced that Haiti was a human rights 'disaster', that there was a 'fundamental problem' with the justice system, that the 'state of the judiciary is so bad that people have lost all hope in it'. He said that an investigation of the soccer massacre had led to the detention of 15 police officers.[7] Most of the officers detained for the massacre, including former division commander Carl Lochard, were released on March 9, 2006.[8] An eyewitness to the massacre and human rights activist, Bruner Esterne, was assassinated on September 21, 2006.[9]

There would be no prosecutions for MINUSTAH's July 6 massacre, however. What was behind this declaration of 'disaster'? Perhaps the international community was preparing yet another option – declaring Haiti ungovernable and unsuitable for elections due to the human rights situation? Another UN official condemned the imprisonment of Yvon Neptune and of Jean-Juste, in late November. Louis Joinet from the UN Commission on Human Rights told the press after a two-week visit that '[i]f the Haitian judiciary does not have the means to try the people it detains, it should be compelled to release them'.[10] It was not so compelled. Shortly after Joinet's report, Jean-Juste was diagnosed with leukaemia in prison, which added urgency to the demands for his release, but progress on political prisoners would have to wait until the coup regime was gone.

At the end of October the international community made a show of support for the electoral process, holding a 'donors' conference' in Brussels at which the donors pledged to unblock a portion of the money they had prevented from being disbursed under Aristide. The Europeans announced the unblocking of $86 million, and the U.S. pledged $230 million. Whether Haiti would see any of the money was another question. Some of it, in any case, was for things like 'civil society participation in the political process' – the same sorts of funding to the same sorts of organizations that had organized and backed the 2004 coup. Other money was to go to the justice system, in the form of training police and paying Canadian police officers to do so. One such project, announced at the end of October, was for a 'reception center for minors in conflict with the law' at a Port-au-Prince police station. Funded by USAID, this initiative would help with the criminalization and eventual incarceration of poor people starting at a very early age, a trend long established in the U.S. and a favourite export.[11]

RENÉ PRÉVAL ENTERS THE RACE

By the end of October, most of the Fanmi Lavalas activists had decided to back René Préval for president,[12] and he emerged as the favourite – indeed the only candidate with any real popular backing. When would the elections be? The ID cards, being prepared by a U.S. firm based in Mexico, were not ready. The electoral list had yet to be finalized, and without it ballots could not be printed. Another delay was announced on November 16, with elections postponed to December 27,[13] and yet another on November 25 to January 8.[14]

At the beginning of November, the coup regime that had lowered the minimum wage, allowed the Marines to shut down the only medical school without protest, and cheered on police and UN massacres of poor people announced that it was suing Aristide for corruption – for misappropriating funds from the public treasury and transferring them to the United States.[15] Most of the charges were related to the telecommunications industry, which, incidentally, was being handed over to private networks Nortel, Digicel, and Ericsson by the coup regime as the charges were being laid.[16] The charges were filed in Miami – perhaps the coup regime knew to whom it really answered. In any case, the charge was so useful that evidence would have been found if it were true. But the most avid investigators could unearth only normal lobbying and legal fees, to people like Aristide's lawyer Ira Kurzban, who replied to the corruption charges in *Haiti Progres*:

> To my understanding, the United States sent seven people from the Treasury Department immediately after the coup to investigate financial wrongdoing, and a number of Haitians have been working day and night to find the money that [the] President supposedly took. But, it's now obvious, there is none. There are no Swiss bank accounts, no yachts, no Trump Tower apartments, all of which there were with Duvalier. There are none of the things that one classically identifies with the claim that a president has abused his authority and stolen money for his own benefit.[17]

In December, U.S. Congresswoman Maxine Waters was to ask an interesting question in a press release: how was the coup regime financing its civil lawsuit against Aristide? Legal costs could go into the hundreds of thousands of dollars, after all.[18]

MINUSTAH and the police continued to attack Cité Soleil, as they would throughout the pre-electoral period. On November 15 they killed four people in the neighbourhood, and arrested 29 'suspected gang members'. Several days before they had killed another 'suspect' and arrested nine others. In the third week of November, three more residents were shot and killed during MINUSTAH operations.[19] One Brazilian MINUSTAH soldier told a reporter: 'This place is not a policing operation anymore. It's low-intensity warfare,' which again raised the question of the political status and protections of the combatants and non-combatants – a question that did not arise in the public discussions of any of the UN or other international bodies involved in Haiti. A Doctors Without Borders clinic said they had seen six people die from gunfire in their clinic.[20] The police announced some statistics in mid-November: in the previous two weeks, 4 individuals were shot dead, 12 bodies discovered, 18 abducted, and 172 arrested in the Port-au-Prince area.[21] Police also shot protesters in Port-au-Prince who rallied against treatment of fellow Haitians in the Dominican Republic, where Haitians were being blamed for violence and killed by mobs, as well as deported in large numbers.[22] Three were wounded in a protest at the presidential palace where the Dominican president was meeting officials of the Haitian coup regime.

The more it began to look as if elections might actually occur, the more the coupsters got nervous. One leader of one of the pro-coup parties, Micha Gaillard, called for all the coup forces to unite, perhaps behind wealthy white businessman Charles Baker, to prevent Préval from coming to power.[23] But the spoils of power were too tempting for any of the coupster candidates to withdraw from the race and throw their support to Baker. The coup regime was in a race to lock the future government in to as many constraints as possible. It announced a budget in the fall. In December, it fired five Supreme Court judges and replaced them in violation of the Constitution. Judges and lawyers went on strike. One lawyers' group, led by pro-Lavalas lawyer Mario Joseph, pointed out that this action came rather late: 'Justice died well before now' he wrote.[24] But coup Prime Minister Latortue swore in January 2006 that he would step down on February 7 regardless of whether an election occurred.[25] At a CARICOM meeting at the end of January, Latortue argued that, with elections coming, it was time for the Caribbean nations to let Haiti back in the fold. As for the coup regime's human rights record, political prisoners, and specifically the case of Jean-Juste, Latortue suggested that it was Lavalas, not his own government, that was keeping Jean-Juste imprisoned: 'We have no interest to get Jean-Juste in jail,' he said, arguing that 'efforts to keep him in jail "at all costs" are part of an opposition strategy to embarrass the government'.[26] Two days later (January 29) Jean-Juste was, indeed, released, conditionally, for medical care. Charges against him were not dropped until June 19, 2008, and he died less than a year after that, on May 27, 2009.

As for Préval, he built his campaign outside of the capital and through direct contact. The country's media and the international media were cut off from most Haitian voters in the countryside. These voters were Préval's constituency and by talking directly to them, he did not rely on private media that would distort his message and his image. He avoided making any major media splash, remaining low-key as he had done for years, including during the 2004 coup. He need not have made any massive promises in any case. Given his record and the competition, he needed only to stay in the race and do what he could to prevent the election from being stolen from him. In a speech in Jacmel in late December, Préval announced that he would be friendly to the private sector. He would put donors and Haiti's business community at ease as much as possible.[27] But as election day approached, Préval also tried to cool things down in Cité Soleil, telling the press that there was no 'military solution' there, but addressing social and economic problems would help.[28]

Another candidate, Dany Toussaint, a former member of

Lavalas who joined the 2004 coup, was briefly detained at the beginning of January for having a couple of unlicensed, loaded automatic pistols in his car.[29]

On January 6, the UN Security Council met to discuss Haiti. On January 7, the head of MINUSTAH, Brazilian General Urano Teixeira Da Matta Bacellar, was found dead – shot, probably suicide – in his hotel room in Port-au-Prince.[30] Teixera had replaced Gen. Augusto Heleno Ribeiro Pereira in September 2005 after Heleno had asked to be replaced and told the press he didn't want to have to answer for war crimes charges. Teixeira was eventually replaced by Chilean General Eduardo Aldunate Herman, who had served in Chile's military under Pinochet.

A State Department diplomatic cable leaked by Wikileaks suggested that then Dominican President Fernandez was sceptical of the idea that Teixera's death was a suicide:

> Fernandez inquired about the circumstances surrounding the death of Brazilian Army General Urano Teixeira da Matta Bacellar. DAS Duddy confirmed that all indications pointed to suicide. Fernandez expressed skepticism. He had met General Bacellar; to him, suicide seemed unlikely for a professional of Bacellar's caliber. Fernandez said he believes that there is a small group in Haiti dedicated to disrupting the elections and creating chaos; that this group had killed MINUSTAH members in the past (a Canadian and a Jordanian, and now the Brazilian General); and that there would be more violence against MINUSTAH forces as the election date approaches. The President said he knew of a case in which a Brazilian MINUSTAH member had killed a sniper. Although he allowed that Bacellar's death might be due to an accidentally self-inflicted wound, he believes that the Brazilian government is calling the death a suicide in order to protect the mission from domestic criticism. A confirmed assassination would result in calls from the Brazilian populace for withdrawal from Haiti. Success in this mission is vital for President Lula of Brazil, because it is part of his master plan to obtain a permanent seat on the U.N. Security Council.[31]

Teixeira's death came after public statements by business community representative Reginald Boulos calling for MINUSTAH to carry out another cleansing operation in Cité Soleil.[32] If MINUSTAH would not carry out such a cleansing, then Haitians should go on a general strike. 'We believe the political management of the UN has not decided yet to provide the security environment that they were meant to provide,' Boulos said at a news conference. 'The general population is tired, very tired of this insecurity. Elections cannot take place in this kind of environment.'[33]

This was a last-ditch attempt at preventing elections. The 'general strike' Boulos called for took place on January 9, and faded quickly. A Canadian activist in Haiti described the 'general strike' as follows:

> I was driving around Port-au-Prince today during the so-called general strike. Many of the big businesses – Texaco, Shell, upscale grocery stores, fancy restaurants (mostly situated in the Petionville area) – were closed, but the marketplaces were bustling with people. So it seemed like folks working the 'informal economy', which is a lot of people, couldn't afford to take the day off because Boulos and Apaid said so.[34]

On January 8, UN representative Juan Gabriel Valdes hit back at Boulos, denouncing a 'campaign of hatred and lies'.[35] That same day the final (and actual) date for the Haitian election was announced: February 7, 2006. Days before the poll, candidates were telling the press that this was the worst run election in Haitian history, which says something about the value and efficiency of international tutelage.[36]

Valdes may have responded to Boulos with anger on the airwaves, but UN forces were responding positively to Boulos's call for 'cleansing' in Cité Soleil, with dozens of people killed there by UN forces in the first nine days of January.[37] People in Cité Soleil marched against the abuses on January 12.[38] On January 17, two Jordanian MINUSTAH soldiers were killed in an ambush at a checkpoint.[39] A week later the electoral council announced it would not be putting polling stations in Cité Soleil – voters would have to leave the neighbourhood to vote, which, in the event, they did do.[40]

Haiti Progres, a left-wing newspaper, wrote an editorial outlining the three possible scenarios for the election. First was the possibility of an election day massacre to stop elections from happening – this had occurred in Haiti's 1987 election. Second, there was the possibility of a 'selection' – rigging the vote to pick someone other than Préval, who, towards the end, everyone knew was going to win if the election was fair. Third, *Haiti Progres* raised the possibility of Préval being a 'figurehead', elected under foreign occupation without any real power to rule.[41] *Haiti Progres* concluded from this that people should boycott the election. The number of voting stations was going to be drastically reduced, according to counterinsurgency logic of 'force concentration' and 'force protection'. The 2000 elections had 2,000 voting stations. The United Nations argued to the electoral council, successfully, that MINUSTAH could only protect a drastically smaller number of stations – about 800.[42] This would make voting access difficult – but it might also prevent a repeat of the 1987 election day massacre, unless MINUSTAH itself was going to perpetrate such a massacre. This was unlikely, but, after MINUSTAH's behaviour the previous July, not to be ruled out.

The day before the election, I asked Marguerite Laurent, a tireless and insightful Haitian activist based in New York, whether she agreed with these scenarios and what she thought would happen. She said the following:

> Tomorrow the people, across Haiti, will be wearing ONE color to show the corporate press that's in Haiti who exactly they are voting for. Moreover, Haitians talk to one another and tomorrow will THEMSELVES be declaring who's the winner!!! Haitian have an unparalled political acumen and sense, a history of oppression and the historical and social legacy that validates the poor's heroic struggles and willingness to go face to face with the world's tyrants. The last two years have proven the masses' willingness to die so that their voices will count. That determination is what René Préval is benefiting from today … But our enemies are implacably racists, so Justin, what I do know for sure is that these elections, if they go forward, will be contested one way or the other, no matter the outcome.

Events bore out Laurent's predictions.

Early on Tuesday February 7, 2006, the press sent wire reports of election day 'glitches'. Long lines, delayed openings, a lack of voting materials, cards that didn't match registers, culminated in anger and the widespread sense that the election was being stolen. 'They're trying to keep out the people and give the election to [the] bourgeoisie,' one Haitian told a *Washington Post* reporter.[43] Voters stormed a voting station in Petionville. UN envoy Valdes said that '[t]he people have voted massively'. The electoral council reported that voting in the countryside was much more regular than in the capital. They also reported that there had been four deaths from violence – with a Haitian policeman killing a voter, a mob killing the policeman, and two men who collapsed in line. Préval, meanwhile, was suggesting patience and caution to Haitians, through the press: 'We will not be able to do everything right away,' he said, 'but we are determined to do our best and raise the standard of living for the people of Haiti.'[44]

Haitians certainly did show patience, in the first instance with the very slow, and highly suspicious vote count. Estimates were that about 63 per cent of voters, or 2.2 million, had submitted a ballot – no estimates were available of how many tried and failed to vote because of all the election day chaos, which served those trying to prevent Préval from power or from having a clear mandate. The question was whether Préval could win over 50 per cent of the total vote and thus avoid a runoff election a month later, which would be another chaotic event, another opportunity for electoral theft, another logistical ordeal, and another opportunity for sabotage. In early partial counts, Préval was comfortably above 50 per cent and his nearest rival, Leslie Manigat, was at around 12 per cent. Coupsters like Hans Tippenhauer were already denouncing the elections, saying that people voted multiple times. Tippenhauer cited no evidence, and all accounts suggested the problem was that people were prevented from voting, not voting too much.[45]

ATTEMPTS TO RIG THE ELECTION AGAINST PRÉVAL

When five days passed and the counts were still incomplete, this electoral intervention, on which tens of millions of dollars were spent and for which all the countries and electoral NGOs and corporations of the world were mobilized, had become truly suspect. One of the members of the electoral council, Pierre Richard Duchemin, told the press on February 13 that 'there's a certain level of manipulation'. The president of one electoral district, Jean-Henoc Faroul, was more specific. He said tally sheets from Préval strongholds had vanished. 'The electoral council is trying to do what it can to diminish the percentage of Préval so it goes to a second round,' he told the press. UN spokesman David Wimhurst 'said tally sheets with vote results have been found in the garbage, but he said the discovery was not necessarily evidence of fraud as they may have been simply mishandled by election workers', and that '136 tally sheets containing the results of possibly thousands of votes were still unaccounted for in Port-au-Prince'. Vanished tally sheets combined with the wholesale declaration of vast numbers of ballots 'invalid because of irregularities' – 125,000 ballots, or 7.5 per cent of the votes cast. 4 per cent of the ballots could not be found. Another 4 per cent of the ballots, 85,000–90,000 of them in total, were 'kept' in the total despite being blank, keeping Préval's margin lower.[46] Max Mathurin, the president of the electoral council, later told Reuters that '[t]he blank ballots were probably introduced into the ballot boxes in a fraudulent manner ... in some polling stations, blank ballots totaled a quarter of the votes, and in some others, one third of the votes'. Elsewhere, half-burned votes marked for Préval were found in a garbage dump.[47] It was a carefully calibrated fraud, bringing Préval just below the 50 per cent he needed to prevent a runoff. The elections were, indeed, being stolen before the eyes of Haitians and the world.

Haitians reacted one way, the world – at least as represented by the UN mission in Haiti – reacted another. Haitians mobilized to protest the fraud. They took the streets, put up barricades in some areas, and finally took over the Hotel Montana. One of the places the Haitian coup was planned and the occupation implemented, the place where the wealthy and where elite journalists and internationals would stay, the hotel was an important symbol of elite power and foreign intervention in the country. UN helicopters evacuated guests from the roof of the hotel while Haitians went for a swim in the exclusive pool (which, according to *LA Weekly*, the Hotel Montana drained the next day). Elsewhere, MINUSTAH soldiers opened fire on demonstrators, killing one and wounding four.[48]

The next day Préval himself decided to join the fight. He said the vote counts were marked by 'gross errors and probably gigantic fraud' and demanded respect for the will of the Haitian people.[49] The internationals – the UN and U.S./France/Canada – tried to get Préval to agree to some accord with the second-place winner, Leslie Manigat (who had won about 12 per cent of the vote).[50] The very idea of a deal was preposterous: the UN/U.S./France/Canada bargaining position was based on fraud, while Préval's was based on having won the election. In the event, however, Préval also relied on popular mobilization and splits within the electoral council that exposed the fraud – Haitians, in both cases. Préval did not have to accept a power-sharing deal with the people he had defeated, and in the end even MINUSTAH countries like Brazil recommended that his victory be recognized. Préval was declared the winner, in the first round, with 50.15 per cent of the vote – certainly a smaller share than was actually cast for him. The calls of congratulations began to arrive – first from Hugo Chávez and Thabo Mbeki, but before long also from Canada's Stephen Harper and others. Haiti's people had won a victory against all odds, winning the election back from those who had stolen it from them. Given the balance of forces, such a victory could only be partial. But that partial victory had overturned much of what the coupsters had hoped to accomplish.

PRÉVAL TAKES OFFICE

Préval took office on May 14, 2006. He took over a country still under foreign military occupation through MINUSTAH. He inherited a police force that had been systematically corrupted, subverted, and remade in the image of the coupsters and their international sponsors. It had absorbed the ex-FADH and ex-FRAPH paramilitaries that had terrorized the country through two coups. Préval's personal security was in the hands of this very police force. The police were the worst example, but the same applied to other institutions of government and their loyalties. The Haitian business community was still at large. The NGO and media infrastructure that had helped make the coup was still thriving, and foreign money was still pouring in to coupster forces. The Haitian economy was still destroyed, its environment still devastated, its people still dependent on precarious foreign aid and expensive exports to meet their basic needs. Préval's power was so constrained that his officials could travel to the U.S. or Canada only at their own peril: several discovered they were on secret black lists when they tried to enter Canada in May 2006. Préval's prime minister, Jacques Eduoard Alexis, was denied a visa,[51] for which Canada's foreign minister, Peter Mackay, later apologized. Canada eventually granted PM Alexis a temporary visa.[52]

But Préval had a mandate, and the pressure of the violence was eased, somewhat. Some of the high-profile political prisoners – Yvon Neptune, Annette Auguste, and others, were released. Movements had a chance to meet and organize again. Préval opened diplomatic and economic channels to Venezuela and Cuba and returned Haiti to CARICOM. Some of the most important efforts, such as a 'social appeasement fund' that could have addressed some of the causes of the social crime and violence in the slums, Préval could not implement because the donors refused to release the funds. Still, Haitians had long since proved their ability to use whatever space they had won to expand their organizations and their capacities. Préval's victory had brought them some of that space, although events would show that Préval's own space of manoeuvre was very limited.

ASSESSING THE MINUSTAH/LATORTUE
GOVERNMENT OF 2004–06

Before discussing the continuities and discontinuities between Préval's government and the MINUSTAH/Latortue government of 2004–06, an accounting of Latortue's government, compared with Aristide's, is in order. The interim (coup) government was a transition to dictatorship.

James Gordon Meek of the *New York Daily News* spent some time with Gérard Latortue in June 2006 as he returned to his home in Boca Raton, Florida.[53] 'I'm proud to say my mission was completed,' said Latortue. Meek hails Latortue for a peaceful handover of power (which Aristide also did), 'firing corrupt customs officers and police and taking steps to help free the civil service of political cronyism. He claimed cooperation with the U.S. Drug Enforcement Administration on counternarcotics efforts, got $1.3 billion in foreign aid and enlisted European Union support to rebuild roads.' On the other side, there's 'rash of kidnappings and a Justice Ministry "witch hunt" against Aristide supporters during his tenure'. While the New York newspaper gives a view from Latortue's Florida home, a better-informed assessment is provided by Alex Dupuy, a critic of Aristide who called the ousted President a 'false prophet'. Dupuy criticizes Aristide, but he is no proponent of the 2004–06 government:

> From the outset, the Latortue government made it clear through its actions that justice was political and partisan and would be administered in the pursuit of objectives that corresponded to the class and political interests of those in power and their foreign backers.[54]

Dupuy points out that MINUSTAH chose to co-exist with the armed paramilitaries who were committing abuses but took a much more aggressive approach with the ghetto populations.[55]

CORRUPTION

The Latortue government brought Haiti to the top of Transparency International's corruption table, although the report only came out after Préval had come to power.[56] Under Aristide, Haiti had been high on Transparency's table as well, but Aristide's opponents, who claimed that they overthrew him because of corruption, brought corruption to new heights during their term in power. The allegations of corruption against Aristide have never held up, as lawyer Brian Concannon wrote in response to the *Wall Street Journal* in August 2006: 'There is not a single criminal or civil complaint outstanding against Mr. Aristide, in Haiti, the U.S. or anywhere else. None of the reported foreign bank accounts have ever been found.'

HUMAN RIGHTS

As with corruption, so too with human rights. The U.S. State Department's own assessment of the coup government, released March 8, 2006, identified the following human rights problems:[57]

- arbitrary killings by the Haitian National Police (HNP)
- disappearances committed by the HNP
- overcrowding and poor sanitation in prisons
- prolonged pretrial detention and legal impunity
- use of excessive – and sometimes deadly – force in making arrests or controlling demonstrations, often with impunity
- self-censorship practised by most journalists
- widespread corruption in all branches of government
- violence and societal discrimination against women
- child abuse
- internal trafficking of children and child domestic labour.

The best study of the human rights situation under the coup government was the 2006 *Lancet* study by Kolbe and Hutson.[58] Using household surveys and cluster sampling, they found evidence for 8,000 murders and 35,000 rapes in the 22 months following the coup. Most of the violence was attributed to the police (21.7 per cent), the demobilized army (13.0 per cent), and anti-Lavalas gangs (13.0 per cent). While Lavalas supporters committed violence, there were no systematic political atrocities. As one of the authors told *Democracy Now!*:

> We didn't find any – we didn't detect – any Lavalas atrocities with regards to murder or sexual assault. We did detect some physical assaults by Lavalas members and some threatening behavior by Lavalas members. So they're not completely exonerated from any human rights abuses. However, as the questioner noted, a vast majority of the atrocities that weren't committed by criminals, but by others, were from groups affiliated in some fashion with anti-Lavalas movements.[59]

Coup proponents attempted to discredit the study by pointing out one of its authors had worked in Haiti previously as a journalist and volunteer, writing favourably about Aristide. *The Lancet* reviewed the study and its methods and found no flaws in it as a piece of research.[60] The study was also not a systematic comparison of the coup government's human rights record to the Aristide government's record. Given the balance of evidence, however, any such comparison would show the coup government to be vastly worse.

CRIME

MINUSTAH's mandate in the coup government period was fundamentally confused. A UN peacekeeping mission made sense in a civil war context, where, for example, a government faced an armed rebel force. The UN would interpose itself between the two sides, prevent firefights from breaking out, and broker a peace deal, perhaps incorporating the rebels into the army. In Haiti, there was no civil war and no armed rebellion, only an armed government that had overthrown a movement-linked government, and the ousted movement, trying to assert itself using primarily the same means that brought it to power – popular mobilization. The UN interposed itself on the side of the government, and, lacking any rebel force, began to concentrate on disarmament of gangs, citing violent crime as a problem that the UN would address through its DDR programme. The problem was that neither weapons nor crime were big problems in Haiti the way they were in many other jurisdictions. Charles Arthur, writing in 2006, pointed out that Haiti's murder rate was less than half the Dominican Republic's, less than Guyana's, less than Trinidad and Tobago's, and less than one-fifth that of Jamaica.[61] On Wikipedia's list of countries by intentional homicide rate for the 2000s, Haiti comes in around 20th, below El Salvador, Honduras, Guatemala, Venezuela, Colombia, South Africa, and, interestingly, Brazil[62] – the very country supplying thousands of troops to keep Haitian crime in check.

AID AND DEVELOPMENT

Did the post-coup government do anything to improve the economic situation of Haitians? Haiti's first census in 24 years, conducted in May 2006, provides some useful context for understanding Haiti's development challenges. The $8 million census, sponsored by the EU, Japan, the IDB, the UN, and Belgium, as well as the Government of Haiti, revealed that half the population was under 20, 33 per cent were unemployed, and HIV prevalence was between 4 and 5 per cent.[63] According to World Bank figures, 52.7 per cent of Haiti's GDP came from remittances in 2004, while 80 per cent of Haitians with college degrees live abroad. Lavalas had an economic programme aimed at moving the majority from absolute misery to poverty with dignity. By contrast, the coup government's strategy was primarily aimed at getting international aid monies flowing after the donor countries had choked Lavalas of funding. How effective was this?

Since the coup got international aid flowing again, one might think that there would be some economic benefit to the people. This does not seem to be so. As usual with aid to Haiti and other jurisdictions, much more was promised than delivered. What was delivered was primarily oriented towards consolidating the coup, and in any case ended up largely back in the donor countries. Aid, which was 65 per cent of Haiti's government budget, for all the promises, remained at about $100 million per year.

To give some sense of donor priorities, of the first $15 million Canada announced in 2006, $5 million would go to a Police Reform Programme and $5 million for a Community Security Programme.[64] No doubt security was a high priority for Haiti and for economic development, but these funds completely failed, as the police committed worse abuses in the coup period than before. Most such funds go to pay the Canadian (or U.S.) trainers, in any case, as Abe Sauer wrote on post-earthquake reconstruction: 'A report on U.S. contracts for reconstruction found that only $1.60

of every $100 awarded goes to Haitian firms, essentially meaning that the brunt of Haiti funding actually functions as stimulus for economies elsewhere.'[65]

Haiti also remained crippled by international debt under the coup government. When this debt was finally cancelled, it was in 2009, under the Préval government. The coup government accomplished nothing here either.

On corruption, human rights, crime, and aid and development, the coup government was worse than the government it replaced. The overthrow of Haiti's elected government and its replacement by a UN occupation operating alongside a Haitian coup regime was a disaster by every measure. Perhaps worse than the coup government's performance, however, is that it institutionalized a set of structures that transferred the power of governance away from Haitians and into the hands of a diverse set of foreign actors. Some writers, like Alex Dupuy, hoped that Préval's government would be a new phase in the transition to democracy, which had been derailed 'by both Aristide and his enemies'. This democracy would open up possibilities for the people to struggle and not be betrayed again by false prophets.[66] Unfortunately, Dupuy's hopes were not borne out. The structures of Haiti's new dictatorship have endured since the coup government was replaced by the elected government of René Préval, as the next chapters show.

8 THE PRÉVAL REGIME, 2006–10

In 2009, three years into Préval's regime, U.S. Ambassador Sanderson described him as 'Haiti's indispensable man. Legitimately elected, still moderately popular, and likely the only politician capable of imposing his will on Haiti – if so inclined'. Sanderson continued: 'Managing Préval will remain challenging during the remainder of his term yet doing so is key to our success and that of Haiti.'[1] Imagine a Haitian (or Colombian, or Venezuelan, etc.) ambassador talking about 'managing Obama', and the relationship between the U.S. and Haiti even under Préval becomes clear.

Préval's government had greater legitimacy than the Latortue regime, but it was nearly powerless in the face of the internationally constituted dictatorship. Dependent on donors for finances and the UN and the Haitian Police for security, Préval's government had very little room to manoeuvre. It was also struck by multiple disasters, including the economic crisis in 2008 and, much worse, the earthquake of 2010. It was slightly better than what preceded it, but it was not a sovereign government with the power to make independent decisions: the coup had been consolidated from 2004 to 2006.

From 2010 to 2011, Wikileaks made available a huge archive of cables from U.S. Embassies around the world. For Haiti, these cables cover the period from late 2004 to early 2010, and provide an interesting view into Préval's highly constrained government. There are also several frequently recurring themes in the cables that are more likely to reflect U.S. preoccupations than Haitian realities. These include:

• The two contradictory notions, frequently repeated, that the Lavalas movement is 'finished' and lacks any capacity to mobilize large numbers of people, and also that it is a major political 'threat', in that it might win elections. Related, a detailed analysis of Lavalas's weakness because of Aristide's absence on the one hand, and the insinuation that Aristide is manipulating Haitian politics from South Africa on the other.[2]

- A preoccupation with Venezuela's president Hugo Chávez, his growing influence in the country, and the contradictory notion that his promises are empty and that Haitians are 'beginning' to realize this (the notion that U.S. agencies have ever made any empty development promises does not seem to make its way into the cables).

- An implicit understanding that to remain popular, Préval has to adopt some of the elements of Lavalas's pro-poor policies and be lenient, instead of punitive, towards Lavalas activists and politicians, while simultaneously lamenting when he does so and celebrating when he does not. This includes even grudging acceptance that Lavalas charities are 'well-run, politics aside'.[3]

- A similar criticism that '[p]olitical parties, motivated more by strong personal agendas than by political ideologies, still struggle for greater involvement in the government and political life',[4] along with the contradictory fear that Haiti's relationship with Venezuela and Cuba could be 'ideological' in nature.

Like any communications, the cables reflect the ideological biases and interests of their writers. But they also contain a great deal of very interesting information about the real governance of Haiti during Préval's presidency.[5]

PACIFICATION OF THE POOR NEIGHBOURHOODS

Préval had argued in public and in private, to the U.S. Embassy, that the key to reducing violence in the poor neighbourhoods was negotiation, not violent crackdowns. U.S. Embassy Charge d'Affaires and former Ambassador to Haiti Timothy Carney wrote after a November 2, 2005, meeting with Préval that the latter 'seeks to end the current impasse which has trapped the general population between the ganglords and MINUSTAH, and he fears that any new operations by MINUSTAH will produce disastrous casualties in the close, crumbling neighborhood'. Carney's comment on Préval's proposal: 'MINUSTAH is wary of engaging with gang leaders, as the political class has strongly criticized such engagement in the past. However, Préval carries a level of credibility that

could advance disarmament while simultaneously yielding significant electoral reward for him ... Préval clearly seeks to take credit
for eliminating gang violence in the area.'[6] According to the U.S.,
the dangers to the communities clearly had to be balanced against
the danger of Préval taking credit for ending the violence.

Unfortunately, Préval's proposed approach was not taken up,
even when he got into office. MINUSTAH continued to fight
'bandits' in the slums. Brazilian troops had taken over command
in Cité Soleil from the Jordanians in May, and demonstrated
their arrival with aggression. On June 8, 2006, Radio Metropole
reported that 'violence erupted' in Cité Soleil the previous day and
'at least six people were killed'. On the following day, three other
radio stations (Radio Ginen, Radio Melodie, Radio Vision 2000)
reported that MINUSTAH denied that anyone had died and was
unable to confirm any victims.[7]

Préval's lack of 'fire in the belly' for his 'reluctance to give public
endorsement to forceful MINUSTAH action in Cité Soleil' was a
continuing source of tension between him, MINUSTAH, and the
U.S.[8] But it paid off in several temporary truces, including one that
lasted for most of August 2006.[9] Préval was convinced over the
course of the following weeks to authorize a MINUSTAH attack
on Cité Soleil, and gave an ultimatum to the gangs to 'disarm or
die' on August 9.[10]

Another UN attack, also with unconfirmed victims, was
witnessed by an international delegation in Simond Pele, Cité Soleil
on August 24. Brazilian troops fired into the neighbourhood from
tanks.[11] Other operations included Solino (Sept 7/06, 2 arrested)
and Cité Soleil (Oct 19/06, 2–3 killed).[12] It was not MINUSTAH
policy to check where all its bullets landed, despite the high density
and flimsy construction of housing in the community of some
200,000.

A more concerted set of UN attacks on Cité Soleil occurred,
with Préval's approval, in December of 2006. On December 22,
a major attack with some 400 MINUSTAH troops and Haitian
police left at least nine people dead.[13] Five days later on December
27, another attack killed at least five.[14] The UN kept up 'anti-gang'
raids in 2007, wounding six in a Cité Soleil raid on January 24
and killing five the following day.[15] Those concerned about civilian
deaths could be comforted: MINUSTAH's spokesperson said that
those killed were 'likely gang members'. MINUSTAH attacked
again on February 9/07 and reported that two of their soldiers
were wounded.[16] These operations created a kind of siege of Cité

Soleil, disrupting what miniscule church-based and other social services, education, feeding programmes, and health services as were available to this desperately poor community.[17] By March 2007, the U.S. Embassy summarized the situation in Cité Soleil as follows:

> MINUSTAH, by all accounts, does have control of Cité Soleil. Nevertheless, that does not mean that the average Cité Soleil resident has been liberated from gangs and now feels safe to go about his or her daily life free from extortion, harassment and threats of physical harm. From a military perspective, the emerging gang leaders pose no threat, but on the community level they continue to harass and terrorize the population.[18]

The government and UN tried combining these attacks with fairly minimalist 'social appeasement' – offering job training and cash to up to 1,000 people who disarmed. USAID had a joint project with MINUSTAH, called the Haiti Transition Initiative, worth about $5.5 million, to fund soccer games and basketball courts, of which Préval was dismissive.[19] The benefits could be cashed in by people who turned in arms and accepted ID cards. The World Bank announced $1.25 million in grants for Cité Soleil. In February 2007 the U.S. announced an additional $20 million for job creation in Cité Soleil.[20] The UN envoy in charge of the programme, Edmond Mulet, revealed the contradiction central to the UN presence in Haiti in his announcement of the programme: 'This is not a traditional disarmament that you would see anywhere else in the world where you have a clear leadership or a subversive group or a military insurgency that you can make deals with. This is more like a one-on-one approach. Each (gang member) has different motivations.'[21]

Unsolved crimes also abounded. Haitian Police reported that their people were being killed – ten agents in May 2006.[22] Yet another massacre occurred in Grand Ravine, when assailants whose identities are unknown killed at least 21 people. UN personnel suggested that the violence was aimed at destabilizing Préval's government.[23] Like the August 2005 Martissant massacre and the subsequent murder of eyewitness Bruner Esterne, these killings were likely the work of a gang called the 'Lame Ti Manchet' or 'Little Machete Army'. Lame Ti Manchet's August 2005 massacre was co-ordinated with Haitian police, and their crimes have gone unpunished.[24] Another mysterious assassination occurred on

April 14, 2007, when Johnson Edouard, a journalist with New York-based *Haiti Progres* and a Lavalas spokesman, was killed in his bed in Gonaives. Journalist Jean-Rémy Badio had been assassinated in January 2007.[25] Lavalas activist Lovinsky Pierre-Antoine disappeared on August 12, 2007 and was not seen since.

By the end of February 2007, MINUSTAH's commander, Major General Carlos Alberto dos Santos Cruz, was declaring a kind of victory: 'Now it's possible to walk in Boston [a neighbourhood in Cité Soleil] without fear, without problems, without criminals circulating freely.'[26] The 'gang leaders' had apparently fled to the countryside.[27] MINUSTAH justified its assaults by citing a survey by the U.S. State Department's Haiti Stabilization Initiative in November 2007, which found that 67 per cent of Cité Soleil residents believed that the UN mission had improved their situation, that 78 per cent of residents believed that their living conditions had improved after the crackdown, and 89 per cent of residents believed that the Préval government was doing everything possible to provide services to the community. Another poll by the United States Institute for Peace in 2008 found that 52 per cent of Cité Soleil residents reported that family members, friends, or neighbours were killed or wounded in MINUSTAH's anti-gang operations.[28] Given the timing and the questions, however, the polls must be interpreted carefully. Coming after intense fighting, the polls may show mostly exhaustion with the anti-gang operations and relief that they had ended. The poll results cannot be used to justify the operations, given the latter's violence and questionable legality.

The pacification had worked: a year later, as other parts of the capital were rioting in hunger, Cité Soleil experienced 'graveyard quiet', according to one reporter: '"Many people just don't have the energy to take to the streets and demonstrate here the way they used to," said Sergo Pierre, a Cité Soleil shop owner.'[29]

THE PRISON SYSTEM AND THE JUSTICE SYSTEM

Between MINUSTAH's arrests and the unsolved crimes, there was no relief in sight for Haiti's prison system. With the national prison in Port-au-Prince holding some 2,500 prisoners (operating at eight times its capacity), with the majority suffering from preventable diseases and infections, and 10 per cent of the total prison population of 5,500 convicted, the prisons were described by the ICG as a 'powder keg awaiting a spark'.[30]

Préval's inauguration on May 14, 2006, coincided with a riot at the National Penitentiary, which gave U.S. Ambassador Sanderson cause to comment on the problems of the prison by way of explanation of the undetermined number of prisoners who died in the suppression of the riot:

> The National Penitentiary currently holds over double its intended capacity. Only five percent of the total population at the prison have been formally sentenced while the remainder await habeas corpus proceedings in overcrowded, unsanitary conditions. The facility itself is antiquated and poorly maintained, and the prison guards lack the proper non-lethal training and equipment. The unfortunate timing of the riot serves as a reminder of the immediate challenges facing Préval's government in the judicial system.[31]

Amnesty International estimated in July 2006 that of the 2,000 people being held without trial, 100 of them were political prisoners, among them 'well-known supporters of former Haitian president Jean-Bertrand Aristide'. Préval's regime did slowly free many of the high-profile political prisoners. Jocelerme Privert, interior minister until the 2004 coup, was finally released in June 2006. Yvon Neptune, prime minister, was released in July, with charges against him dropped in April 2007. Annette 'So Ann' Auguste, a Lavalas activist, was freed on August 15, along with Yvon Antoine, Paul Raymond, and George Honore. Upon their release, Kevin Pina of the Haiti Information Project prepared a list of 126 of 'Haiti's forgotten women prisoners', the majority of whom had never seen a judge. Many died of malnutrition before seeing a judge – including vitamin-B deficiency linked to U.S.-processed rice, where Haitian rice might have kept people alive.[32]

HAITI'S ECONOMY UNDER PRÉVAL'S GOVERNMENT

Préval was constrained from the beginning in several familiar ways. As outgoing governments tend to do, the post-coup government, according to an IMF official, went on a spending spree before leaving office. The U.S. Embassy commented that 'Interim Government of Haiti (IGOH) spending could leave President-elect Préval with empty coffers just as he is about to take office ... giving

Préval the opportunity to blame the international community for Haiti's economic failure'.[33]

U.S. Embassy cables summarize some of that country's thinking on Haiti's economy. 'Despite local challenges, Haiti offers low wages and a close proximity to the U.S., both of which make Haiti competitive in the face of increased international textile production.'[34] That competitiveness has not been realized, according to the U.S., because of high-interest loans (around 30 per cent) and local deficiencies in security. The real reasons are deeper, having to do with an inability to raise capital or increase productivity locally. The textile sector in Haiti is not truly a manufacturing sector – most of the value added is done elsewhere, and hardly any of the profits are made in Haiti, leaving little capital available for reinvestment. When added to the political punishment imposed on Haiti for the past few decades in the form of embargoes, dropped loans, and denials of development assistance, the failure of the garment sector to provide employment or development is explained.

A related structural weakness is the lack of government revenue. The Haitan government collected $500 million in fiscal year 2006, with 80 per cent of that coming from customs revenue,[35] about $63 per capita. Canada, in the same period, raised about $257 billion, or $8,500 per capita.

By 2008, the global economic crisis hit Haiti hard in the form of higher fuel and food prices. Since most Haitians were at the edge of survival, many were pushed over. There were public demonstrations, food riots, and transportation strikes related to the price hikes.[36] Like its other systems, Haiti's food system had long since been devastated by international policy. Unable to protect its agriculture with a tariff, Haiti imported staple foods, especially rice. Where local production would have provided some insulation against global commodity price fluctuations, Haitians were at the mercy of the global market. On Flag Day in 2008, Préval made a speech calling for strengthening the domestic Haitian economy against the forces of globalization. The U.S. Embassy cable reassured Washington that 'so far it is just rhetoric … Nevertheless, the anti-globalization message will be a theme to watch.'[37] After the 2008 hurricanes, Préval also criticized the 'charity paradigm' of aid to Haiti.[38]

Economist Amartya Sen, who won the 1998 Nobel Prize, is famous for his analysis of famines. With Jean Dreze, he found that no famine has taken place in a relatively democratic country with a free press, because people do not starve for a lack of food, but for a lack of entitlements to food. Sen and Dreze found that a democratic system can force a government to act to protect its citizens from starvation.[39] The near-famine in Haiti in 2008, and the chronic hunger suffered by a large proportion of the population, demonstrates the lack of democracy in Haiti. But the Préval government in its response was more democratic than the Latortue/MINUSTAH regime of 2004–06. The government subsidized rice on an emergency basis, but suffered politically for acting late. Préval, an agronomist, recognized that subsidizing imported food was not a permanent answer – but it did hold the line against threatening starvation.[40] Préval also quietly provided fuel through tax relief and price ceilings, apparently without telling the U.S., who found out months later from the news.[41]

Later that year, Haiti was devastated by hurricanes Gustav and Hanna. As the earthquake of 2010 would show, natural disasters hit vulnerable areas like Haiti much harder than more affluent societies with better infrastructure. Preliminary estimates were that the food security of about 100,000 families was harmed by the storms. Key bridges and roads were damaged or destroyed, as well as housing.[42]

A fuel crisis in 2009 showcased the monopoly control over imports by the 'gang of eleven'. As Richard Morse, the owner of the famous Hotel Olofson, put it: 'If it was the street gangs blocking the sale of gas, the UN troops would have a mandate to restore stability, they would have a mandate to restore public order, they would have a mandate to shoot if necessary. Unfortunately the UN doesn't have a mandate to address office gangs, the business elite, the economic monopolies.'[43]

With the legitimate economy in such disarray, informal and illicit economies proliferated. The use of Haiti as a transshipment point to the U.S. drug market was a preoccupation of both Haitian and the U.S. governments. The U.S. approach, the 'War on Drugs', involved imprisoning people for drug crimes in the U.S. and intervening in countries like Bolivia, Colombia, and Haiti to interdict and destroy drugs. To Préval, the central problem was not the sources or transshipment points, but the demand for drugs in the U.S., a problem the U.S. had chosen not to deal with. He told Canadian Governor General Michaelle Jean that 'trafficking through Haiti is not a Haitian problem but an American problem, and one the U.S. has failed to deal with. Drugs feed corruption in the political process and corruption eats away at Haiti's fragile stability.'[44] He also pointed out to Ambassador Sanderson that the U.S. spends more 'stopping illegal migrants from Haiti sailing to the U.S. than we do to stop the flow of drugs to Haiti'.[45]

Towards the end of 2009, a fight over Haiti's minimum wage began. Given the Prévalence of the informal and agricultural sector, minimum wage increases could only affect a very small minority of workers. Préval was ambivalent about the minimum wage increase, fearing that it would reduce Haiti's desirability as an investment destination.[46]

PRÉVAL IN THE AMERICAS: HAITI'S RELATIONS WITH CUBA, VENEZUELA, THE U.S., AND BRAZIL

Préval's ability to stay in office at all depended on maintaining U.S. goodwill, while trying to offer some economic and political progress to his voters. All too often, these two goals were in conflict, so that in international relations as in domestic ones, Préval was in a very precarious situation, one which may quickly have left him depressed and despondent. U.S. Deputy Chief of Mission Thomas Tighe reported on Préval's 'maudlin' attitude in a meeting on August 24, 2006:

> Préval warned that Lavalas could win the next parliamentary elections (February 2008) gain control of the government, select the next prime minister and police chief, all without Aristide's return, if he was not able to jump-start the economy. Maybe, Préval said mockingly, he too will end up in South Africa. He must get people back to work and convince his people that Haiti will change. If not, his future is questionable.[47]

One thing the U.S. expected was that Préval distance himself from the exiled President Aristide. Initially, Préval fulfilled expectations: when several Lavalas politicians won legislative elections, U.S. Ambassador Sanderson commented in a cable that 'the president elect has indeed kept his distance from Lavalas elected officials'.[48]

When Canadian Prime Minister Stephen Harper visited Haiti on July 20, 2007, Préval had invited Lavalas activist Annette 'So Anne' Auguste, the grandmother who was arrested by U.S. Marines during the 2004 coup and released by Préval after he came to power. Préval had 'invited Auguste as a display of [the government's] willingness to reach across party lines and reconcile with political opponents. The Canadians, however, made arrangements so that Harper never interacted with Auguste. Palace staff kept her away from Préval to prevent photographers from associating him with Aristide collaborators.'[49]

The U.S. also expected Préval to distance himself from Venezuela and Cuba, and according to their own communications, they were initially pleased. 'Préval has declined invitations to visit France, Cuba, and Venezuela in order to visit Washington first. Préval ... has stressed to the Embassy that he will manage relations with Cuba and Venezuela solely for the benefit of the Haitian people, and not based on any ideological affinity toward those governments.'[50] Such ideological affinities would be dangerous indeed to the new president.

All the same, Préval accepted their help in various moments, risking U.S. disapproval to do so. In April 2006 he announced his intention to join Chávez's PetroCaribe initiative, which would enable Haiti to obtain gas at preferential rates. U.S. Ambassador Sanderson accompanied the memo reporting the PetroCaribe announcement with a disappointed comment: 'In previous meetings, [Préval] has acknowledged our concerns and is aware that a deal with Chávez would cause problems with us.'[51] In a later cable, Sanderson explained, 'The chance to score political points and generate revenue he can control himself proved too good an opportunity to miss.'[52] When Venezuela and Cuba prepared to build three electricity plants in Haiti at the end of 2007, the U.S. Embassy described them as 'taking advantage of Haiti's electricity gap'.[53]

When Venezuela (unsuccessfully) sought a seat on the UN Security Council in 2006, with CARICOM support, the U.S. campaigned to prevent it. Ambassador Sanderson reported on Préval's diplomacy: 'He [Préval] repeatedly pressed me [Sanderson] on why the U.S. is so concerned about Chávez's government being on the Council.' Sanderson concluded that 'Préval's efforts to be coy notwithstanding, Haiti will, I am certain, join the CARICOM consensus to vote for Venezuelan candidacy. Préval is not enamoured of Chávez; however, he does believe he needs Venezuelan support – as well as American – to move Haiti forward. Thus his effort, transparent though it may be, to carefully walk the line.'[54] In 2007, the U.S. Ambassador bemoaned Préval's 'obliviousness to the impact and consequences his accommodation of Chávez has on relations with us', and suggested that there was 'a common trait among Haitian officials in misjudging the relative importance that

U.S. policy makers attach to Haiti versus Venezuela and Chávez's regional impact'.[55]

Préval was much more ambivalent towards MINUSTAH than the U.S., for whom '[t]he UN Stabilization Mission in Haiti is an indispensable tool in realizing core USG (U.S. government) policy interests in Haiti'.[56] United Nations peacekeeping operations can have different mandates – a 'Chapter 6' mandate requires more consent from the host country and encourages negotiated solutions, while a 'Chapter 7' mandate, which MINUSTAH has, enables UN soldiers to engage in more aggressive operations. Préval considered trying to change MINUSTAH's mandate from a Chapter 7 to a Chapter 6, on grounds that the Chapter 7 'sends the signal to investors that Haiti is a "war zone," and ups insurance rates'. Ambassador Sanderson, after discussion with her 'Chinese, Canadian and French colleagues', found that they 'all agree[d] that from our vantage point here this is a terrible idea which opens a Pandora's box of issues better left closed'.[57]

An overall assessment of Préval's administration must take into account the fact that the president of Haiti does not determine the country's security, economy, or political realities. In this context, Préval's contribution was probably positive. He helped 'cool down' conflicts in Haiti and at several moments struck a course somewhat independent from what the U.S. wanted. That he was not able to do more for the Haitian people probably says more about the structural constraints of Haiti's new dictatorship than it does about Préval's inclinations.

Senatorial elections in 2009 had low turnouts and procedural irregularities. Various tricks were used, less heavy-handed than during the interim government, to keep Lavalas out of the running. Préval's Lespwa party won most seats. Haiti's CEP tried to exclude Lavalas from the February/March 2010 elections as well – but the earthquake threw electoral politics into disarray.

9 THE EARTHQUAKE AND HAITI'S POLITICS OF DISASTER, 2010/11

On January 12, 2010, a 7.0 Richter-scale earthquake with its epicentre about 25 km from Port-au-Prince, struck Haiti. The earthquake killed about 250,000 and displaced 1.5 million. Property damage was estimated at $14 billion, or about 46 years of Haiti's national budget.

THE EARTHQUAKE

An earthquake rated 7.0 is very serious, and the Haiti earthquake was closer to the surface than other quakes that have had lower death tolls, but social factors were a major cause of the horrific death toll. The quality of housing construction and the lack of enforcement of building codes, dense populations living in these unsafe buildings near the epicentre of the earthquake, and the lack of infrastructure for response were more important in the final toll than the geological aspect of the disaster. The relative importance of social compared to biological factors is demonstrated by comparison with the February 27, 2010, earthquake off the coast of Chile, with a Richter scale rating of 8.8 and a death toll of about 521.

Other shocking comparisons reveal Haiti's relative lack of resources. In China's 2008 earthquake, rated 7.9, 1 in every 595 affected died and 1 in every 690 affected was rescued; in Haiti's 2010 earthquake, 1 in every 15 died, and 1 in every 16,588 was rescued.

THE EMERGENCY RESPONSE

Among the 250,000 buildings destroyed was the presidential palace. For all the reasons outlined in this book, the Haitian government was unable to respond quickly to the earthquake and needed international help. The help that came from the U.S. was of the type Haiti was used to: militarized, controlled from without, and given in such a way as to undermine Haitian capacity and sovereignty.

The U.S. military took over the Port-au-Prince airport on January 13 and immediately gave priority to its own military flights, turning away World Food Program flights, medical supplies from Doctors Without Borders, including an inflatable surgical hospital on January 16. The search for survivors was called off on January 22, which is also when Haiti, the U.S., and the UN signed an agreement granting the U.S. control of ports, airports, and roads.

An analogy can be made between famine and the response to emergencies like the earthquake. As Amartya Sen's analysis (discussed above in Chapter 8) showed, famines do not occur in countries with democratic governments and freedom of the press. Similarly, dictatorships with concentrated wealth and a lack of sovereign, democratic decision-making handle natural disasters much worse, and have higher levels of vulnerability because they lack infrastructure. Decisions, even about the details of emergency response, were influenced by the dictatorship. An example of this was the unusual recourse to amputation in post-earthquake emergency response.

One emergency physician, François-Xavier Verdot, described this disgusting reality as follows to a *Le Monde* reporter two weeks after the quake:

> Amputation is an act of rescue to save a life when a limb is crushed or in sepsis. The Americans have made it almost routine, without trying to imagine an alternative, proud of the slaughter that lets them rack up impressive numbers of patients ... I've seen simple arm fractures treated with amputation when they could have been fixed. I've seen the result of guillotine amputations, where the limb is cut as by a cigar cutter. The risk of infection is huge because the bone is exposed, and the procedure was done without scheduling a second surgery to fasten a stump that could serve to fix a prosthesis.[2]

Was this a situation where such amputations were an emergency medical requirement? Not for everyone – the Cuban doctors in Haiti had impressive numbers of surgeries (2,728, including 1,297 high-complexity surgeries) and only carried out 380 amputations of upper limbs and 644 of lower limbs. The Cubans had been there before the quake and would remain afterwards.[3]

THE INTERNATIONAL AID REGIME AND THE FAILURES OF REBUILDING

As the emergency phase wound down, effective military control of Haiti was returned to the MINUSTAH mission from the U.S. Marines. Six months after the earthquake, experts estimated it would take years to even clear the rubble. A year after the quake, in 2011, 90 per cent of the rubble had yet to be cleared and around 800,000 people were still living in about 1,000 camps around the capital (*Miami Herald*, Jan 21/11). While Haitians attempted, in some cases with considerable success, to self-organize to support one another in the camps, power in the camps was exercised by a combination of NGO funders, landowners, and the UN. Journalist Ansel Herz documents stories of well-run camps being dismantled overnight.[4] Haiti advocates Bill Quigley and Jeena Shah reported some of the terrible facts of displacement a year after the earthquake:

- Of 1,268 displacement camps, 29 per cent were forcibly closed.
- By December 2010, 2,074 of the 180,000 destroyed homes had been repaired.[5]

A cholera epidemic infected 170,000 and killed 3,600 over the course of 2010. From a public health perspective, a cholera epidemic, like amputations, is usually a sign of serious errors or a severe lack of needed resources. A report by Mark Schuller at the City University of New York a year after the earthquake argued that the cholera epidemic was a failure of the international donor community. Published by the Institute for Justice and Democracy in Haiti (IJDH), the report followed a previous study that used a random sample of Haitians in 108 camps, and found that 1 in 4 camp residents had left since the epidemic struck. Researchers found that a year after the quake, 37.6 per cent of camps did not have water, and 25.8 per cent did not have a toilet.[6]

The reality turned out to be much worse than the early reports feared. Cholera, new to Haiti in 2010, was in fact introduced by Nepali MINUSTAH soldiers at the Mirebalais base who had their

"cholera imported from Nepal"

waste dumped into the Artibonite river by contractors. At the time, Nepal was fighting a severe outbreak of cholera. The strain of cholera matched those found in Nepal, and the Haitian cases were all downstream of the dump sites on the Artibonite river, but MINUSTAH continued to deny that there was any conclusive proof that the UN had introduced cholera in Haiti. The massive affront of a UN mission introducing a disease that killed thousands was compounded by the official denials to enrage Haitian public opinion. Demonstrations for MINUSTAH's departure continued to gather supporters.

The difference between international goodwill and the priorities of the institutions that rule Haiti is illustrated by the difference between pledged and delivered donations. As Isabel Macdonald documented in a *Nation* article on January 11, 2011, of the $5.3 billion pledged in March 2010, $1.28 billion had been delivered a year later. Disaster Accountability Project (DAP) estimates were of $11 billion pledged and half or less spent. Stark examples include Catholic Relief, which had spent 32 per cent of the $192 million it raised, and the Red Cross, which raised $500 million and was treating interest on the money as 'unrestricted revenue'. An Oxfam report noted that U.S. aid pledged to Haiti was less than the annual subsidy for U.S. rice production.[9] No significant progress on reconstruction had been made.

A report by COHA Associate Samantha Nadler cited the Disaster Accountability Project report on aid failings:

> The Disaster Accountability Project (DAP) recently published its 'One Year Report on the Transparency of Relief Organizations Responding to the 2010 Haiti Earthquake.' After auditing 196 organizations that received donations for disaster relief, only 38 have completed follow-up surveys. The more than 80 percent that did not respond is a telling indicator of the lack of accountability among aid groups over the past twelve months. DAP's Executive Director, Ben Smilowitz, concluded: 'The fact that nearly half of the donated dollars still sit in the bank accounts of relief and aid groups does not match the urgency of their own fundraising and marketing efforts and donors' intentions, nor does it convey the urgency of the situation on the ground. This may be a disincentive for future giving by individuals and other governments.'[10]

In an article shortly after the earthquake, Jeffrey Sachs argued that Haiti required about $10–20 billion over ten years in a single bank account at the Inter-American Development Bank working 'closely with a professional executive team made up of native and diaspora Haitian professionals with relevant expertise'. Sachs argued that the economic plan should focus on peasant agriculture, reconstruction, infrastructure, small-scale manufacturing, and public services, and that the international response needed to be harmonized.[11] This was at least a thought-out proposal. Nothing like it occurred. Instead, the U.S. set up the Interim Haiti Recovery Commission (IHRC), placing control of Haiti's finances and reconstruction in the hands of this body, chaired by Bill Clinton and Haitian Prime Minister Max Bellerive. The IHRC 'effectively displaced the Haitian government and is in charge of setting priorities for reconstruction', according to Haitian-American economist Alex Dupuy, who continued:

So far (Jan 9/11), the IHRC has not done much. Less than 10 percent of the $9 billion pledged by foreign donors has been delivered, and not all of that money has been spent. Other than rebuilding the international airport and clearing the principal urban arteries of rubble, no major infrastructure rebuilding – roads, ports, housing, communications – has begun. According to news reports, of the more than 1,500 U.S. contracts doled out worth $267 million, only 20, worth $4.3 million, have gone to Haitian firms. The rest have gone to U.S. firms, which almost exclusively use U.S. suppliers.[12]

In contrast to Sachs's ideas, the reconstruction plan emphasises the industrial zones over agriculture, and as with all international economic plans, denies Haiti the ability to build its domestic market and its possibilities for food security.

The implementation of the plan maximized revenues for donors and donor countries at the expense of Haitians. Abe Sauer provided a very illustrative example in the New York website The Awl:

In November, 2010, Lewis Lucke, a former U.S. ambassador to Swaziland and former USAID official in Haiti, filed suit against Haiti Recovery Group Ltd. for some $500,000 in unpaid fees for the tens of millions of dollars in contracts Lucke secured for the group in the days after the earthquake. After leaving his USAID position, Lucke immediately signed a $30,000 a month 'consulting' contract with the Haiti Recovery Group, a

(Haiti Recovery Group)

conglomerate formed by several American contractors with the specific goal of securing U.S. funding. Lucke used the contacts developed while at USAID to score the conglomerate over $20 million in contracts. Then it canned him ...[13]

These tendencies were criticized by OAS Special Representative Ricardo Seitenfus in an interview with Swiss newspaper *Le Temps* on December 21, 2010.[14] Seitenfus said, 'Haiti is not an international menace. We are not in a civil war situation ... we are confronted with a struggle for power between political actors who don't respect democratic rules.' He argued that Haiti was the victim of negative international attention, seeking to have the UN make Haitians into 'prisoners on their own island'. On the economic plans for Haiti, Seitenfus said that 'to make Haiti a capitalist country, an export platform for U.S. market is absurd. Haiti must return to what it is, that is to say, a predominantly agricultural country.' Haiti was evidence of the failure of the international community, he argued. International aid could not replace the functions of the state, and to every infrastructural problem from roads to unemployment, the UN's response has been to send more troops. 'It is unacceptable from the moral standpoint to consider Haiti as a laboratory ... It seems that a lot of people come to Haiti ... to do business. For me as a Latin American it is a disgrace, an affront to our conscience.' A few days later, Seitenfus was removed from his job.

Another interesting point made by Seitenfus was that 'when the level of unemployment is 80 per cent, it is unbearable to deploy a stabilization mission. There is nothing to stabilize and everything to build.' If the Haitian elections of 2010 were indeed a part of this 'stabilization mission', they mostly helped stabilize the situation of absolute misery for the majority of the population.

A stark reminder that Haiti has not been rebuilt is the hundreds of thousands of people still living in tents in camps in Port-au-Prince. As of October 2011, estimates were that there were still 595,000 people living in camps. Close to two years after the quake, such large camp numbers were indicative of a structural housing crisis. In part, this was due to an absolute shortage of good housing in the city.[15] On the other hand, there was also a problem with affordable housing. With the majority employed outside the official economy, Haitians lacked sufficient income to pay for rental housing. The destruction of so many housing units raised the price of what remained.

important point (margin annotation)

In most countries it would be appropriate to analyze reconstruction successes and failures as the government's successes and failures. But since, in Haiti, most resources are controlled by NGOs and foreign governments, it is the performance of these entities that must be evaluated. Anthropologist Mark Schuller, a scholar of international aid regimes and NGOs focusing on Haiti, prepared a series of reports on NGO performance in Haiti. In the camps, NGOs failed to provide basic services to residents and failed to involve majorities to participate in decision making.[16]

check footnote (margin annotation)

Anthropologist Tim Schwartz, author of the 2010 book *Travesty in Haiti*, described some of the possible paths that could have been taken to rebuild Haiti had a more rational system been in place:

> One of the biggest expenditures in the wake of the earthquake was rubble clean up ... With the money made available we could have orchestrated a cleanup that involved the some 3 million unemployed Haitian men – and women as well. We could have simply bought rubble at disposal sites and let the Haitian poor bring the rubble in with wheel barrows and their own little trucks and horse carts. The international community paid an average of US$40 per cubic meter for rubble. If it was just wheel barrows doing the clean up then at 6 cubic feet in a standard wheel barrow and 10 million cubic meters of total rubble, that would have been 40 million wheel barrows of rubble. So If 1 million men pushed one wheel barrow per day to the dump site, cleanup would have taken about 40 days; and it would have put US$400 million directly into the hands of the Haitian poor. It is also worth pointing out that those poor would have made US$9 per day in the process, that's twice what the UN was paying participants in their cash for work programmes (US and UN cash for work programmes never amounted to more than a small fraction of the rubble removal. For example, in the first year USAID invested 17 million in cash for work versus some 100 million in rubble removal. Moreover, much of the cash for work activities were frivolous such as cleaning the streets and picking up trash).
>
> [...]
>
> An economy would have emerged around the sale of rubble. It would have included small and large local trucks, people carrying buckets on their head, men would have been retrieving

far more than one wheel barrow per day and the money for the rubble would have been pumped straight into the bottom of the Haitian economy creating a massive economic stimulus. Instead, the money went into the pockets of foreign corporations that specialize in disaster cleanup, such as DRC and AshBritt and to Haitian millionaire entrepreneurs such as Gilbert Bigio who partnered with those organizations. It also went to the for profit consultant agencies DAI and Chemonics and to the NGO CHF that handled the administration of the rubble cleanup. They took two years to clean up. They're still cleaning up.

Instead, Schwartz said, 'the bulk of the Haitian urban population sat there, unemployed or engaged in petty economic activities and watched US and Canadian and Haitian Elite-owned dump trucks gathered up and brought in the rubble. As Haitians on the street were saying at the time, "rubble could have been gold".'[17]

NGOs are, ultimately not accountable to the people they serve. There is also no accountability in the literal sense of the word. In Schwartz's words:

> Anyone who tries to do the research will find themselves bogged down in a quagmire of reports, prevarications, and refusals to provide information. The NGOs and UN agencies are structured and regulated in such a way that they simply will not provide specifics. Try to get the information yourself. They will not tell you ... There is no one person or no one thing that forces the NGOs and UN agencies to give us good accounting for their expenditures.[18]

Without good accounting, NGOs invite back-of-the-envelope calculations, like Tim Schwartz's calculation of how billions of dollars of aid money disappeared without any benefit to Haitian earthquake victims:

> All you have to do is perform the basic math. Journalists are fond of saying that there are 10,000 NGOs in Haiti ... let's be conservative and say there were 10,000 aid workers in Haiti after the quake. Now figure that every one of them is making $200 per day. Some less, some a lot more. But if we take $200 as an average that's 730 million per year. Per diem is at least another average of 100 per day (some get a lot more); that's another 365 million. A vehicle and driver cost $150 per day,

so let's say that for every two foreign aid workers there is one vehicle. That's another 750,000 per day; 274 million per year. So now we are at 1.369 billion per year and we have not even begun to talk about all the educated nationals who are working for aid agencies, the secretaries, administrators, and then the security guards and cooks and cleaners. Nor have we mentioned the inflated rents (~$3,000 per apartment; $6,000 to 10,000 for an office), hotel rooms ($100 per night and up), air line flights (those to the DR tripled in cost after the quake, going from US$150 per round trip to US$500), then all the equipment for offices, the trucks ... Nor have we said anything about the 20% to 50% of the money that went back to the home office to cover the considerable administrative expenses there. So if we're spending at least 1.3 billion per year or more on administration and there was 2.7 billion in charity spent over a period of 2 years ... This is rough accounting but it's a good approximation and it's enough to say with confidence – and without the aid agencies giving us the information that they won't give – that most of the money did not and does not get to the poor Haitians for whom we intended it. The same process is duplicated to a much greater extreme in the national and international agencies that received money from governments ... a UN consultant gets a per diem of US$284 per day. That's before salary. Again no one has had the energy or disposition to get into the actual expenditures on the poor, but that's another type of shame.[19]

Schwartz has proposed a mechanism for the public accounting and evaluation of NGO programmes in Haiti, but such a mechanism could only succeed in a sovereign, democratic context. The NGO economy, with all its failures, is a consequence of the way Haiti is governed, a consequence of the dictatorship.

important stance

10   THE 2011 ELECTIONS AND MICHEL MARTELLY

Beatrice Lindstrom pointed out the financial disproportion of the UN mission in an article arguing for fresh elections:

> Four days after the elections, the U.N. proposed a 2011 budget for MINUSTAH of $853 million, or $2.3 million a day. This amount nearly surpasses total aid distributed by Haiti's top 30 donors and represents five times the budget the U.N. requested to combat cholera.
>
> New elections would cost a fraction of this – just $29 million, or 12½ days of MINUSTAH's operations in Haiti – and would render MINUSTAH's continued operations unnecessary.[1]

U.S. INTERFERENCE IN THE ELECTIONS

Préval's term was set to expire. The election was planned for November 28. As usual, Lavalas was banned by the Provisional Electoral Commission (CEP), as were 15 other parties. This was perhaps more surprising than under the interim government in 2006, but it does reveal the continuity and the lack of independence of Préval's administration.

There was a brief interlude when singer Wyclef Jean announced his candidacy for the presidency. He was in the news for a few weeks,[2] was excluded by the CEP, and left the scene.

Nadler summarizes election day (November 28, 2010) as follows:

> On Election Day, voters faced numerous barriers to cast their ballots. To begin, there were fewer than 1,000 polling stations set up across the country. More than a million internally displaced people were not issued proper identity cards, leaving

them disenfranchised. The list of registered voters (used in the country's electoral commission) predated the earthquake and contained the names of at least 250,000 deceased Haitians. Observers witnessed and reported ballot stuffing, accounts of intimidation at numerous voting stations, and other widespread irregularities. Overall, it was estimated that only 27 percent of registered voters went to the polls (compared to the 59.3 percent turnout in the 2006 elections).[3]

Given the margin of error needed in one of the worst electoral situations in history, the elections were close: Mirlande Manigat (wife of the second-place candidate in the 2006 election) won 31.37 per cent, Jude Celestin 22.38 per cent, and Michel Martelly 21.84 per cent. Celestin was Préval's chosen candidate. The U.S. insisted on continuing with a second round, and the OAS manipulated the results to try to exclude Celestin. Mark Weisbrot put some of the data together in the UK *Guardian*:

> As it turns out, the OAS 'experts' did a very poor job on their election analysis. They threw out 234 tally sheets, thus changing the election result. According to the OAS, the government candidate, Jude Celestin, was pushed into third place and, therefore, out of the runoff election. This leaves two rightwing candidates – former first lady Mirlande Manigat, and popular musician Michel Martelly – to compete in the runoff. The OAS has Martelly taking second place by just 3,200 votes, or 0.3% of the vote.

The first problem with the OAS mission's report is that there were more than 1,300 ballot sheets, representing about 156,000 votes, that went missing or were quarantined. This is about six times as many ballot sheets as the ones that the mission eliminated. Since these areas were more pro-Celestin than the rest of the country, he would very likely have come in second if the missing tally sheets had been included. The mission did not address this problem in its report.

The second problem is that the mission examined only 919 of the 11,181 tally sheets to find the 234 that they threw out. This would not be so strange if they had used statistical inference, as is commonly done in polling, to say something about the other 92 per cent of ballot sheets, which they did not examine. However, this is not included in the leaked report.[4]

Préval was also very concerned about being sent into exile by the U.S., no idle fear given Aristide's fate.

THE CANDIDATES

Who were the candidates? Jude Celestin was Préval's chosen successor. Préval represented a leader who, while he had cooperated with the U.S. since 2006, was not entirely under their control. As Ambassador Sanderson had cabled, 'managing Préval' had always been a challenge. The new elections were an opportunity to get someone easier to manage.

Not that Celestin was a good choice from the perspective of the popular movement. Activist Patrick Elie described Celestin as

> a very poor choice as a candidate. Mr. Celestin had not been part of the democratic popular movement. He was almost like a rabbit pulled out of a hat. And also, I never understood what was the ideological or political cement holding that platform called 'Inite' … it was doomed from the beginning. Now of course the international community, especially the U.S., also helped to doom it. Not because of Mr. Celestin himself, but because in some indirect way, this would have meant a continuation of the Lavalas experience. Not because Mr. Celestin was Lavalas, but because whether he claims it or not, Mr. Préval originates from this movement.[5]

U.S. pressure during the second round of elections was to try to get Celestin to withdraw or for Préval and the CEP he controlled to exclude Celestin, leaving the runoff vote to two candidates completely favourable to the U.S.

Journalist and Haiti scholar Jeb Sprague wrote about Michel Martelly in December of 2010,[6] including a note on a press conference where Martelly 'spoke nostalgically of the Duvalierist era, when François "Papa Doc" Duvalier and later his son Jean-Claude "Baby Doc" enforced their iron rule with gun and machete wielding Tonton Macoutes'.

DUVALIER RETURNS

In this context, Baby Doc Duvalier returned to Haiti on January 17, 2011, in between the first and second round of elections. His return was tacitly supported by the U.S. In an op-ed arguing that Aristide should have been the one to return, Mark Weisbrot quoted the U.S. State Department: 'Asked about the return of Duvalier, who had thousands tortured and murdered under his dictatorship, State Department spokesman P.J. Crowley said, "this is a matter for the Government of Haiti and the people of Haiti", but when asked about Aristide returning, he said "Haiti does not need, at this point, any more burdens."'[7]

Baby Doc was questioned by Haitian authorities the day after his arrival, charged with corruption, theft, and misappropriation of funds, though without any clarity about whether he would be brought to trial.[8] On January 21, Duvalier stated that he felt 'profound sadness' for those harmed by his dictatorship, stated he would help rebuild the country, and called for national reconciliation.[9]

Isabeau Doucet, writing in the *Guardian*, summarized the situation after Baby Doc's return most clearly:

> What is certain is that Baby Doc's return is merely the starkest manifestation yet of a basic political fact: after the interlude of 1990–2004, Haiti has once again become a de facto dictatorship. Its affairs are at the mercy of the international community, and this latest, so-called democratic election is double-speak for a process that effectively ensures the near-total disempowerment, exclusion and pacification of the Haitian people.[10]

ARISTIDE RETURNS

On March 18, 2011, Jean-Bertrand Aristide returned to Haiti. He was greeted by thousands of people who waited for him at Port-au-Prince's airport. For Aristide to return, seven years after the coup, was still to defy the United States. The State Department tweeted that 'Aristide is the past. Haitians must look to the future.'

Aristide gave an inspiring speech at the airport, linking Lavalas's exclusion from political life to the exclusion of the majority of Haitians from meaningful participation:

> The problem of exclusion, its solution is inclusion. The exclusion of Fanmi Lavalas is the exclusion of the majority. The exclusion of the majority is tantamount to cutting the branch on which we sit. The problem of exclusion, its solution is the inclusion of all Haitians without favoritism.[11]

Aristide then proceeded to avoid public life almost completely. For years he had been saying that he wanted to avoid politics and focus on education, and his behaviour after his return suggests supports his claim. He also continued to avoid providing details about the coup itself. When asked by Amy Goodman about it in the air heading toward Haiti, Aristide said: 'Maybe one day I will talk about it, but if you don't mind, if you allow me, today I would prefer to concentrate and to focus on the positive.'[12]

Given Aristide's silence, the timing of his return is a matter of speculation. He returned in the very short window of time after the first round of presidential elections and before the run-off. Préval was still president, but he was going to hand power over to one of the candidates. Préval's favourite candidate, Celestin, had just been dropped.

If Préval had feared some kind of international action against him or his administration in retaliation for allowing Aristide to return, by this point he had little to fear. He was leaving office anyway, and his candidate was out of the running. With the runoff about to start, a coup to force him into exile would be both wasteful and excessive. Had he waited any longer, however, he might not have had the authority. That Aristide arrived, quietly despite the inevitable celebrity welcome, suggests some careful planning and subtle defiance to the international community by both Aristide and Préval.

On the other hand, it was seven years later, the coup had been consolidated, and the subtle international dictatorship was firmly established. Aristide could be allowed back home to play an educational role, whereas if he had been able to return sooner, and return to politics, the coup might have been reversed and the democratic government restored.

MARTELLY'S CHAOTIC PRESIDENCY

The idea of a new election gained ground in early 2011, but a new election might mean new rules. Would the banning of Fanmi Lavalas and the exile of Aristide continue to hold in a new election? Could the U.S. and donors risk such an outcome? The OAS desire to declare the election fraudulent was tempered by these risks. The U.S. suggestion would be to put Préval's chosen candidate, Celestin, out of the running without any procedural basis for doing so, a tactic which eventually succeeded on February 3, 2011, when the CEP announced that the runoff would be between Manigat and Martelly, who Mark Weisbrot pointed out had won 'around 6.4 and 4.5 per cent of registered voters, respectively'.[13] Haiti needed a legitimate government, but it was not to be.

In their excellent blog 'Haiti Relief and Reconstruction Watch', the Center for Economic and Policy Research (CEPR) noted the second-round victory of Michel Martelly was not the landslide it was purported to be:

> Preliminary results announced by the CEP last night showed Michel 'Sweet Micky' Martelly with 67.6 percent of the vote, while Mirlande Manigat received 31.5 percent. While news headlines focus on the 'landslide' victory for Martelly, he actually received the support of only 16.7 percent of registered voters – far from a strong mandate – as early reports show Martelly with just 716,986 votes to Manigat's 336,747. Reports indicate that turnout was even lower than in the first round, when it was a historically low 22.8 percent, and Martelly's percent of votes (as well as Manigat's) would have been even smaller were it not for the use of new electoral lists which removed some 400,000 people from the rolls.[14]

In his first months in office, Martelly had the same sorts of difficulties previous governments have had, but his connections to the Duvalier dictatorship added a different dimension. The first task of the president is to appoint a prime minister, who then must be ratified by the Chamber of Deputies and the Senate. Martelly's first choice, Bernard Gousse, was rejected. His second choice, Garry Conille, was ratified in October 2011, five months after he assumed the presidency. Conille resigned four months later, in February 2012, too soon to have accomplished anything. Martelly announced several programs in 2011, including a schools programme and a camps-to-homes project, but even a year into his term, he had fulfilled neither the hopes of his supporters nor the fears of his opponents. Instead, Martelly's early months in power featured deadlocks in Parliament and dangers of constitutional crisis.

Haiti activist and *Haiti Liberte* publisher Kim Ives identified two different factions in Martelly's government: a pro-Washington faction dedicated to maintaining international control of Haiti, and neo-Duvalierists seeking to use old strategies to enrich themselves while subordinating international forces. Conille's resignation in February 2012 was a loss for the pro-Washington faction in Haitian politics – recall that Garry Conille was a former member of Bill Clinton's staff and was appointed with the promise of focusing Clinton's attention on Haiti. The loss of the PM's office by the pro-Washington faction was a gain by the neo-Duvalierists, who 'seek to establish Haiti as a sort of chasse gardee for their business interests and corruption, rejecting oversight by Washington and the international institutions'.[15] According to this analogy, 'Martelly is trying to replay some of Duvaliers' tactics, working to re-establish the Macoutized Army and flirting with the Venezuela-led ALBA alliance, much as Papa Doc would get his way by threatening Washington that he might ally with Cuba.'[16]

It is unlikely that Martelly can succeed with 'neo-Duvalierist' strategy in this decade. Haiti's new dictatorship is based on international control, not control by Martelly or someone like him. In trying to turn the clock backward, however, Martelly appears likely to plunge Haiti into further political chaos, exacerbating the economic and social chaos wreaked by the coups, the earthquake, and the exclusionary model of development imposed on Haiti from without.

CONCLUSION

Replacing dictatorship with sovereignty

In October 2011, I spent some time in Port-au-Prince, mostly looking into the housing situation. Some Lavalas activists I talked to put on a brave face, while others were more afraid for the future than they had been even immediately after the 2004 coup. But the affront to Haiti's sovereignty was felt well beyond Lavalas, including politicians, like Senator Steven Benoit, who want nothing to do with Lavalas.

> Haiti is this country where if you want to experiment, you go to Haiti. Brazil, for example, had never had – I love Brazil, but let's tell the truth. Brazil had never had an international peacekeeping force. Brazil is preparing itself to be a leader in the UN, which is no problem, good for them, they have over 150 million people, and they are a huge country, so it's only normal that they are part of the UN with the right to veto, and this is their goal, and this is why they are in Haiti, to prove to the world that they are just like the Americans, the French, or the Russians or the Chinese.
>
> [...]
>
> So Brazil's thinking of Brazil. Brazil's not thinking of Haiti. Argentina's thinking of Argentina. So it's time for Haiti to think of Haiti. The international community has never helped a country become a success story. If you can remember one country, please let me know. Only us Haitians can save Haiti.
>
> [...]

Keep in mind after 200 years, the French are here. How would you feel if the British had come back to the U.S. after 200 years? When an American is watching this, they need to feel my grief right now. Because how would you feel if the British were in Manhattan and reclaiming Manhattan? The French are back in Haiti, the Americans are back in Haiti, Sri Lanka is in Haiti, Nepal is in Haiti. We say thank you, but no thank you. Haitians need to take charge of Haiti.[1]

At the time, there were demonstrations against the UN presence for a number of reasons: a videotaped sexual assault by Uruguayan soldiers against an 18-year-old boy, a growing body of proof that the cholera epidemic that killed thousands of Haitians was introduced by UN troops, and years of violence against demonstrations all had eroded the prestige of the fundamentally confused UN mission. There was discussion of MINUSTAH's mandate eventually ending, to be replaced by a reconstituted Haitian Army (this was Benoit's preference). Whenever the UN mandate ends, the mission will have played a dishonourable role in suppressing political movements and exercising social control.

Whenever a democratic government is toppled by externally sponsored violence, the sponsors use a defined strategy. Understanding the strategy in a particular case may help resistance the next time. On the other hand, if we fail to learn, if we accept the notion that even though the same thing keeps happening it is the unique fault of some uniquely corrupt leader, we may be condemned to repeat the past.

The Haiti coup of 2004 and the coup regime of 2004–06 were experiments in a new kind of imperialism. Labelling a coup against a democratic regime the overthrow of a tyrant was an old trick. Finding proxies to do the dirty work and then call for imperial backup when they got in trouble was also a practice that went back to ancient times.

What was new was how successfully 'human rights' communities, progressives, and radicals were co-opted into this violent coup by a few thousand dollars and some cheap rhetoric. These progressives ended up supporting a coup and occupation that was, by every single standard, far more brutal than the regime it overthrew. If they can look at this history and recognize that they were duped, perhaps they can be on the right side the next time this sort of thing is attempted. If, by contrast, they decide to try to defend and rationalize their errors, they will contribute to further irrelevance of leftists and progressives to the difficult situations faced by the victims of imperial foreign policy.[2]

The coup was a successful experiment in dividing and confusing solidarity movements and progressives, who ought to have been the first constituency to respond and the constituency with the clearest understanding of what had occurred. It was also a highly successful experiment in winning progressive Latin American regimes over to local collaboration with imperialism. In the case of Lula's Brazil (and to a lesser extent Chile), blunting its foreign policy independence and getting it to go along, willingly, with the suppression of the sovereignty of another country in the Americas, was a significant achievement for the U.S. Haitians paid for it, but so would everyone in the Americas and in the world. Smashing Haiti also provided the forum for the U.S., Canada, and France to patch up their disagreements over Iraq. The contempt for Haitians implied here, in making their lives and deaths an arena for patching up differences between powerful countries, is striking.

Although I disagree completely with Philippe Girard's point of view as expressed in his history of Haiti, I do agree with him on some of the prescriptions at the end of his book:

> the answer to this oft-mentioned question – what the U.S. should do to help Haiti – is simple: as little as possible. U.S. farmers do not need to donate rice to hungry Haitians – this will undercut the local rice industry. U.S. taxpayers do not need to bankroll the Haitian government – this will make the business of running Haiti too lucrative and desirable. U.S. troops do not need to patrol the streets of Port au Prince – this will give rise to an understandable nationalist outcry. U.S. ambassadors do not need to select politicians they deem to be best suited for Haiti's future – it is up to Haitians to set up their own government.[3]

What would sovereignty look like? Let us imagine sovereignty in three spheres: Haiti's electoral and political processes, in Haitian financial and economic affairs, and in social matters.

In electoral processes, international observers, and the international media, should be welcome in any and all elections. Such electoral observers might be helpful in keeping the electoral authority (the CEP in Haiti) honest. Having such international observation need not prejudice Haiti's independence in electoral matters. The banning of the most popular party (Lavalas) on procedural grounds would be a clue that normal processes are not being followed. So would the heavy involvement of the embassies of the U.S., Canada, and France.

All of the elected governments of the past decade – Aristide, Préval, Martelly – have had difficulties making policy because of the super-majority requirements of Haiti's constitution. Whereas the government, to spend its small share of the money, needs massive amounts of consensus won through expensive electoral processes, NGOs and private businesses can operate without any of these mechanisms. Perhaps Haitians will choose to change the constitution in future years. If they do, it will be incumbent on Haiti's friends to support them in doing so.

In economic matters, ultimately, Haiti will finance its activities from tax revenues raised on work and business activities done at good wages, not through donations and aid. This does not preclude France paying back the indemnity that it extorted from Haiti ($21 billion in 2004, but the interest continues to accrue). It does not preclude reparations for the damage done by slavery, successive occupations, and international debt payments. To become self-sufficient, Haiti will need capital, and this will have to come from other countries. Understanding that this is not aid or charity but Haiti's due will be key in changing the relationship between Haiti and the countries that are currently running the dictatorship over it.

Insightful writers on Haiti have argued that aid needs to get to Haiti in a way that builds up the public sector, in a way that is controlled democratically, and in a way that is accountable to the public.[4] But it is important to note that even with all the aid, the absolute amount of economic resources available to Haitians is tiny compared to most poor countries, to say nothing of rich countries. It is easy to talk about billions of dollars in aid and where did it go, but billions in aid, delivered to millions of people over years or decades, amounts to tens or hundreds of dollars per capita. The citizens of wealthy countries have thousands or tens of thousands of dollars per capita, raised as taxes from the public and spent by elected governments on them every year. This simple point cannot be repeated strongly enough. What looks like corruption or backwardness or cultural practice is actually adaptation to scarcity. That scarcity was violently imposed and continues today only through violence and terror.

To address social problems, given that Haiti's murder rates are lower than many of the MINUSTAH countries, it is strange that these countries are there, costing more than Haiti's annual budget, in order to protect Haitians from gangs and crime. Haiti's problems of crime and violence can be traced to inequality, which could be addressed through economic programmes enacted by a sovereign and democratic government. There would still be a need for police, but without an unequal order to enforce, the police would have a very different role and function.

Haiti's new dictatorship was imposed from the outside, and is maintained from the outside. It is unlikely that it can be replaced from the outside. Instead, Haitians will have to replace it. This would be easy enough for Haitians to do if those who were imposing the dictatorship on them would stop doing so. To begin with, we could stop believing the lie that Haiti is a site of heroic foreigners struggling against local corruption and look at the facts of Haiti's recent history, facts that paint us in an unflattering light.

NOTES

INTRODUCTION

1 Michel-Rolph Trouillot (1990) *Haiti: State Against Nation. The Origins and Legacy of Duvalierism.* Monthly Review Press, New York. The discussion of the idea of dictatorship is on pp. 164–5.
2 Patrick Bellegarde-Smith (2004) *Haiti: The Breached Citadel.* Westview Press, Boulder, CO. pp. 121–2.
3 Trouillot. *Haiti: State Against Nation.* p. 164.
4 Robert Fatton, Jr (2007) *The Roots of Haitian Despotism.* Lynne Rienner Publishers, London.
5 Philippe Girard (2010) *Haiti: The Tumultuous History – From Pearl of the Caribbean to Broken Nation.* Palgrave Macmillan, New York.
6 Erica James (2010) *Democratic Insecurities: Violence, Trauma, and Intervention in Haiti.* University of California Press, Berkeley, CA.
7 James. *Democratic Insecurities.* p. 33.

1 HISTORICAL CONTEXT: HAITI IN THE AMERICAS FROM INDEPENDENCE TO TODAY

1 The best contemporary account is by Fray Bartolome de Las Casas (1999) *A Brief Account of the Devastation of the Indies*, first published in 1552. Penguin Classics, London.
2 Quoted in Robert Heinl and Nancy Gordon Heinl (1996) *Written in Blood: The History of the Haitian People.* University Press of America, Lanham, MD; also quoted in Paul Farmer (2011) *Haiti after the Earthquake.* PublicAffairs, New York. p. 124.
3 C.L.R. James's *The Black Jacobins* is mandatory reading for this incredible story.
4 Toussaint L'Ouverture (1802) 'Letter to Jean-Jacques Desslines'. Available on The L'Ouverture Project website: http://thelouvertureproject.org/index.php?title=Toussaint_Louverture_letter_to_Jean-Jacques_Dessalines. [Accessed November 25, 2011].
5 This follows very closely the description in William Reed. 'Haiti: African Americans' Neighbour in Need'. Black Press Business. April 24, 2005. Available online: http://www.BlackPressInternational.com. [Accessed April 1, 2012].

6   C.L.R. James makes this argument in *The Black Jacobins*.

7   John Brown was a white U.S. revolutionist abolitionist who, prior to the U.S. Civil War, attempted to spark a slave revolt in the U.S. by armed insurrection. He was executed in 1859, but played a major role in the ending of slavery in the United States. There is a John Brown Avenue in Port-au-Prince today.

8   David Nicholls (1996) *From Dessalines to Duvalier: Race, Colour and National Independence in Haiti*. Rutgers University Press, New Brunswick, NJ, cited in 'Keeping the Peace in Haiti?' Harvard Law Student Advocates for Human Rights, Cambridge, MA. March 2005 (henceforth Harvard Human Rights Report, March 2005).

9   James Ferguson (1987) *Papa Doc, Baby Doc: Haiti and the Duvaliers*. Blackwell, Oxford; New York, cited in Harvard Human Rights Report, March 2005.

10 Matthew Smith (2009) *Red & Black in Haiti: Radicalism, Conflict, and Political Change, 1934–1957*. University of North Carolina Press, Chapel Hill, NC. p. 29.

11 Matthew Smith (2009) *Red & Black in Haiti*. p. 31. Junot Diaz's novel *The Brief Wondrous Life of Oscar Wao* refers to these massacres and the Trujillo dictatorship.

12 Smith. *Red & Black in Haiti*. p. 32.

13 All dollar amounts are USD unless stated otherwise.

14 Smith. *Red & Black in Haiti*. p. 36.

15 Smith. *Red & Black in Haiti*. p. 45.

16 Smith. *Red & Black in Haiti*. p. 61.

17 Smith. *Red & Black in Haiti*. p. 82.

18 Smith. *Red & Black in Haiti*. p. 91.

19 Smith. *Red & Black in Haiti*. p. 97.

20 Smith. *Red & Black in Haiti*. p. 99.

21 Smith. *Red & Black in Haiti*. pp. 112–13.

22 Smith. *Red & Black in Haiti*. p. 115.

23 The politics of the coup against Estimé are complex, fascinating, and of special interest to those who followed the 2004 coup against Aristide. The story is told with great skill in Smith, *Red & Black in Haiti*, Chapter 4.

24 Smith. *Red & Black in Haiti*. pp. 164–6.

25 This story is also complex and fascinating, including characters (especially Duvalier's electoral rival Daniel Fignole) who are not mentioned in my account. Please see Smith, *Red & Black in Haiti*, Chapter 5.

26 Robert Debs Heinl, Jr, and Nancy Gordon Heinl (1996) *Written in Blood: The Story of the Haitian People, 1492–1995*. University Press of America, Lanham, MD, cited in the Harvard Human Rights Report, March 2005.

27 This incident is related in William Blum (1998) *Killing Hope: U.S. Military and CIA Interventions Since WWII*. Common Courage Press, Monroe, ME. pp. 145–6.

28 ab Ferguson. *Papa Doc, Baby Doc*, cited in Harvard Human Rights Report, March 2005.

29 Ferguson. *Papa Doc, Baby Doc*, cited in Harvard Human Rights Report, March 2005.

30 Blum. *Killing Hope.*
31 Ferguson. *Papa Doc, Baby Doc,* cited in Harvard Human Rights Report, March 2005.
32 Another well-known figure, assassinated in 1994, was Jean-Marie Vincent.
33 Blum. *Killing Hope.*
34 Blum. *Killing Hope.*
35 Blum. *Killing Hope.*
36 Human Rights Watch (1996) 'Thirst for Justice: A Decade of Impunity in Haiti', cited in Harvard Human Rights Report, March 2005.
37 Blum. *Killing Hope,* citing Paul Farmer (1994) *The Uses of Haiti.* Common Courage Press, Monroe, ME.
38 Kern Delince (1994), cited in ICG Report, May 2005.
39 Harvard Human Rights Report, March 2005, citing Human Rights Watch, 'Thirst for Justice', and Blum, *Killing Hope.*
40 Harvard Human Rights Report, March 2005, citing Human Rights Watch 'Thirst for Justice'.
41 Blum. *Killing Hope,* citing Jean-Bertrand Aristide with Christophe Wargny, tr. Linda M. Maloney (1993) *Jean-Bertrand Aristide: An Autobiography.* Orbis Books, Maryknoll, NY.
42 Harvard Human Rights Report, March 2005.
43 Harvard Human Rights Report, March 2005, citing Human Rights Watch, 'Thirst for Justice'.
44 Harvard Human Rights Report, March 2005.
45 Harvard Human Rights Report, March 2005, citing Human Rights Watch, 'Thirst for Justice'.
46 Allan Nairn. 'Haiti Under the Gun'. *The Nation,* January 8/15, 1996.
47 Harvard Human Rights Report, March 2005.
48 Robert Muggah (2005) 'Securing Haiti's Transition: Reviewing Human Insecurity and the Prospects for Disarmament, Demobilization, and Reintegration'. Small Arms Survey, Graduate Institute of International Studies, Geneva. Available online: http://www.smallarmssurvey.org/fileadmin/docs/B-Occasional-papers/SAS-OP14-Haiti-EN.pdf. [Accessed January 20, 2012].
49 Harvard Human Rights Report, March 2005.
50 John Canham-Clyne and Worth Cooley-Prost. 'The Haiti Aid Scam'. *The Progressive.* September 1995. p. 25.
51 Harvard Human Rights Report, March 2005.
52 Harvard Human Rights Report, March 2005.
53 Blum. *Killing Hope.*
54 Haiti Action Committee (2005) 'We Will Not Forget: The Achievements of Lavalas in Haiti', by Laura Flynn and Robert Roth and published early in 2005. Available at: http://www.haitiaction.net. [Accessed April 1, 2012].
55 Harvard Human Rights Report, March 2005.
56 Muggah. 'Securing Haiti's Transition'. p. 55.
57 From the MADRE 'Haiti Backgrounder'. ZNet. Available online: http://www.zmag.org/content/showarticle.cfm?SectionID=55&ItemID=5043. [Accessed April 1, 2012].

58   Quoted by Justin Felux. 'Imperial Arrogance'. ZNet. March 24, 2004. Available online: http://www.zmag.org/content/showarticle. cfm?ItemID=5207. [Accessed April 1, 2012].
59   Peter Hallward. 'Option Zero in Haiti'. *New Left Review*. May–June 2004 .
60   Hallward. 'Option Zero'.
61   Haiti Action Committee. 'We Will Not Forget'.
62   Harvard Human Rights Report, March 2005.
63   Haiti Action Committee. 'We Will Not Forget'.
64   Muggah. 'Securing Haiti's Transition'.
65   Patrick Elie, who worked in Aristide's post-1994 government and helped establish the PNH, described the PNH as 'a bastard child': 'This police force was created when Haiti was, for all intents and purposes, under military occupation by the US ... so we did not have complete control over the process of setting up the police. The police turned out to be a kind of bastard child that came out of our own will to create a democratic police and the US will to create a police that would have replaced the Army as a tool to secure US interests in Haiti and eventually act as an arbiter of political life in Haiti.' Interview with Patrick Elie, Port-au-Prince, September 26, 2005.
66   Muggah. 'Securing Haiti's Transition'. p. 54.
67   Scott Wilson. 'Popular Haitian Lawmaker Worries U.S.; Onetime Ally, a Suspect in Journalist's Death, Is Also Rival of Aristide'. *Washington Post*. March 4, 2002. p. A14
68   Wilson. *Washington Post*. March 4, 2002.
69   From a 'Foreign Policy in Focus' report by Conn M. Hallinan. 'Haiti: Dangerous Muddle'. IRC Americas Program Policy Report, Interhemispheric Resource Center. March 8, 2004.
70   Harvard Human Rights Report, March 2005. p. 8.
71   Wilson. *Washington Post*. March 4, 2002.
72   Hallward. 'Option Zero in Haiti'.
73   To compare electoral results with Aristide, Bush had 48 per cent of the votes cast on a turnout of 51.3 per cent of the voting population.
74   Cited in Dan Beeton. 'What the World Bank and IDB Owe Haiti'. Global Policy Forum. July 25, 2006. Available online: http://www.globalpolicy.org/component/content/article/97/32135.html. [Accessed April 1, 2012].
75   Cited in Beeton. 'What the World Bank and IDB Owe Haiti'.
76   This is all reported in Paul Farmer's excellent article for *London Review of Books*, 'Who Removed Aristide?' April 2004. Available online: http://www.zmag.org/content/showarticle. cfm?ItemID=5318. [Accessed April 1, 2012].
77   Clara James in *Z Magazine*, June 1997 issue. Available online: http://www.zmag.org/ZMag/articles/june97james.htm. [Accessed April 1, 2012].
78   Hallward. 'Option Zero in Haiti'.
79   For some excellent studies on crime and other problems and their relationship to inequality, see Wilkinson and Pickett (2010) *The*

Spirit Level: Why Greater Equality Makes Societies Stronger. Bloomsbury Press, New York.

80 Peter Hallward (2007) Damming the Flood. Verso, London. p. 155.

2 NARRATIVES, MEDIA STRATEGIES, AND NGO STORIES

1 Paul Farmer uses this term in his 2011 book Haiti After the Earthquake. PublicAffairs, New York.

2 Peter Hallward (2008) Damming the Flood: Haiti, Aristide, and the Politics of Containment. Verso, London; New York. pp. 178–9.

3 See his 2003 book The Uses of Haiti. Common Courage Press, Monroe, ME.

4 Timothy T. Schwartz (2010) Travesty in Haiti: A True Account of Christian Missions, Orphanages, Food Aid, Fraud and Drug Trafficking. Self-published. It's remarkable that Schwartz's book hasn't found a publisher, since it is full of original information, sharp and painful first-hand insight, and good writing.

5 See especially the dialogue in Chapter 6 of Schwartz. Travesty in Haiti. p. 106.

6 Clinton's testimony to the Senate Foreign Relations Committee, March 10, 2010. Quoted in Farmer. Haiti After the Earthquake. p. 150.

7 Timothy Schwartz treats both of these phenomena with important insider detail in Travesty in Haiti.

8 Senator Steven Benoit has argued for the return of the Haitian Army on constitutional grounds. He told me as much in an interview in his Port-au-Prince office on October 5, 2011.

9 Two documentary films provide the most concise insight into these two cases. For Venezuela, Bartley and O'Brien (2003) The Revolution Will Not be Televised. For Honduras, the Real News's Honduran Coup series, starting in 2009, is excellent. Available online: http://therealnews.com/t2/index.php?option=com_content&task=view&id=33&Itemid=74&jumival=408. [Accessed November 28, 2011].

10 Justin Podur. 'A Dishonest Case for a Coup'. ZNet. February 16, 2006. Available online: http://www.zcommunications.org/a-dishonest-case-for-a-coup-by-justin-podur. [Accessed April 1, 2012]

11 Philippe Girard (2010) Haiti: The Tumultuous History – From Pearl of the Caribbean to Broken Nation. Palgrave Macmillan, New York. p. 206.

12 Alex Dupuy (1997) Haiti in the New World Order. Westview Press, Boulder, CO.

13 Peter Hallward. 'Hallward Reviews Alex Dupuy's "The Prophet and Power"'. Haitianalysis.com. August 18, 2007. Available online: http://www.haitianalysis.com/2007/8/18/hallward-reviews-dupuy-s-the-prophet-and-power-jean-bertrand-aristide-the-international-community-and-haiti. [Accessed April 1, 2012].

14 Fatton. The Roots of Haitian Despotism. Lynne Rienner Publishers, Boulder, CO. p. 209.

15 See especially Isabel Macdonald (2007) 'Covering the Coup'. Chapter 2, Table 2.

16 Jeb Sprague. 'Invisible Violence: Ignoring Murder in Post-Coup Haiti'. Fair Extra! July/August 2006. Available online: http://www. fair.org/index.php?page=2937. [Accessed April 1, 2012].

17 Paul Knox. 'Aristide's Haiti Was Just Left to Drift'. *Globe and Mail*. March 10, 2004. A19.

18 Hallward. *Damming the Flood*. p. 188.

19 Hallward. *Damming the Flood*. p. 187.

20 Walt Bogdanich and Jenny Nordberg. 'Mixed U.S. Signals Helped Tilt Haiti Towards Chaos'. *New York Times*. January 29, 2006.

21 Diana Barahona and Jeb Sprague. 'Reporters Without Borders and Washington's Coups'. *Counterpunch*. August 1, 2006.

22 Jeb Sprague. 'Seeking an "Even Playing Field": Washington and UN Work to Undermine Fanmi Lavalas'. *Narcosphere*. April 13, 2006; and Anthony Fenton. 'Declassified Documents: National Endowment for Democracy FY2005'. *Narcosphere*. February 16, 2006. Available online: http://narcosphere.narconews.com/ notebook/anthony-fenton/2006/02/declassified-documents-national-endowment-democracy-fy2005. [Accessed April 1, 2012].

23 Joe Emersberger. 'Amnesty International's Track Record in Haiti since 2004'. ZNet. February 27, 2007. Available online: http:// www.zcommunications.org/amnesty-internationals-track-record-in-haiti-since-2004-by-joe-emersberger. [Accessed April 1, 2012].

24 Terry Buss and Adam Gardner (2008) *Haiti in the Balance: Why Foreign Aid Has Failed and What We Can Do about It*. Brookings Institution Press, Washington, DC.

25 See, for example, John Canham-Clyne and Worth Cooley-Prost. 'The Haiti AID Scam'. *The Progressive*. September 1995. p. 25.

26 Robert F. Fatton, Jr (2002) *Haiti's Predatory Republic: The Unending Transition to Democracy*. Lynne Rienner Publishers, Boulder, CO. p. 126.

3   THE COUP BEGINS: 2000–04

1 Thomas M. Griffin. 'Haiti Human Rights Investigation: November 11–21, 2004'. Center for the Study of Human Rights, University of Miami School of Law.

2 Yifat Susskind. 'Haiti: Insurrection in the Making'. MADRE. Feb 25, 2004. Available online: http://www.madre.org/countries/Haiti. html. [Accessed April 1, 2012]. The backgrounder was reposted to ZNet: http://www.zmag.org/content/showarticle.cfm?SectionID=5 5&ItemID=5043 [Accessed April 1, 2012], and also has valuable 'profiles' on paramilitary leaders Emmanuel Constant, Louis Jodel Chamblain, Jean Tatoune, and Guy Philippe.

3 Quoted by Peter Hallward. 'Option Zero in Haiti'. *New Left Review*. May–June 2004. Available online: http://www.newleftreview.net/ NLR26102.shtml. [Accessed April 1, 2012].

4 Scott Wilson. *Washington Post*. February 12, 2002.

5   Associated Press. December 20, 2001.

6   This was reported in an article by Michel Vastel in the Canadian magazine *L'Actualite* on March 15, 2003. The article is described in another article on the *Haiti Progres* website: http://www.haiti-progres. com/2003/sm030305/eng03-05.html. [Accessed April 1, 2012].

7   The story is related by journalist Anthony Fenton in an April 6, 2004 ZNet article: http://www.zmag.org/content/showarticle. cfm?ItemID=5280. [Accessed April 1, 2012].

8   Related by Griffin. 'Haiti Human Rights Investigation'. Griffin interviewed the participants at the meeting and Apaid himself. Apaid admitted to the meeting and to having influence over Labanye, though Apaid said the meeting took place after Aristide's government was overthrown in the February 29, 2004 coup.

9   *Black Commentator* (www.blackcommentator.com). Issue 62, October 30, 2003. Available online: http://www.blackcommentator. com/62/62_haiti_1.html. [Accessed April 1, 2012].

10 Harvard Human Rights Report, March 2005.

11 *Black Commentator*. Issue 62, November 6, 2003. Available online: http://www.blackcommentator.com/63/63_haiti_2.html. [Accessed April 1, 2012].

12 'The Bush Administration's End Game for Haiti'. *Black Commentator*. Issue 67, December 4, 2003. Available online: http:// www.blackcommentator.com/67/67_pina.html. [Accessed April 1, 2012].

13 *Black Commentator*. January 15, 2004. Available online: http:// www.blackcommentator.com/73/73_haiti_pina.html.   [Accessed April 1, 2012].

14 Isabel Macdonald (2007) 'Covering the Coup: Canadian News Reporting, Journalists, and Sources in the 2004 Haiti Crisis'. MA Thesis. York University.

15 Hallward. 'Option Zero in Haiti'.

16 Peter Hallward (2007) *Damming the Flood: Haiti, Aristide and the Politics of Containment*. Verso, London; New York. pp. 194–8.

17 Related by Justin Felux. 'Witch Hunt Intensifies'. ZNet. June 29, 2004. Available online: http://www.zmag.org/content/showarticle. cfm?ItemID=5798. [Accessed April 1, 2012].

18 Reported by Haiti Action in their report, 'Hidden from the Headlines'. Available online: http://www.haitiaction.net/HidFrame. html. [Accessed April 1, 2012]. Lydia Polgreen. 'Haitian Forces Battling Uprising Report Retaking 3 Towns'. *New York Times*. February 10, 2004.

19 Tom Reeves, writing for ZNet in mid-February 2004, reviewed some of the mainstream coverage of the killings. Available online: http://www.zmag.org/content/showarticle.cfm?SectionID=55&Ite mID=4997. [Accessed April 1, 2012].

20 Reeves (Feb 16, ZNet), quoting Ian James in the Associated Press, Feb 14, 2004.

21 Reeves (Feb 16, ZNet), quoting the *Miami Herald,* Dec 6, 2002.

22 Cynthia McKinney. 'Haiti and the Impotence of Black America'. ZNet. March 21, 2004. Available online: http://www.zmag.org/ content/showarticle.cfm?ItemID=5182. [Accessed April 1, 2012].

23   Some of this information was published in the *San Francisco Chronicle* days after the coup on March 4, 2004, in a story by Steven Dudley, who cites U.S. officials and documents they provided him.
24   Stevenson Jacobs. 'DEA Agents Arrest Former Haitian Rebel Leader'. Associated Press. July 17, 2007.
25   A good reference on paramilitarism and drug traffic focusing on the Vietnam and Afghan cases is Alfred McCoy (2003) *The Politics of Heroin: CIA Complicity in the Global Drug Trade: Afghanistan, Southeast Asia, Central America, Colombia*. Lawrence Hill Press, Chicago, IL.
26   Reported by Haiti Action, April 2004. Available online: http://www.haitiaction.net/HidFrame.html. [Accessed April 1, 2012].
27   Peter Hallward discusses the importance of Gonaives foothold to the rebels in *Damming the Flood*.
28   This is the military assessment presented in Randall Robinson's 2007 book *An Unbroken Agony*. Basic Civitas Books, New York.
29   HRW (http://hrw.org/english/docs/2004/02/14/haiti7476.htm) noticed by Rahul Mahajan in his blog, Empire Notes: http://www.empirenotes.org/archive08feb142004.html. [Accessed April 1, 2012].
30   This takes us away from our subject matter, but it is important that the reader see these connections. Gregory Wilpert of Venezuelanalysis.com prepared an article on HRW's work on Venezuela (June 18, 2004). Available online: http://www.venezuelanalysis.com/articles.php?artno=1200. [Accessed April 1, 2012].
31   Mahajan's assessment is at: http://www.empirenotes.org/archive15feb212004.html [Accessed April 1, 2012], while Wilentz's (March 1, 2004) column is at: http://www.thenation.com/docprint.mhtml?i=20040301&s=wilentz. [Accessed April 1, 2012].
32   These incidents were reported in June 2005 by Ben Terrall, 'Awarding Abuse', in *Fault Lines*, the newspaper of the San Francisco Indymedia Center (indybay.org).
33   Tom Reeves. 'Return to Haiti, the American Learning Zone'. ZNet. April 15, 2004. Available online: http://www.zmag.org/content/showarticle.cfm?ItemID=5335. [Accessed April 1, 2012].
34   Claude Ribbe. 'Aristide, un an Apres'. February 21, 2005. Available online: www.hayti.net. [Accessed April 1, 2012]. The interview was conducted in Pretoria, South Africa.
35   David Pugliese (2002) *Canada's Secret Commandos: The Unauthorized Story of Joint Task Force Two*. Esprit de Corps Books, Ottawa.
36   Marc Carnegie. 'Caribbean Nations Ask UN for Multinational Force in Haiti'. *Agence France Press*. February 26, 2004.
37   'Venezuela donara un milion de dolares a Haiti asi como ayuda en combustibles y medicinas'. *Europa Press*. February 23, 2004.
38   McKinney. 'Haiti and the Impotence of Black America'.
39   Kevin Skerrett. 'Faking Genocide in Haiti'. ZNet. June 23, 2005. Available online: http://www.zcommunications.org/faking-genocide-in-haiti-by-kevin-skerrett. [Accessed April 1, 2012].
40   Ronald St Jean. 2004. A propos du 'Genocide de la Scerie: Exiger de la NCHR toute la verite'. Comite de Defense des Droits du Peuple Haitien (CPDH), Editions Scli. Port au Prince.

41 Aristide's statement is available on ZNet: http://www.zmag.org/content/showarticle.cfm?SectionID=55&ItemID=5097. [Accessed April 1, 2012].
42 The interview is available online at: http://www.zmag.org/content/showarticle.cfm?ItemID=5111. [Accessed April 1, 2012].
43 Paul Farmer. 'Who Removed Aristide?' *London Review of Books*. April 2004.
44 'Aristide: U.S. Forced Me to Leave'. BBC News. March 2, 2004. Available online: http://news.bbc.co.uk/2/hi/3524273.stm. [Accessed January 20, 2012].
45 Robinson. *An Unbroken Agony*. p. 175.
46 Robinson. *An Unbroken Agony*. The quotes from Bozize are from pp. 247–8, and are based on Robinson's interviews with Congresswoman Maxine Waters.

4 THE SLAUGHTER ON U.S. WATCH: TO JUNE 2004

1 Described in Charles Arthur. 'Haiti's Army Turns Back the Clock'. Red Pepper. April 2, 2004. Available online: http://www.zmag.org/content/showarticle.cfm?ItemID=5261. [Accessed April 1, 2012].
2 'International Labor/Religious/Community Fact Finding Delegation to Haiti (April 26–May 2) organized by the San Francisco Labor Council. 'Initial Statement on the Current Situation of Workers, the Labor Movement, and Human Rights in Haiti'. May 4, 2004.
3 Justin Felux. 'The Murder of Cassey Auguste'. ZNet. May 15, 2004. Available online: http://www.zmag.org/content/showarticle.cfm?ItemID=5532. [Accessed April 1, 2012].
4 Justin Felux. 'The Witch Hunt Intensifies'. June 29, 2004. ZNet. Available online: http://www.zcommunications.org/witch-hunt-intensifies-by-justin-felux. [Accessed April 1, 2012].
5 Paul Farmer. 'Who Removed Aristide?' *London Review of Books*. April 2004.
6 Aristide mentioned this in his interview with Amy Goodman, online: http://www.zmag.org/content/showarticle.cfm?ItemID=5111. [Accessed April 1, 2012]. The University then became a headquarters for UN troops, and was not returned to Haitian sovereignty until Préval became president again in 2006.
7 Reported by Tom Driver, April 5, 2004, ZNet. Journalist Anthony Fenton, who was with Driver in Haiti, reported the same pattern in his own article on April 6 on ZNet: http://www.zmag.org/content/showarticle.cfm?ItemID=5280. [Accessed April 1, 2012].
8 Canadian Press, March 20, 2004. Published in the *Toronto Star*.
9 The interview is on ZNet: http://www.zmag.org/content/showarticle.cfm?SectionID=54&ItemID=5121. [Accessed April 1, 2012].
10 His article was first published by the Pacific News Service. Available online: http://www.zmag.org/content/showarticle.cfm?ItemID=5145. [Accessed April 1, 2012].
11 Tom Driver. 'On the Way Home from Haiti'. ZNet. April 5, 2004. Available online: http://www.zmag.org/content/showarticle.cfm?ItemID=5274. [Accessed April 1, 2012].

12 Quoted in Justin Felux. 'Imperial Arrogance'. ZNet. March 24, 2004. Available online: http://www.zmag.org/content/showarticle.cfm?ItemID=5207. [Accessed April 1, 2012].

13 Isabel Macdonald. 'DDR in Haiti: The UN's Cleansing of Bel Air Ahead of Elections'. Haiti Information Project. December 17, 2005. Available online: http://www.haitiaction.net/News/HIP/12_17_5/12_17_5.html. [Accessed April 1, 2012].

14 Jeb Sprague. 'Failed Solidarity: The ICFTU, AFL-CIO, ILO, and ORT in Haiti.' Labor Notes. September 28, 2006. Available online: http://labornotes.org/node/230. [Accessed April 1, 2012].

15 Washington Fact Sheet from the Office of the Spokesman, April 5, 2004.

16 Oriel Jean was eventually jailed in Miami for three years, on involvement in cocaine smuggling. 'Former Aristide Security Chief Jailed'. *Trinidad & Tobago Guardian*. November 20, 2005.

17 'Some 200 Haitians Riot in Dominican Custody'. Associated Press. March 16, 2004.

18 CNN correspondent John Zarella. 'Haiti on the Brink'. Wolf Blitzer, John Zarrella, Lucia Newman. February 24, 2007.

19 'Bush Says International Force Can Go to HAITI after Political Solution'. AFP. February 25, 2004.

20 Amnesty International Press Release, April 8, 2004.

21 'Haiti Human Rights Report'. Let Haiti Live Coalition, vol. 1, ed. 1. April 30, 2004. See the NLG reports, available online: http://www.nlginternational.org/report/Haiti_delegation_report1.pdf and http://www.nlginternational.org/report/Haiti_delegation_report_phaseII.pdf. [Accessed April 1, 2012].

22 Let Haiti Live Coalition. 'Human Rights Report'. April 30, 2004.

23 Tom Reeves. 'Haiti's Disappeared'. ZNet. April 29, 2004. Available online: http://www.zmag.org/content/showarticle.cfm?ItemID=5467. [Accessed April 1, 2012].

24 Alan Pogue, a documentary photographer, reported this in April 2004. Online: www.documentaryphotographs.com. [Accessed April 1, 2012].

25 Brian Concannon. 'Chamblain'. HaitiAction.net. April 29, 2004. Available online: http://www.haitiaction.net/News/BC/bc4_29_4.html. [Accessed April 1, 2012].

26 Amnesty International Press Release, April 8, 2004.

27 Dominique Esser and Kim Ives. 'Haiti and Abu Ghraib'. ZNet. June 17, 2004. Available online: http://www.zmag.org/content/showarticle.cfm?ItemID=5727. [Accessed April 1, 2012].

28 Annette Auguste. 'From a Haitian Prisoner of Conscience'. ZNet. May 23, 2004. Available online: http://www.zmag.org/content/showarticle.cfm?ItemID=5606. [Accessed April 1, 2012].

29 Esser and Ives. 'Haiti and Abu Ghraib'. ZNet.

30 Flashpoints Radio, KPFA, Berkeley CA, May 18, 2004, cited by Tom Reeves. 'Canada in Haiti'. ZNet. June 7, 2004. Available online: http://www.zmag.org/content/showarticle.cfm?ItemID=5665. [Accessed April 1, 2012].

31 Related by Marguerite Laurent and Pierre Labossiere. 'The Raid on

the Mayor'. ZNet. June 18, 2004. Available online: http://www.
zmag.org/content/showarticle.cfm?ItemID=5736. [Accessed April
1, 2012].
32 Haiti Support Group. June 14, 2004.

5 INTERNATIONALIZING THE OCCUPATION: THE
SUMMER 2004 TRANSITION

1   Roberto Manriquez. 'Chile in Haiti and Iraq'. ZNet. June 2,
    2004. Available online: http://www.zmag.org/content/showarticle.
    cfm?ItemID=5637. [Accessed April 1, 2012].
2   Gunnery Sgt Mike Dougherty. 'U.S. Marines Train Chileans for
    Haiti Occupation'. Department of Defense U.S. Marine Corps
    News. March 23, 2005.
3   Reported by EFE. June 25, 2004.
4   Thomas M. Griffin. 'Haiti Human Rights Investigation: November
    11–21, 2004'. Center for the Study of Human Rights, University of
    Miami School of Law
5   Melinda Miles. 'Come to Haiti'. ZNet. November 29, 2004.
    Available   online: http://www.zmag.org/content/showarticle.
    cfm?ItemID=6754. [Accessed April 1, 2012].
6   See Amnesty International. August 16, 2004. AI Index:
    AMR 36/053/2004 (Public). Available online: http://www.
    amnesty.org/en/library/info/AMR36/053/2004/en.   [Accessed
    April 1, 2012].
7   Quoted in Justin Felux. 'Killers and Kangaroo Courts'. ZNet.
    August 18, 2004. Available online: http://www.zmag.org/content/
    showarticle.cfm?ItemID=6058. [Accessed April 1, 2012].
8   Led by Ramsay Clark, who gave this information at a September 6,
    2004 press conference in Port-au-Prince.
9   Reported by Miles. 'Come to Haiti'. ZNet.
10 John Maxwell. 'Hapless Haitians'. ZNet. September 27, 2004.
    Available   online: http://www.zmag.org/content/showarticle.
    cfm?ItemID=6313. [Accessed April 1, 2012].
11 Kevin Pina. 'Flood of Repression'. ZNet. October 1, 2004.
    (Flashpoints Interview September 29, 2004 transcription). Available
    online: http://www.zcommunications.org/flood-of-repression-in-
    haiti-continues-by-kevin-pina. [Accessed April 1, 2012].
12 For background on Labanye and his gang in Cité Soleil, see Chapter
    3, 'The coup begins'.
13 Griffin. 'Haiti Human Rights Report'. 2005.
14 Griffin. 'Haiti Human Rights Report'. 2005
15 'Gunfire erupts in Haiti's slums'. Haiti Information Project. October
    4, 2004. Haiti Information Project is a group of journalists who
    work independently of the state and corporate media. They are pro-
    Lavalas: among the leaders of the project is Kevin Pina.
16 For useful background on 'Operation Baghdad', see Nik Barry-Shaw.
    'Haiti's Big Lie: Operation Baghdad and Imperial Propaganda'. Znet.
    April 30, 2008. Available online: http://www.zcommunications.

org/haitis-big-lie-by-nik-barry-shaw. [Accessed April 1, 2012].

17 'Paramilitaries Shoot Aristide Supporters'. Haiti Information Project. October 3, 2004.

18 'Haiti Human Rights Alert'. Institute for Justice and Democracy in Haiti. October 2, 2004.

19 ICG Haiti Report. November 8, 2004. Note 1, p. 16.

20 Harvard Law Student Advocates for Human Rights & Centro de Justica Global. 'Keeping the Peace in Haiti? An Assessment of the UN Stabilization Mission in Haiti Using Compliance with its Prescribed Mandate as a Barometer for Success'. March 2005. (Henceforth 'Harvard Human Rights Report'). p. 39.

21 Griffin. 'Haiti Human Rights Report'. 2005

22 Haiti Information Project. October 15, 2004.

23 'Peacekeepers, Police Storm Haiti's Bel Air'. Associated Press. October 24, 2004.

24 Harvard Human Rights Report. March 2005. p. 27.

25 Griffin. 'Haiti Human Rights Report'. 2005

26 Haiti Information Project. October 13, 2004.

27 Kevin Pina interviewed by Dennis Bernstein for Flashpoints. Transcript on ZNet, October 25, 2004: http://www.zmag.org/content/showarticle.cfm?ItemID=6490. [Accessed April 1, 2012].

28 The embargo was effectively lifted at this point. It was not officially lifted, however, until two years later, in October 2006. Stevenson Jacobs. 'U.S. Eases off Haiti Arms Embargo'. Associated Press. October 11, 2006.

29 Kevin Pina interviewed by Dennis Bernstein for Flashpoints. Transcript on ZNet, November 1, 2004: http://www.zmag.org/content/showarticle.cfm?ItemID=6546. [Accessed April 1, 2012].

30 Kevin Pina interviewed by Dennis Bernstein for Flashpoints. Transcript on ZNet, November 9, 2004: http://www.zmag.org/content/showarticle.cfm?ItemID=6613. [Accessed April 1, 2012].

31 Kevin Pina interviewed for Flashpoints. Transcript on ZNet, November 11, 2004: http://www.zmag.org/content/showarticle.cfm?ItemID=6631. [Accessed April 1, 2012].

32 Harvard Human Rights Report. March 2005. p. 23.

33 AFP. October 24, 2004.

34 Griffin. 'Haiti Human Rights Report'. 2005

35 Harvard Human Rights Report. March 2005. p. 32.

36 Griffin. 'Haiti Human Rights Report'. 2005

37 Harvard Human Rights Report. March 2005. p. 31

38 Reed Lindsay. 'Massacre in the "Titanic"'. *Toronto Star*. December 20, 2004.

39 Carlo Dade and John W. Graham. 'The Role for Canada in Post-Aristide Haiti: Structures, Options, and Leadership'. FOCAL. December 2004. (www.focal.ca).

40 Kevin Pina interviewed by Flashpoints, transcript on ZNet, December 7, 2004: http://www.zmag.org/content/showarticle.cfm?ItemID=6816. [Accessed April 1, 2012].

41 Harvard Human Rights Report. March 2005. p. 28. The child's body was taken by MINUSTAH, who told the parents to go to the morgue. When the parents went to the morgue, they were told to go

to another morgue. They filed a complaint with MINUSTAH, but never saw the remains of their son and never had the chance to bury him.

42 Haiti Information Project. December 14, 2004.
43 Haiti Information project. December 16, 2004.
44 Haiti Information Project. December 29, 2004.
45 Harvard Human Rights Report. March 2005. p. 36.
46 Thomas Griffin's team interviewed these police officers. See his 'Haiti Human Rights Report'. 2005. p. 49.
47 Harvard Human Rights Report. March 2005. p. 40.
48 Tamara Lush. 'Haitians Worry They Are a Target'. *St. Petersburg Times.* January 1, 2005.
49 *South Florida Sun-Sentinel.* December 29, 2004.
50 '38 Haitians rescued near Jamaica'. Associated Press. December 31, 2004.

6   OCCUPATION YEAR TWO: 2005

1 Haiti Information Project. December 31, 2004. Available online: http://www.haitiaction.net/News/HIP/12_31_4.html. [Accessed April 1, 2012].
2 Agence Haitiene de Presse. January 4, 2005. Agence Haitien de Presse is affiliated with the Port-au-Prince radio station Radio Solidarite. It is a pro-Lavalas organization.
3 Haiti Information Project. January 7, 2005.
4 Haiti Information Project. January 5, 2005.
5 Agence Haitiene de Presse. January 17, 2005.
6 Haiti Information Project. January 8, 2005.
7 Agence Haitien de Presse. 'AJH Secretary General: Police Executed Journalist Abdias Jean'. Jan 19, 2005. UNESCO Director-General Koichiro Matsuura condemned the killing in a Jan 28, 2005 press release, available online: http://portal.unesco.org/en/ev.php-URL_ID=24855&URL_DO=DO_PRINTPAGE&URL_SECTION=201.html. [Accessed April 1, 2012].
8 'BBC Monitoring International Reports'. Caribbean Media Corporation. January 23, 2005.
9 Harvard Human Rights Report. March 2005. p. 33.
10 Agence Haitien de Presse. January 24, 2005.
11 Agence Haitien de Presse. January 19, 2005.
12 'Haiti Action Alert'. January 25, 2005. Available online: http://haitiaction.net/News/HAC/1_25_5.html. [Accessed ?]; and Flashpoints Radio interview with Kevin Pina. January 24, 2005. Available online: http://www.zmag.org/content/showarticle.cfm?ItemID=7135. [Accessed April 1, 2012].
13 Harvard Human Rights Report. March 2005. p. 26.
14 Sasha Kramer. 'Walking a Tightrope'. Portland Indymedia. March 17, 2005.
15 Lyn Duff. 'Killings of Haitian Street Kids Soar'. Pacific News Service. January 16, 2005. Available online: http://www.zmag.org/

content/showarticle.cfm?ItemID=7035. [Accessed April 1, 2012].

16   Naomi Klein. 'The Rise of Disaster Capitalism'. *The Nation*. May 2, 2005.

17   Fluor Corporation. February 9, 2005. Available online: http://investor.fluor.com/news/20050209-155419.cfm. [Accessed April 1, 2012].

18   'Hydro-Quebec Line Crew Returns from Haiti Mission'. Canada Newswire. March 10, 2005.

19   The embassy contract is mentioned in SNC-Lavalin's annual reports of 2002 and 2003, but not 2004.

20   Agencia Brasil, Brasilia, March 10, 2005, via BBC Monitoring Latin America Global News Wire.

21   Center for Justice and Accountability. Press Release. January 14, 2005. Available online: http://www.cja.org/cases/ConstantDocs/Constantpr1.14.04.htm. [Accessed April 1, 2012].

22   Kirk Semple. 'Ex-militia Chief from Haiti Is Sentenced to up to 37 Years for Fraud'. *New York Times*. October 28, 2008. Available online: http://www.nytimes.com/2008/10/29/nyregion/29toto.html?_r=1&ref=emmanuelconstant. [Accessed April 1, 2012].

23   Agence Haitien de Presse. January 24, 2005.

24   Reuters. January 22, 2005.

25   Agence Haitien de Presse. January 24, 2005.

26   Agence Haitien de Presse. January 24, 2005

27   Agence Haitien de Presse. February 2, 2005

28   Agence Haitien de Presse. January 4, 2005.

29   Thomas Griffin. 'Haiti Human Rights Report'. p. 35 (interview with Julien).

30   Agence Haitien de Presse. February 8, 2005.

31   *Haiti Progres*. February 9–15, 2005. vol. 22, no. 48. (www.haitiprogres.com).

32   Reuters. January 20, 2005.

33   *Haiti Progres*. February 9–15, 2005. vol. 22, no. 48. (www.haitprogres.com).

34   Haiti Human Rights Alert. February 4, 2005.

35   Judy DaCruz, based on eyewitness reports, February 6, 2005.

36   *South Florida Sun-Sentinel*. February 8, 2005.

37   Joseph Guyler Delva. Reuters. February 28, 2005.

38   Peter Prengaman. 'Haitian Police Search Compound for Rebel'. Associated Press. February 10, 2005.

39   AFP. February 25, 2005.

40   Judy Dacruz, Independent Human Rights Lawyer. 'Cité Soleil: A Wretched Forgotten Land'. February 18, 2005. Available online: http://ijdh.org/articles/article_urgent_human_rights_alerts-february18-2.htm. [Accessed April 1, 2012].

41   'Bahamas Deports Haitians'. Reuters. March 3, 2005.

42   'Bahamas: Haitian Boat People Intercepted at Sea'. *South Florida Sun-Sentinel*. February 7, 2005.

43   'Jamaica Rescues 58 Foundering Haitians'. UPI. February 17, 2005.

44   Marina Jimenez. 'Haitians Languish in Squalor Awaiting Trial'. *Globe and Mail*. February 7, 2005.

45 Peter Prengaman. Associated Press. February 19, 2005.

46 UN News Service. February 22, 2005.

47 Reed Lindsay. 'Answers as Elusive as Prison Escapees in Port-au-Prince'. Newsday. February 23, 2005.

48 Kevin Pina reported having interviewed Bellizere on Flashpoints Radio, transcript posted to ZNet. February 28, 2005. Available online: http://www.zmag.org/content/showarticle.cfm?ItemID=7335. [Accessed April 1, 2012]. Bellizere later went into hiding.

49 Claude Ribbe. 'Precisions sur l'attaque de la prison de Port-au-Prince le 19 Fevrier 2005 et sur la pretendue "evasion" de MM. Neptune et Privert'. February 23, 2005.

50 Yvon Neptune, February 24, 2005, open letter from prison.

51 Inter Press Service. February 22, 2005.

52 Lyn Duff. 'Haiti Rapes'. ZNet. February 24, 2005. Available online: http://www.zmag.org/content/showarticle.cfm?ItemID=7305. [Accessed April 1, 2012].

53 Joseph Guyler Delva. 'Haiti Still Torn by Violence a Year after Aristide'. Reuters. February 28, 2005. The National Protestant Coalition for the Promotion and Respect of Human Rights (CNPRDH) published the names of 11 victims of the police raids from February 23–28, among them Ernst Gay, Alex Michel, Dieubetite Juste, Fritz Delva, Alex Jerome, Junior Joseph, Herard Maxo, Jeff Joseph, Dor Berman, Dane St-Vil, and Celistin Adrien.

54 BBC World Monitoring, Radio Vision 2000, February 26, 2005. Kevin Pina (Flashpoints interview, posted to ZNet, February 28, 2005) reported 12 deaths, and eight killings by police in Village de Dieu the day before (Feb 24).

55 Reed Lindsay. 'Stability Still Eludes Haiti'. Newsday (republished in ZNet, March 9, 2005). Available online: http://www.zmag.org/content/showarticle.cfm?ItemID=7398. [Accessed April 1, 2012].

56 Lindsay. 'Stability Still Eludes Haiti'; Harvard Human Rights Report. March 2005. p. 40; Guyler Delva. 'Haiti Still Torn'. Reuters.

57 AUMOHD (Association of University Graduates Motivated for a Haiti with Rights) Report. March 28, 2005.

58 Agence Haitiene de Presse. March 4, 2005.

59 Agence Haitiene de Presse. March 7, 2005.

60 Associated Press. March 8, 2005.

61 Sasha Kramer. 'Walking a Tightrope'. Portland Indymedia. March 17, 2005.

62 Kramer. 'Walking a Tightrope'. Portland Indymedia.

63 World Bank News Release. March 8, 2005.

64 CCN Mathews Canadian Corporate Newswire. March 16, 2005.

65 Joe Mozingo. 'Citing Aristide Ties, Haiti Bars U.S. Attorney from Entering Country'. *Knight Ridder Newspapers*. March 7, 2005.

66 Maxine Waters. Press Release. March 7, 2005.

67 Kramer. 'Walking a Tightrope'. Portland Indymedia.

68 'UN Troops Clash with Ex-Soldiers in Haiti; One Peacekeeper Killed'. Associated Press. March 21, 2005.

69 'Haitian Journalist Dies of Gunshot Wounds Suffered in Clash Last Month'. Associated Press. April 5, 2005.

70 'UN Troops Take Control of Town from Ex-Soldiers'. Associated Press. March 22, 2005.
71 'Police, Protesters Clash during Pro-Aristide Protest in Haiti'. Associated Press. March 25, 2005.
72 'UN Troops Clash with Gangs in Haitian Slum'. Associated Press. April 4, 2005.
73 'Cops Short of Weapons, Haitian PM Says'. Associated Press. March 31, 2005.
74 'Gunmen Ambush Police, Killing Two Officers and a Driver'. Associated Press. March 31, 2005.
75 Andrew Buncombe. *Independent* (UK). April 17, 2005.
76 Press Release from Congresswoman Maxine Waters, April 27, 2005.
77 Kevin Pina interviewed by Flashpoints Radio. April 12, 2005. Transcript on ZNet: http://www.zmag.org/content/showarticle.cfm?ItemID=7624. [Accessed April 1, 2012].
78 Andrew Buncombe. *Independent* (UK). April 17, 2005.
79 'Gov. Bush Lauds Recommendations on Helping Caribbean Nation'. *Florida Sun-Sentinel*. April 12, 2005.
80 'Shootouts Leave 10 Dead in Haiti'. AFP. April 12, 2005. Published at Independent Online.
81 Agence Haitiene de Presse. April 15, 2005.
82 Agence Haitiene de Presse. April 15, 2005.
83 Claire Schaeffer-Duffy. 'Violence, Repression Endanger Prospects for Fair Elections in Haiti'. *National Catholic Reporter*. April 29, 2005.
84 Haiti Action Alert. April 21, 2005.
85 Letter from Yvon Neptune. April 27, 2005.
86 Ariana Cubillos. 'Ex-Haiti PM Reportedly Flying into Exile'. Associated Press. May 1, 2005.
87 'UN Says Former Haitian PM Jailed Illegally'. Reuters. May 5, 2005.
88 Independent Online. South Africa. May 11, 2005.
89 'Haiti Murder Convictions Quashed'. BBC News. May 11, 2005. Available online: http://us.f800.mail.yahoo.com/ym/login?.rand=4d3p98s42p38f. [Accessed April 1, 2012].
90 RNDDH press release. May 9, 2005.
91 Peter Prengaman. *Montreal Gazette*. June 11 2005.
92 AHP. December 7, 2005.
93 Haiti Information Project. April 25, 2005.
94 Agence Haitiene de Presse. April 26, 2005.
95 Amnesty International Press Release. April 29, 2005.
96 Associated Press. April 27, 2005.
97 Agence Haitiene de Presse. May 4, 2005.
98 Haiti Information Project. May 20, 2005.
99 'Jean', interviewed by the Ezili Danto Witness Project of the Haitian Lawyers Leadership Network. May 19, 2005.
100 Haiti Information Project. May 25, 2005.
101 Haiti Information Project. May 31, 2005.
102 Haiti Information Project. June 5, 2005.
103 Radio Metropole, June 5, 2005, via BBC monitoring international news.

104 'Haiti Police in Deadly Gang Raids'. BBC News. June 5, 2005.

105 Reuters. June 4, 2005; Agence Haitiene de Presse. June 5, 2005.

106 'Haiti Police in Deadly Gang Raids'. BBC News. June 5, 2005.

107 AHP News. June 7, 2005.

108 Haiti Information Project. June 12, 2005.

109 BBC News. June 8, 2005; Reuters. June 8, 2005.

110 Haiti Information Project. June 12, 2005.

111 'Canada to Support Haitian Elections'. *Montreal Gazette*. June 17, 2005.

112 'Class Battles Wrack Haiti'. *Toronto Star*. June 5, 2005.

113 'Cogent Systems Awarded 2.5 Million Contract for AFIS to Support Haiti's Electoral Process'. Cogent Systems Press Release. May 31, 2005.

114 'Montreal Woman Freed by Haitian Kidnappers'. *Montreal Gazette*. June 16, 2005.

115 'Haiti's Kidnappings'. AHP. July 1, 2005. Also see Anthony Fenton. 'Have the Latortues Kidnapped Democracy in Haiti?' ZNet. June 26, 2005.

116 Stevenson Jacobs. 'Peace Corps Suspends Haiti Operations'. Associated Press. June 16, 2005.

117 'Haiti's Interim Justice Minister Submits Resignation'. Haiti-Info. June 15, 2005.

118 Haiti Information Project. June 17, 2005.

119 'Haiti Needs More Police for Elections – Minister'. Reuters. June 17, 2005.

120 Minister Pettigrew Pleased With UNSC Decision on MINUSTAH Renewal'. Canadian Department of Foreign Affairs News Release 114. June 22, 2005. '

121 'UN Envoy in Haiti Wants Jailed Ex-PM Released'. Reuters. June 24, 2005.

122 Sue Ashdown. 'Outsiders Plan Haitian Elections: No Voters? No Problem'. San Francisco Bay View. June 29, 2005.

123 Stevenson Jacobs. 'Violence, Delays Hamper Crucial Haiti Vote'. Associated Press Writer. July 1, 2005.

124 Colum Lynch. 'Annan Makes Plea for Troops in Haiti'. *Washington Post*. June 30, 2005.

125 AHP. July 6, 2005.

126 'UN Occupation Forces Carry Out Massacre of Poor in Port-au-Prince'. Labor/Human Rights Delegation to Haiti: Press Release. July 8, 2005.

127 Joseph Guyler Delva. 'UN Troops Accused in Deaths of Haiti Residents'. Reuters. July 15, 2005.

128 Haider Rizvi. 'UN to Probe Deadly Raid'. IPS. July 25, 2005.

129 Vivian Sequera. 'Brazilian General Denies Accusations of Human Rights Violations in Haiti'. Associated Press. November 23, 2005.

130 Andrew Buncombe. 'UN Admits Civilians May Have Died in Haiti Peacekeeping Raid'. *Independent* (UK). January 10, 2006.

131 Charles Arthur. 'Murder in the Caribbean – How Does Haiti Compare?' Eye on the Caribbean/Alterpresse/Haiti Support Group. February 3, 2006.

132 AHP. July 8, 2005

133 'At Least 6 Persons Killed during a Police Operation in the Populist Neighborhood of Solino.' AHP. July 18, 2005.

134 'Kevin Pina Interviews Georges Honorat'. Flashpoints Radio, KPFA. July 14, 2005.

135 Alfred de Montesquiou. 'Haiti – Priest Detained'. AP. July 19, 2005.

136 'New Reaction to Journalist Jacques Roche's Murder'. AHP. July 18, 2005.

137 'The Interim Government Accuses Lavalas of Responsibility in the Death of Cultural Journalist Jacques Roche'. AHP. July 14, 2005.

138 'AJH Executive Secretary Denounces... Muzzling of the Press'. AHP. July 18, 2005.

139 Leonardo Aldridge. 'Council: Bar Aristide Party from Election'. AP. July 17, 2005.

140 'Haitian Activists Deported from the Dominican Republic'. Haiti Action Committee, Urgent Action Alert. July 21, 2005.

141 Marina Jimenez. 'Haiti Braces for Its Ballot'. *Toronto Globe and Mail*. February 4, 2006.

142 Alfred de Montesquiou. 'Witnesses: Haiti Police Kill 5 in Raid'. Associated Press. August 10, 2005.

143 Joseph Guyler Delva. 'U.S. Envoy Criticizes Release of Haiti Rebel'. Reuters. August 12, 2005.

144 Reed Lindsay. 'Play for Peace Soccer Match Turns Into Massacre'. *Toronto Star*. August 28, 2005; also, Tom Luce (Tr.). '5000 Soccer Fans Witness Machete/Hatchet Lynching by Haitian Police and Civilian Murderers'. AUMOHD report. August 25, 2005. The massacre was also reported on *Democracy Now!* on August 26. The IJDH circulated a preliminary report on August 29, 2005.

145 'Jailed Priest in Haiti Plans to Run for President with Ousted Leader's Support'. Associated Press. August 24, 2005.

7 THE ELECTORAL GAME OF 2006

1 AHP. September 5, 2005.

2 'Aristide To Stay in South Africa until after Elections in Haiti'. Reuters. September 8, 2005.

3 The report is called 'Estimation de la population eligible aux elections de 2005 en Haiti', by Dr Dominique Agossou, Consultant, Aout 2005.

4 Alfred de Monstesquiou. 'Police in Haiti Arrest Two Journalists'. Associated Press. September 9, 2005.

5 Brian Concannon Jr. 'Electoral Cleansing in Haiti Violates Human Rights and Democracy'. Americas Program, International Relations Center (IRC). September 29, 2005.

6 On February 7, 1986, the Duvalier dictatorship ended.

7 Alfred de Montesquiou. 'Haiti's Human Rights a Disaster, UN Says'. Associated Press. October 14, 2005.

8 Lyn Duff. 'Machete Massacre Perpetrators Released from prison – Political Prisoners Still Locked Up'. *San Francisco Bay View*. April 2, 2006.

9   'Haiti: Activist's Killing Shows Need for Disarmament Programme'.
     Amnesty International Press Release. September 28, 2006.
10   'UN Official Slams Haitian Courts'. Associated Press. November
     29, 2005.
11   'Inaguration for a Reception Center for Minors in Conflict with the
     Law'. AHP. October 31, 2005.
12   AHP reported a demonstration 20,000 strong of Fanmi Lavalas
     backing Préval on November 3, 2005.
13   'A CEP Official Announces that the First Round of the Presidential
     and Legislative Elections Will Be Held on December 27'. AHP.
     November 16, 2006.
14   Alfred de Montesquiou. 'Haiti Sets New Dates for Elections'.
     Associated Press. November 25, 2005.
15   'Haiti's Interim Government Sues Aristide'. Associated Press,
     Miami. November 3, 2005.
16   'HaiTel expands wireless network in Haiti with Nortel Technology'
     Nortel press release. November 6, 2005; 'Digicel, Ericsson Building
     First-Rate GSM Network in Haiti'. Digicel press release. November
     7, 2005.
17   'Kurzban Rebuts De Facto Lawsuit Against Aristide'. *Haiti Progres*.
     vol. 23, no. 35. November 9, 2005.
18   Press Release: 'Congresswoman Waters Demands to Know How
     the Interim Government of Haiti is Paying for its Lawsuit Against
     President Aristide'. December 1, 2005.
19   This is according to a bulletin sent by the U.S. activist group the Haiti
     Action Committee on November 29, 2005 based on testimonies
     they received: there were no press reports on these deaths.
20   'UN Troops Kill 4 in Haitian Low Intensity Warfare'. Associated
     Press. November 15, 2005.
21   'Four Fatal Shootings, 16 Corpses Discovered and 18 Cases of
     Kidnapping Have Been Recorded over the Past Two Weeks,
     According to the PNH'. AHP. November 16, 2005.
22   'At Least 3 Haitians Shot during Protest'. Associated Press.
     December 12, 2005.
23   'Leaders from the Former Opposition to President Aristide Issue an
     Appeal for Unity Among All Sectors to Prevent Préval from Winning
     a Second Term as President'. AHP. November 16, 2005.
24   Mario Joseph. Bureau des Avocats Internationaux. Press Notice.
     December 20, 2005.
25   'Latortue Says He Will Step Down as Haiti's Prime Minister on Feb.
     7'.Haiti Info. January 5, 2006.
26   Peter Richards. 'Haiti Seeks Return to Caricom Fold'. Inter-Press
     Service. January 27, 2006.
27   'Presidential Candidate René Préval Affirms His Will to Listen to
     the Haitian Population'. AHP. December 14, 2005.
28   Carlos Valdez. 'Restore Peace to Slum, Haiti Front-Runner Says'.
     Reuters. February 3, 2006.
29   'Haiti: Former Senator Detained after UN Mission Finds Illegal
     Weapons'. UN News Centre. January 3, 2006.
30   Joseph Guyler Delva. 'UN Commander in Haiti Kills Himself – UN
     Officials'. Reuters. January 7, 2006.

31 State Department cable 17.01.2006: Dominican President Receives State DAS for Caribbean. Published on Aftenpolten.no. Available online: http://www.aftenposten.no/spesial/wikileaksdokumenter/article3992007.ece. [Accessed April 1, 2012]. See also Kim Ives. 'Wikileaks Points to U.S. Meddling in Haiti'. *Guardian* (UK) *Comment is Free*. January 21, 2008. Available online: http://www.guardian.co.uk/commentisfree/cifamerica/2011/jan/21/haiti-wikileaks?INTCMP=SRCH. [Accessed April 1, 2012].

32 Boulos made this call in a Radio Metropole interview on January 5, 2006. Translation by BBC Worldwide Monitoring. 'Haitian Businessman Slams UN over Lack of Security, Calls for Strike'. January 7, 2006.

33 'Haiti Business Strike Urged to Protest Kidnappings'. Associated Press. January 6, 2006.

34 Aaron Lakoff to the Canada Haiti Action Network (CHAN) list, January 9, 2006.

35 'MINUSTAH Director Denounces a Hatred Campaign against the Mission on the Air of Radio Stations'. AHP. January 8, 2006.

36 Joseph Guyler Delva. 'Haiti Election Could Be Worst-Run Ever'. Reuters. February 3, 2006.

37 Haiti Action Committee Urgent Action Alert. January 9, 2006.

38 'Haitians March as Violence Mounts'. Associated Press. January 12, 2006.

40 'Two Jordanian UN Peacekeepers Killed in Haiti'. Reuters. January 17, 2006.

41 Joseph Guyler Delva. 'No Voting Stations for Haiti's Largest Slum'. Reuters. January 25, 2006.

42 'The Question of René Préval's Candidacy'. *Haiti Progres*. February 2, 2006.

43 Jose De Cordoba. 'Aristide Ally Favored in Haitian Vote'. *Wall Street Journal*. February 6, 2006.

44 Manuel Roig-Franzia. 'Haitians Outraged by Voting Glitches'. *Washington Post Foreign Service*. February 7, 2006.

45 Andrew Selsky. 'Haitians Vote as UN Provides Security'. Associated Press. February 7 2006.

46 Jacqueline Charles and Joe Mozingo. 'Préval Looks Ready to Take Presidency'. *Miami Herald*. February 11, 2006.

47 Stevenson Jacobs. 'Haitian Election Official Suspects Vote Tampering'. Associated Press. February 13, 2006.

48 Joseph Guyler Delva. 'Haiti Election Authority Says Fraud Tainted Vote'. Reuters. February 17, 2006. The OAS denied fraud.

49 Stevenson Jacobs. 'Gunfire Erupts in Haiti'. Associated Press. February 13, 2006.

50 'Haitian Election Marked by "Gigantic Fraud", Frontrunner Says'. CBC News. February 14, 2006.

51 'Officials Try to Broker Deal between Préval and Manigat on Runoff'. Newsday. February 14, 2006.

52 Joseph Guyler Delva. 'Haitian Officials Say They're Barred from Canada'. Reuters. May 1, 2006.

53 Stevenson Jacobs. 'Canada Foreign Minister Regrets Handling of

Visa Denial for Haitian Prime Minister'. Associated Press. June 4, 2006.

54   James Gordon Meek. 'Interim Haitian Prime Minister Relieved to Leave Office'. *New York Daily News*. June 10, 2006.

55   Alex Dupuy (2007) *The Prophet and Power: Jean-Bertrand Aristide, the International Community, and Haiti*. Rowman & Littlefield, Lanham, MD. p. 179.

56   Dupuy. *The Prophet and Power*. pp.191–2.

57   'Haiti Tops World Corruption Table'. BBC News. November 6, 2006. Available online: http://news.bbc.co.uk/2/hi/business/6120522.stm. [Accessed April 1, 2012].

58   U.S. State Department Bureau of Democracy, Human Rights, and Labor. March 8, 2006. Haiti. Available online: http://www.state.gov/g/drl/rls/hrrpt/2005/61731.htm. [Accessed April 1, 2012].

59   Kolbe and Hutson. 'Human Rights Abuse and Other Criminal Violations in Port-au-Prince, Haiti: A Random Survey of Households'. *The Lancet*. September 2, 2006.

60   'Shocking Lancet Study: 8,000 Murders, 35,000 Rapes and Sexual Assaults in Haiti during U.S.-Backed Coup Regime after Aristide Ouster'. *Democracy Now!* August 31, 2006. 'Available on: http://www.democracynow.org/2006/8/31/shocking_lancet_study_8_000_murders. [Accessed April 1, 2012].

61   Horton and Summerskill. 'Clarification: Human Rights Abuse and Other Criminal Violations in Port-au-Prince, Haiti.' *The Lancet*. February 3, 2007. Available online: http://www.thelancet.com/journals/lancet/article/PIIS0140-6736(07)60169-X/fulltext. [Accessed April 1, 2012].

62   Charles Arthur. 'Murder in the Caribbean – How Does Haiti Compare? Eye on the Caribbean'. Republished in Alterpresse. February 3, 2006. Available online: http://www.alterpresse.org/spip.php?article4074. [Accessed April 1, 2012].

63   Wikipedia: http://en.wikipedia.org/wiki/List_of_countries_by_intentional_homicide_rate. [Accessed April 1, 2012]. See also this 2007 report by the World Bank, 'Crime, Violence, and Development: Trends, Costs, and Policy Options in the Caribbean'.

64   'Haiti's First Census in 24 Years Uncovers Pressing Problems, UN Agency Says'. UN News Centre. May 10, 2006.

65   'Canada Announces Important Contributions to Two Key Haiti Security Programs'. Government of Canada. February 5, 2007. Available online: http://www.news.gc.ca/cfmx/view/en/index.jsp?articleid=3D274079. [Accessed April 1, 2012].

66   Abe Sauer. 'Our Government-Funded Mission to Make Haiti Christian'. *The Awl*. January 20, 2011.

67   Dupuy. *The Prophet and Power*. p. 203.

8   THE PRÉVAL REGIME, 2006–10

1   U.S. Embassy Cable 09PORTAUPRINCE575 'Deconstructing Préval'. Wikileaks. June 16, 2009. Available online: http://wikileaks.

org/cable/2009/06/09PORTAUPRINCE575.html. [Accessed April 1, 2012].

2   U.S. Embassy Cable 08PORTAUPRINCE1389 'Haiti: Rumors Abound Regarding Aristide's Possible Move to Venezuela'. Wikileaks. October 3, 2008. Available online: http://wikileaks.org/cable/2008/10/08PORTAUPRINCE1389.html. [Accessed April 1, 2012]. This cable is an excellent illustration of the contradictory logic.

3   U.S. Embassy Cable 08PORTAUPRINCE399 'GOH Children's Shelter Well Run, Politics Aside'. Wikileaks. March 11, 2008. Available online: http://wikileaks.org/cable/2008/03/08PORTAUPRINCE399.html. [Accessed April 1, 2012].

4   U.S. Embassy Cable 08PORTAUPRINCE341 'Haiti in 2008: Four Years after Aristide'. Wikileaks. February 29, 2008. Available online: http://wikileaks.org/cable/2008/02/08PORTAUPRINCE341.html. [Accessed April 1, 2012].

5   Journalists working with *Haiti Liberte*, *The Nation*, and Wikileaks, published a series of reports based on these cables before Wikileaks published all cables to the public. See 'Wikileaks Haiti: The Nation Partners with Haiti Liberte on Release of Secret Haiti Cables'. *The Nation*. 2010. Available online: http://www.thenation.com/article/161009/wiki-haiti. [Accessed April 1, 2012].

6   U.S. Embassy Cable 05PORTAUPRINCE2766 'René Préval Asks for Help with Disarmament'. Wikileaks. November 8, 2005. Available online: http://wikileaks.org/cable/2005/11/05PORTAUPRINCE2766.html. [Accessed April 1, 2012].

7   The U.S. Embassy cable on the topic (July 10, 2006, 06PORTAUPRINCE1220, http://wikileaks.org/cable/2006/07/06PORTAUPRINCE1220.html [Accessed April 1, 2012]) suggests that no one – not the U.S., not the Haitian government, and not the UN – had solid information on what occurred at the time. BBC media monitoring of Haitian local radios headlines – 8 June 2006, 9 June 2006.

8   U.S. Embassy Cable 06PORTAUPRINCE1336 'GOH and MINUSTAH Prepare to Take On Gangs; Manuel'. Wikileaks. July 21, 2006. Available online: http://wikileaks.org/cable/2006/07/06PORTAUPRINCE1336.html. [Accessed April 1, 2012].

9   U.S. Embassy Cable 06PORTAUPRINCE1342 'New Truce Quells Gang Violence – For Now'. Wikileaks. July 24, 2006. Available online: http://wikileaks.org/cable/2006/07/06PORTAUPRINCE1342.html. [Accessed April 1, 2012].

10 U.S. Embassy Cable 06PORTAUPRINCE1481 'Préval to Gangs: Disarm or Die'. Wikileaks. August 10, 2006. Available online: http://wikileaks.org/cable/2006/08/06PORTAUPRINCE1481.html. [Accessed April 1, 2012].

11 From the delegation's press release: 'Eyewitness Account of UN Firing into Densely Populated Cité Soleil'. August 24, 2006. *Democracy Now!* reported it on August 31, 2006. Available online: http://www.democracynow.org/2006/8/31/eyewitnesses_account_un_forces_open_fire. [Accessed April 1, 2012].

12 Joseph Guyler Delva. 'At Least Three Said Killed in Clash in Haiti Slum'. Reuters, October 20, 2006.
13 'At Least 5 Dead as UN Moves against Haitian Gangs'. CBC News. December 22, 2006. Available online: http://www.cbc.ca/world/story/2006/12/22/haiti.html. [Accessed April 1, 2012]; Joseph Guyler Delva. 'Nine Killed in Haitian Slum Raid'. Reuters. December 23, 2006.
14 'UN Forces Battle Gangs in Slum; Five People Shot'. AFP. December 28, 2006.
15 Clarens Renois. 'UN Forces Raid Gang's House in Haiti; Six Wounded'. AFP. January 24, 2007; '5 Killed in Haitian Clashes'. BBC Caribbean. January 25, 2007.
16 'UN Peacekeepers Raid Haiti Slum'. AP. Feb 9, 2007.
17 See Dr John Carroll. 'A Journey through the World's Most Miserable Slum'. *Counterpunch*. February 12, 2007. Available online: http://www.counterpunch.org/carroll02122007.html. [Accessed April 1, 2012].
18 US Embassy Cable 07PORTAUPRINCE523. 'Gangs of Cité Soleil: Back to Basics'. Wikileaks. March 16, 2007. Available online: http://wikileaks.org/cable/2007/03/07PORTAUPRINCE523.html. [Accessed April 1, 2012].
19 U.S. Embassy Cable 6PORTAUPRINCE5950 'USAID-MINUSTAH Partnership Advances Peace in Haiti's Slums'. Wikileaks. April 3, 2006. Available online: http://wikileaks.org/cable/2006/04/06PORTAUPRINCE595.html. [Accessed April 1, 2012]. Préval dismissed these programmes and sought a more comprehensive plan at a donor's conference in July. See cable: 06PORTAUPRINCE1389.
20 'Haiti Contact Group Endorses Extension of UN Peacekeeping Force MINUSTAH'. AFP. February 1, 2007.
21 Stevenson Jacobs. 'Haiti, U.N. to Disarm Gang Members'. Associated Press. September 4, 2006.
22 Anthony Fenton. Media monitoring of Haitian local radios headlines – 8 June 2006, 9 June 2006.
23 Reed Lindsay. 'Massacre Ends Fragile Haiti Truce'. Newsday. July 14, 2006.
24 Jeb Sprague. 'Lame Ti Manchet Accused of Role in Killing Photojournalist'. January 26, 2007. Available online: haitianalysis.com; and: counterpunch.org. [Accessed April 1, 2012].
25 Stevenson Jacobs. 'Gunmen Kill Haiti Journalist with NYC Paper'. Associated Press. April 14, 2007.
26 Nick Caistor. 'Poverty and Gangs Curb Haiti Progress'. BBC. February 28, 2007.
27 'UN Helicopters Fly over Haiti Rural Areas Searching for Fleeing Gangs'. Caribbean Media Corporation via BBC Monitoring Service. March 1, 2007.
28 Cited in Michael Dziedzic and Roberto M. Perito (2008) 'Haiti: Confronting the Gangs of Port-au-Prince'. United States Institute of Peace Special Report.
29 Tom Brown. 'Graveyard Quiet of Huge Haiti Slum Signals Progress'. Reuters. May 11, 2008.

30 International Crisis Group. 'Haiti: Prison Reform and the Rule of Law'. Latin America/Caribbean Briefing No.15. May 4, 2007. Available online: http://www.crisisgroup.org/en/regions/latin-america-caribbean/haiti/b015-haiti-prison-reform-and-the-rule-of-law.aspx. [Accessed April 1, 2012].

31 U.S. Embassy Cable 06PORTAUPRINCE865 'Haiti: Inaguration Day Prison Riot'. Wikileaks. May 15, 2006. Available online: http://wikileaks.org/cable/2006/05/06PORTAUPRINCE865.html. [Accessed April 1, 2012]. Cable 07PORTAUPRINCE1695 contains more gruesome detail about prison conditions.

32 Jeb Sprague and Eunida Alexandra. 'Mysterious Prison Ailment Traced to U.S. Rice'. Inter Press Service. January 17, 2007.

33 U.S. Embassy Cable 06PORTAUPRINCE542 'Haiti: Spending and Finance Gap Growing Concerns'. Wikileaks. March 23, 2006. Available online: http://wikileaks.org/cable/2006/03/06PORTAUPRINCE542.html. [Accessed April 1, 2012]. As with the other Embassy Cables made available by Wikileaks in 2010/11, the Haiti cables include both interesting information and a sense of the thinking of the U.S. officials who have more power to determine events in Haiti than the Haitian government.

34 U.S. Embassy Cable 06PORTAUPRINCE1858 'Haiti's Textiles: Competitive Prospects for a Struggling Sector'. Wikleaks. September 28, 2006. Available online: http://wikileaks.org/cable/2006/09/06PORTAUPRINCE1858.html. [Accessed April 1, 2012].

35 U.S. Embassy Cable 06PORTAUPRINCE2304 'Haiti: Revenue Collection'. Wikileaks. December 1, 2006. Available online: http://wikileaks.org/cable/2006/12/06PORTAUPRINCE2304.html. [Accessed April 1, 2012].

36 U.S. Embassy Cable 08PORTAUPRINCE583 'Ten Days in April; Haiti's Food Riots'. Wikileaks. April 22, 2008. Available online: http://wikileaks.org/cable/2008/04/08PORTAUPRINCE583.html. [Accessed April 1, 2012].

37 U.S. Embassy Cable 08PORTAUPRINCE753 'Préval Takes Anti-Globalization Stance'. Wikileaks. May 23, 2008. Available online: http://wikileaks.org/cable/2008/05/08PORTAUPRINCE753.html. [Accessed April 1, 2012].

38 U.S. Embassy Cable 08PORTAUPRINCE1388 'Haiti: President Préval Rejects International "Charity"'. Wikileaks. October 10, 2008. Available online: http://wikileaks.org/cable/2008/10/08PORTAUPRINCE1388.html. [Accessed April 1, 2012].

39 Amartya Sen and Jean Dreze (1989) *Hunger and Public Action*. Clarendon Press, Oxford.

40 Reed Lindsay. 'Inside Haiti's Food Riots'. Al Jazeera English. April 15, 2008.

41 U.S. Embassy Cable 08PORTAUPRINCE874 'Haiti: Subsidizing Oil'. Wikileaks. June 16, 2008. Available online: http://wikileaks.org/cable/2008/06/08PORTAUPRINCE874.html. [Accessed April 1, 2012].

42 U.S. Embassy Cable 08PORTAUPRINCE1314 'Storm Aftermath in Haiti: Devestating (sic) Agricultural Damage'. Wikileaks. September 15, 2008. Available online: http://wikileaks.org/cable/

2008/09/08PORTAUPRINCE1314.html. [Accessed April 1, 2012].
Also cable 08PORTAUPRINCE1356 offered a dollar estimate of
$190 million in agricultural losses.

43 Richard Morse. 'Haiti's Gas Gang'. *Counterpunch*. January 9,
2009.

44 U.S. Embassy Cable 09PORTAUPRINCE73 'You Can Go Home
again: Canadian Governor General Shines in Haiti'. Wikileaks.
January 23, 2009. Available online: http://wikileaks.org/cable/
2009/01/09PORTAUPRINCE73.html. [Accessed April 1, 2012].

45 U.S. Embassy Cable 09PORTAUPRINCE109 'President Préval's
Trip to Washington'. Wikileaks. February 2, 2009. Available online:
http://wikileaks.org/cable/2009/02/09PORTAUPRINCE109.html.
[Accessed April 1, 2012].

46 U.S. Embassy Cable 09PORTAUPRINCE530 'Haiti: Students
and Police Face-Off over Minimum Wage Bill'. Wikileaks. June
4, 2009. Available online: http://wikileaks.org/cable/2009/06/
09PORTAUPRINCE530.html. [Accessed April 1, 2012].

47 U.S. Embassy Cable 06PORTAUPRINCE1597 'Préval Coming
to DC/Pensive with Ambassador'. Wikileaks. August 25,
2006. Available online: http://wikileaks.org/cable/2006/08/
06PORTAUPRINCE1597.html. [Accessed April 1, 2012].

48 U.S. Embassy Cable 06PORTAUPRINCE832 'Lavalas Feels Left
Out by Préval'. Wikileaks. May 5, 2006. Available online: http://
wikileaks.org/cable/2006/05/06PORTAUPRINCE832.html.
[Accessed April 1, 2012].

49 U.S. Embassy Cable 07PORTAUPRINCE1276 'Haiti/
Canada Relations Enhanced by PM Visit'. Wikileaks. July 26,
2007. Available online: http://wikileaks.org/cable/2007/07/
07PORTAUPRINCE1276.html. [Accessed April 1, 2012].

50 U.S. Embassy Cable 06PORTAUPRINCE559 'Préval in Washington:
Seeking Status'. Wikileaks. March 23, 2006. Available online:
http://wikileaks.org/cable/2006/03/06PORTAUPRINCE559.html.
[Accessed April 1, 2012].

51 U.S. Embassy Cable 06PORTAUPRINCE692 'Préval Announces
Haiti to Join PetroCaribe'. Wikileaks. April 19, 2006. Available online:
http://wikileaks.org/cable/2006/04/06PORTAUPRINCE692.html.
[Accessed April 1, 2012].

52 U.S. Embassy Cable 06PORTAUPRINCE758 'Préval Will
Sign PetroCaribe Deal on May 15'. Wikileaks. April 28,
2006. Available online: http://wikileaks.org/cable/2006/04/
06PORTAUPRINCE758.html. [Accessed April 1, 2012].

53 U.S. Embassy Cable 07PORTAUPRINCE1989 'Venezuelan and
Cuban Construction of 3 Electricity Plants in Haiti'. Wikileaks.
December 12, 2007. Available online: http://wikileaks.org/cable/
2007/12/07PORTAUPRINCE1989.html. [Accessed April 1,
2012].

54 U.S. Embassy Cable 06PORTAUPRINCE1258 'Préval Tries
to Dodge Issue of Venezuela and UNSC'. Wikileaks. July 12,
2006. Available online: http://wikileaks.org/cable/2006/07/
06PORTAUPRINCE1258.html. [Accessed April 1, 2012].

55 U.S. Embassy Cable 07PORTAUPRINCE781 'Préval Going

to ALBA Summit: Returning with a Check?' Wikileaks. April 26, 2007. Available online: http://wikileaks.org/cable/2007/04/07PORTAUPRINCE781.html. [Accessed April 1, 2012]. Préval also resisted voting with the U.S. on the Cuban Embargo: Cable 07PORTAUPRINCE1743.

56 U.S. Embassy Cable 08PORTAUPRINCE1381 'Why We Need Continuing MINUSTAH Presence in Haiti'. Wikileaks. October 1, 2008. Available online: http://wikileaks.org/cable/2008/10/08PORTAUPRINCE1381.html. [Accessed April 1, 2012].

57 U.S. Embassy Cable 08PORTAUPRINCE1405 'Préval Seeks Change in MINUSTAH Status Prior to Mandate Renewal'. Wikileaks. October 3, 2008. Available online: http://wikileaks.org/cable/2008/10/08PORTAUPRINCE1405.html. [Accessed April 1, 2012].

9 THE EARTHQUAKE AND HAITI'S POLITICS OF DISASTER, 2010/11

1 Lucy Rodgers. 'Why Did So Many People Die in Haiti's Quake?' BBC News. February 14, 2010. Available online: http://news.bbc.co.uk/2/hi/americas/8510900.stm. [Accessed April 1, 2012].

2 Annick Cojean. 'A Port-au-Prince, des amputations par milliers...' *Le Monde.* January 29, 2010. Available online: http://www.lemonde.fr/cgi-bin/ACHATS/acheter.cgi?offre=ARCHIVES&type_item=ART_ARCH_30J&objet_id=1113587&clef=ARC-TRK-D_01. [Accessed April 1, 2012].

3 Maria Laura Carpineta. 'Vamos a estar cuando todos se hayan ido'. *Pagina 12.* February 4, 2010. Available online: http://www.pagina12.com.ar/diario/sociedad/3-139567-2010-02-04.html. [Accessed April 1, 2012].

4 Ansel Herz. 'Haut-Turgeau, Haiti: The Camp that Vanished and the Priest Who Forced Them Out'. Inter Press Service. March 9, 2010. Available online: http://www.mediahacker.org/2010/03/haut-turgeau-haiti-the-camp-that-vanished/. [Accessed April 1, 2012]. Herz has several excellent reports on the camps at his mediahacker.org website.

5 Bill Quigley and Jeena Shah. 'One Year After Quake, Million Plus Remain Homeless and Displaced in Haiti'. ZNet. January 11, 2011. Available online: http://www.zcommunications.org/one-year-after-quake-by-bill-quigley. [Accessed April 1, 2012].

6 Mark Schuller. 'Met Ko Veye Ko: Foreign Responsibility in the Failure to Protect against Cholera and Other Man-Made Disasters'. January 22, 2011. Published on Institute for Justice and Democracy in Haiti. Available online: http://ijdh.org/archives/16896. [Accessed April 1, 2012].

7 Reported in Health Roots Student Organization, Harvard School of Public Health, October 2011. 'MINUSTAH: Keeping the Peace or Conspiring against It? A Review of the Human Rights Record of the United Nations Stabilization Mission in Haiti 2010–11'.

8 Isabel Macdonald. 'Haiti: Where's the Money?' *The Nation.*

January 11, 2011. Available online: http://www.thenation.com/article/157646/haiti-wheres-money. [Accessed April 1, 2012].

9 Abe Sauer. 'Our Government-Funded Mission to Make Haiti Christian: Your Tax Dollars, Billy Graham's Son, Monsanto and Sarah Palin'. The Awl. January 20, 2011. Available online: http://www.theawl.com/2011/01/our-government-funded-mission-to-make-haiti-christian-your-tax-dollars-billy-grahams-son-monsanto-and-sarah-palin. [Accessed April 1, 2012].

10 Samantha Nadler. 'Post Quake Haiti: The Year in Review'. Council on Hemispheric Affairs. January 21, 2011. Available online: http://www.coha.org/post-quake-haiti-the-year-in-review/. [Accessed April 1, 2012].

11 Jeffrey Sachs. 'Haiti's Road to Recovery'. *Guardian* (UK) 'Comment Is Free'. January 31, 2010. Available online: http://www.guardian.co.uk/commentisfree/cifamerica/2010/jan/31/haiti-road-to-recovery. [Accessed April 1, 2012].

12 Alex Dupuy. 'Foreign Aid Keeps the Country from Shaping Its Own Future'. *Washington Post*. January 9, 2011. Available online: http://www.washingtonpost.com/wp-dyn/content/article/2011/01/07/AR2011010706511.html. [Accessed April 1, 2012].

13 Abe Sauer. 'Our Government-Funded Mission to Make Haiti Christian: Your Tax Dollars, Billy Graham's Son, Monsanto and Sarah Palin'. The Awl. January 20, 2011.

14 Amaud Robert. 'Haiti est la preuve de l'echec de l'aide internationale: Interview avec Ricardo Seitenfus, representant de l'OEA en Haiti'. Republished in Alterpresse. Available online: http://www.alterpresse.org/spip.php?article10439. [Accessed April 1, 2012].

15 Interview with Jean-Bernard Chassagne, vice-mayor of Tabarre municipality in Port-au-Prince. October 7, 2011.

16 See Mark Schuller. 'Unstable Foundations: Impact of NGOs on Human Rights for Port-au-Prince's Internally Displaced People'. Published on Institute for Justice and Democracy in Haiti. October 4, 2010. Available online: http://ijdh.org/archives/14855. [Accessed April 1, 2012].

17 Tim Schwartz. 'Help that Hurts: An Interview with Tim Schwartz about Haiti'. Interviewed by Justin Podur. Z Communications, March 18, 2012. Available online: http://www.zcommunications.org/help-that-hurts-by-justin-podur. [Accessed April 1, 2012].

18 Schwartz. 'Help that Hurts'. Z Communications.

19 Schwartz, 'Help that Hurts'. Z Communications.

10 THE 2011 ELECTIONS AND MICHEL MARTELLY

1 Beatrice Lindstrom. 'Beyond the Blue Helmets: Stability in Haiti Requires New Elections'. CIP Online. January 13, 2011. Available online: http://www.cipamericas.org/archives/3869. [Accessed April 1, 2012].

2 'Haiti Rejects Wyclef Jean's Presidency Bid'. BBC News. August 21, 2010. Available online: http://www.bbc.co.uk/news/entertainment-arts-11034608. [Accessed April 1, 2012].

3 Samantha Nadler. 'Post Quake Haiti: The Year in Review'. Council on Hemispheric Affairs. January 21, 2011. Available online: http://www.coha.org/post-quake-haiti-the-year-in-review/.   [Accessed April 1, 2012].

4 Mark Weisbrot. 'Haiti's Democracy in the Balance'. *Guardian* (UK) 'Comment Is Free'. January 18, 2011. Available online: http://www.guardian.co.uk/commentisfree/cifamerica/2011/jan/18/haiti-usa. [Accessed April 1, 2012].

5 Interview with Patrick Elie. Port-au-Prince, October 5, 2011. Transcript archived online here: http://killingtrain.com/node/814. [Accessed April 1, 2012].

6 Jeb Sprague. 'Martelly in Haiti'. ZNet. December 20, 2010. Available online: http://www.zcommunications.org/stealth-duvalierism-by-jeb-sprague. [Accessed April 1, 2012].

7 Mark Weisbrot. 'Aristide Should Be Allowed to Return to Haiti'. *Bellingham Herald* (WA). January 20, 2011. Available online: http://www.cepr.net/index.php/op-eds-&-columns/op-eds-&-columns/aristide-should-be-allowed-to-return. [Accessed April 1, 2012].

8 An interview with Kim Ives. 'Did Baby Doc Return to Haiti to Pressure Préval in the Election?' *Democracy Now!* January 19, 2011. Available online: http://www.democracynow.org/2011/1/19/did_baby_doc_duvalier_return_to. [Accessed April 1, 2012].

9 'Duvalier Apologizes to Victims, Urges Unity'. MSNBC. January 21, 2011. Available online: http://www.msnbc.msn.com/id/41197566/ns/world_news-haiti/. [Accessed April 1, 2012].

10 Isabeau Doucet. 'Baby Doc's Return Haunts Haiti'. *Guardian* (UK). January 17, 2011. Available online: http://www.guardian.co.uk/commentisfree/cifamerica/2011/jan/17/jean-claude-baby-doc-duvalier-haiti. [Accessed April 1, 2012].

11 Aristide's speech. March 18, 2011. One link to the speech is on YouTube: http://www.youtube.com/watch?v=INV8sVz-V0M. [Accessed April 1, 2012].

12 Exclusive Interview with Jean-Bertrand Aristide: 'If Haiti's Military is Restored, "We are Headed Back to Misery"'. *Democracy Now!* March 21, 2011. Available online: http://www.democracynow.org/2011/3/21/democracy_now_exclusive_interview_with_jean. [Accessed April 1, 2012].

13 '"Big Setback" for Haitian Democracy as U.S. Gets Its Way; Forces Runoff Elections Between Two Right-Wing Candidates, CEPR Co-Director Says'. Center for Economic and Policy Research, Press Release. February 3, 2011. Available online: http://www.cepr.net/index.php/press-releases/press-releases/big-setback-for-haitian-democracy-as-us-gets-its-way. [Accessed April 1, 2012].

14 'Martelly's Historically Weak Mandate'. Haiti: Relief and Reconstruction Watch blog. April 5, 2011. Available online: http://www.cepr.net/index.php/blogs/relief-and-reconstruction-watch/martellys-historically-weak-mandate. [Accessed April 1, 2012].

15 Kim Ives. 'Class Analysis of a Crisis: What Lies Behind PM Conille's Resignation?' *Haiti Liberte,* vol. 5, no. 33. February 29, 2012.

Available online: http://www.haiti-liberte.com/archives/volume5-33/Class%20Analysis.asp. [Accessed April 1, 2012].

16 Ives. 'Class Analysis of a Crisis'. *Haiti Liberte*.

CONCLUSION: REPLACING DICTATORSHIP WITH SOVEREIGNTY

1 Interview with Steven Benoit, October 6, 2011.

2 See Nicolas Guilhot's excellent book, *The Democracy Makers: Human Rights and International Order* (Columbia University Press, New York), for some history of the process of co-optation of the concepts of 'human rights' and 'democracy' to serve imperial foreign policy goals.

3 Philippe Girard. (2010) *Haiti: The Tumultuous History – From Pearl of the Caribbean to Broken Nation.* Palgrave Macmillan, New York. p. 229.

4 Timothy Schwartz. (2010) *Travesty in Haiti: A True Account of Christian Missions, Orphanages, Fraud, Food Aid and Drug Trafficking.* Self-published; and Paul Farmer (2011) *Haiti after the Earthquake.* PublicAffairs, New York.

INDEX